GERMANY'S HITLER

Herr Heinz A. Heinz' aim has been to draw a picture of the *Führer* from details supplied at first hand by those friends and helpers and comrades of his who believed in him from the first, who joined him at the beginning, stood by him through the darkest days, and have lived to see one of the most astounding achievements of modern times.

HITLER'S LOVE FOR CHILDREN IS WELL KNOWN. HE OFTEN
INVITES DOZENS OF THEM FOR TEA AT WACHENFELD

GERMANY'S HITLER

By

HEINZ A. HEINZ

WITH 29 *ILLUSTRATIONS*

LONDON
HURST & BLACKETT, LTD.

Reprinted 2004 by
Liberty Bell Publications
PO Box 890
York, SC 29745
www.libertybellpublications.com

ISBN: 1-59364-010-2

DEDICATED

TO MY SINCERE ENGLISH

AND AMERICAN FRIENDS

I am very much indebted to Herrn
Hans Rolf Hoffmann, Munich, for
his kind support.

THE AUTHOR

CONTENTS

LIST OF ILLUSTRATIONS

GERMANY'S HITLER

CHAPTER I

BIRTH AND BOYHOOD

MIDWAY between Vienna and Munich lies
Linz on the Danube, in Upper Austria. One
changes here to a small branch line on the railway
tending north, and comes presently to a beautiful
hilly and wooded district called the " Waldgebiet."
The character of the country gives it the name.
The foothills and mountains are covered with forest,
only broken here and there by the fields and patches
of cultivation which have been cleared by Bavarian
peasants who with toil and hardihood have wrung
a frugal living from the soil in this region for over a
thousand years. It has, indeed, bred a sturdy and
dogged race, used generations long to a fierce fight
with the forces of nature. Every clod of soil, every
foot of arable land had to be wrested from the
forest at the cost of human sweat and sinew. The
country folk of the Waldgebiet have gone back no
whit to-day from the toughness of their ancestors,
neither in physique nor character.

One observes in the rugged weather-beaten face of
a man of these parts, bright defiant eyes like those
of a falcon under a rugged forehead, and finds himself
in the presence of a typical " German," wrought by a
lifetime of struggle to the temper of stoutest finest

steel. The realisation forces itself upon one what it is that has enabled these people to resist the hardships of a thousand years. They have isolated themselves here in the recesses of the forest from easy access, and the race has been kept absolutely clear of any Slavonian admixture. In the Waldgebiet to-day, albeit a part of the racial " mish-mash " of the one-time Austrian Empire, the Bavarian dialect is spoken, and life is wholly German still.

In the Upper Austrian Waldgebiet, utterly lost to the world, lies a tiny village called Walterschlag.

In one of the white wooden houses in the recesses of this forest, and to a father and mother wearing the lovely old German costumes of Grimm's fairy-tale pictures, a baby was born in 1672 who bore the name of Stephan Hitler. He grew up in the Waldgebiet, and came in time to possess the cottage and the clearing which had been his father's, when the latter died. Stephan's son, Johannes, followed him ; there was an Uncle Martin—all " Bauern," small peasant proprietors of the soil, and Waldgebiet peasant farmers at that.

Martin Hitler's son Georg, however, became the village miller. It was but a poor living he made, very toilsome, and with little result. When he grew too old to carry on any more, he had not enough put by to prevent his becoming a charge on the little community in general.

This Georg, however, possessed a son, Alois, with a streak of originality and ambition in him. Something marked him out among the village children. At the age of thirteen Alois Hitler had made up his mind to clear out of the still and lonely forest and see something of life outside and the big world for himself. He bundled his few little possessions together, and set off on foot for Vienna "to make his fortune," three gulden in his pocket from his mother.

This was in the year 1850. We see a sturdy youngster clad in short leathern breeks, curiously laced at the knee, with green suspenders and an embroidered band across the breast over a linen shirt, low thick heavy nail-studded shoes, and a green Jäger hat with a tuft of chamois hair—a "Gemsbart"—in it, trudging through the sombre aisles of the pine forest as hundreds and hundreds of boys, from Whittington's time onward, have trudged to the great city with dreams all about their heads.

Vienna in 1850 was a very different place from what it is to-day. The young Emperor Francis Joseph, then only about twenty years of age, had not long acceded to the throne abdicated by his uncle. There had been, in this big outside world, a short-lived revolution going on, and Kossuth's attempt to wrest Hungary away had already called down upon the Emperor's youthful head the terrible curse of the Countess Karolyi which was to pursue him, and the strange Habsburg House, relentlessly for nearly seventy years, and who knows—perhaps to this very day.

Vienna in 1850 was the brilliant capital of an extraordinary Empire which was never a nation at all in the same sense as geographical and national characteristics and aspirations made a nation of the French or of the English. Austria-Hungary was just a medley of races which chiefly detested each other, bound loosely together for the convenience of the rest of Europe as Napoleon left it, and unified only by the fact that the Habsburgs, everywhere,

were dominant. The Vienna to which young Alois
Hitler came in 1850 was the Vienna so soon to be
graced by that strange figure of imperial beauty,
moodiness and tragedy, the Empress Elizabeth. He,
however, cannot be presumed to have had much to
do with the great world of the Ballplatz and the
Ringstrasse. At that time and in that place humanity
was held only to " begin at the baron." The peasant
boy from the Upper Austrian hinterland was absorbed by the common folk living in the old picturesque, but ever windy Gassen of the working-class
parts of the city.

He bound himself apprentice for a couple of years
to a shoe-maker, but when his time was out, resolved
to try, yet again, for something better. Nothing but
poverty and struggle seemed to offer him as a hand-
worker in imperial Vienna.

The boy's ambition was by no means satisfied by
this. Away back at home in the forest it had seemed
to him that the village priest's position was a pretty
good one, but now he saw that to become a State
official offered still more distinction. Such then
became the goal of Alois Hitler's striving desires—
to become a non-commissioned officer of the Austrian
Customs. With all the purpose and tenacity born
in a boy of the Waldgebiet he struggled forward to
this end, and indeed, he did succeed at last in
qualifying for and obtaining a post in this force.

Years ago, as he left Walterschlag, Hitler had
sworn never to turn up there again until he had made
something of himself—got somewhere—but now,
when this really seemed to have been accomplished
the young fellow was proud and free to recall the girl
he had left behind him ! So now he said good-bye
to Vienna, returned home, married Klara Pölzl, the

daughter of a neighbour there with whom he had been playmates, and found himself appointed as Customs Officer to the small Austrian frontier town of Braunau on the Inn.

A daughter was born to the couple, and then, a good many years later, came a boy.

Barely two months before, mysterious and shocking tragedy had overtaken the Crown Prince Rudolph at his hunting box at Meyerling in the forest not many miles north of Vienna. The whole German world was still ringing with the scandal and wrought up to a fever pitch of curiosity about it.

To recall it, and in connection with the absolutely obscure and unimportant birth of a child to an equally obscure and unimportant functionary in the Customs Service is to contrast the world into which Adolf Hitler came on April 20th, 1889, with the world as he was to refashion it forty-four years later. An heir had appeared, but it was not such an heir as had disappeared! The consequences of the death of Rudolph were to be as nothing compared to the consequences of the birth of Adolf!

This little Adolf was a likely youngster, true to stock and type, who throve lustily under his mother's care.

But few particulars, really, are available about his childhood. The Führer himself has made only the scantiest reference to matters of purely family or biographical interest in *Mein Kampf*, and obviously attaches little importance to them. It were gratuitous to seek for more, and indeed, vain at present now that the German frontier is closed against Austria, and when the Hitler relatives in Austria are in concentration camps.

No relatives have the same name now. The

Reichskanzler's elder sister, a widow, Frau Angela Raubal, keeps house for him in the Salzburg mountains in the famous retreat Haus Wachenfeld (of which more later). His mother, Frau Clara Hitler, had a sister who married a farmer somewhere near Linz, and it is her children, among them Herr Ludwig Schwatz, farmers also, who are the cousins and relations in Austria to-day.

We know this much, that in the course of a few years, Alois Hitler was posted to a more important town, Passau, at the junction of the Inn and the Danube. Foreseeing, however, that he might constantly be shifted from pillar to post, and being unwilling to incur the expense of removing his household every time, Hitler bought a small holding, a " Bauerngut," in a village called Hafeld, and there established them in modest comfort. For himself he remained in Passau, perforce contenting himself from time to time with such visits to Hafeld as time and duty permitted.

Here, then, in Hafeld, near Passau, young Adolf grew to boyhood. His mother looked after the little farm, and no doubt the child ran wild about the lovely country-side, played in the meadows and paddled in the brook with others of his age. Hafeld is one of those villages which appear to be bigger than they really are, owing to the houses being widely separated from each other by fields or fruit gardens. The Hitler house stands on a little elevation. It is a pretty, small, one-story house absolutely hidden in an orchard. Another orchard runs up by the side. Like all the other dwellings in Hafeld it has stabling built on to it for one or two horses or cows, and over this is the hayloft—always a happy hunting-ground where children are concerned.

THE REALSCHULE, LINZ, ATTENDED BY HITLER AS A BOY

HOME OF THE HITLER FAMILY AT LAMBACH-AM-TRAUN. THE CORNER HOUSE IN CENTRE

When Alois Hitler reached the age of sixty he was pensioned off. Doffing the two-peaked hat of official-dom, he reverted to the old garb of the Waldgebiet, and betook himself to his little place at Hafeld, there to revert to the life and occupations of the " Bauer." Hence his son wrote of him many years later : " So it came about that after a long life of work and duty, my father reverted to his original standing."

Previous to this, however, the family had spent two years in Lambach, a small town between Linz and Salzburg with some important-looking buildings. Adolf, now eight or nine years old, was sent to school at the eleventh-century Benedictine Monastery there. Here it was that he learnt the rudiments of music. He figured as a chorister on occasions of festive or of religious solemnity, and naturally aspired to become a prior. Hitler, senior, need not have disturbed himself so much about this notion as he seems to have done. New ideas, new contacts, new experi-ences soon drove all thought of this sort out of Adolf's head.

It is interesting to recall these singing practices of his at Lambach, though, in view of the Reichs-kanzler's well-known passion for music. A good sketcher, indeed, he did become, and a man of immensely wide and deep reading, but the monastery probably represents all the technical instruction he ever had the opportunity of receiving in music. The modern monastery is a widespread picturesque building in simple and restrained Renaissance style, with a deep roof and a well-proportioned clock tower and belfry rising in the midst over an ornate main entrance. It consists of three stories, with rows of eight plain windows the whole length of the façade.

B

In the courtyard of this institution there is a
well with a massively built stone archway over it, the
keystone of which displays a shield with a date,
1860, on the upper half, and a swastika below. The
swastika figured elsewhere at Lambach, noticeably
as the central device in a coat of arms surmounting
an elaborately carved *prie-dieu*. The Superior here
in 1859 had adopted the swastika, and it may be that
the force of this boyhood association had something
to do with the Führer's thought of it when designing
the flag for his Party, later. But it is well known
that his final decision to adopt the swastika for the
symbol of his movement resulted chiefly from his
intensive study of racial development in the history
of the world.

The house in which the Hitlers lived in Lambach
was but a stone's-throw from the school. It was a
solidly built well-designed block of buildings on the
corner of the Linzerstrasse and the Kirchengasse,
facing an irregular picturesque square.

The next milestone was reached for Adolf when,
rummaging one day through his father's collection
of books, he came across some bound copies of an
old illustrated newspaper of the time of the Franco-
Prussian War. He seized upon these with avidity
and made off into the fields, to lie upon his
stomach in the sun by the singing brook, as was
his wont, there to pore over the fascinating pages
undisturbed.

The story gripped the boy's imagination and filled
it with heroic aspiration. And to this encounter
may be ascribed the beginning of Hitler's *Kampf*
after union with Austria. The first thing that
occurred to the child, poring over the story of '70
and '71, was why had Germany to fight alone ?

Why hadn't the Austrians fought too? Were they not also Germans?

The figure of Bismarck claimed a passionate hero worship, and then it dawned upon this little Austrian Adolf that not every German could pride himself on belonging to the Reich! Disturbing as this was, the problem proved far too abstruse at that period for him to unravel. But it stayed with him, and occupied his thoughts and worried him, for there seemed no jot of difference to him between an Austrian and a German, or rather between one German and another German—with just a frontier between.

With the idea of sending Adolf to the Realschule in Linz, Hilter moved to a village called Leonding, in the neighbourhood of that place. Linz at this period was the chief town of Upper Austria, very beautifully situated on an open plain on both sides of the Danube. Ambitious as he was for the boy, he judged it better to send him to the Realschule than to the Gymnasium, deeming it waste of time to spend years over the dead languages, and imagining that Adolf's newly evinced turn for drawing would be better fostered in the more practical type of school. He had set his heart on his son obtaining a desk of some sort in one of the Ministries, " becoming something," as he himself had become, and considered everything to that end.

It never entered into his head to consult Adolf's own inclinations. A boy of his age was not entitled to have anything at all to say in the matter, but just to do as he was bid, and allow his father to know best. Alois Hitler belonged to the old school of authoritative martinet parents, and like many another, was destined to encounter fierce, tenacious opposition.

It suddenly appeared that Adolf had no intention whatever of embracing the career designed for him. He was going to be an artist ! At eleven he decided that, and launched himself with characteristic impetus into a terrific, if tacit, struggle on the question. It was a case of will against will, neither ready to yield one inch. Adolf was lightning quick at school, and learned with astonishing facility. This fact afforded him ample leisure to spend his time otherwise than at his desk. He was forever running about in the woods, glorying in fresh air and freedom, and hardening his resolve never to shut himself up in a stuffy office all day, say what his father might !

They scarcely argued it out. " You're going to be an official, my boy," insisted old Hitler, and would have enlarged on the theme. " I'm not," exploded Adolf, " I'm going to be a painter ! " But it was useless to try and explain. " Never, as long as I've a ha'porth of authority in my own house," countered the father, to which all the reply he got was : " You just wait and see ! "

Here, then, was where the mother stepped in to heal the breach. These altercations, as obstinate on the one side as on the other, somewhat disturbed the peace of the family for more than a year. It was only because he hated to see his mother distress herself that young Adolf would " shut up " with as good a grace as he did. He devised another means of bringing it home to his father that his mind was set on painting and on nothing else. Purposely he neglected his schoolwork in order that the ever-recurring plaints of " insufficiency " recorded on the pages of his exercise-books, might convince his parent that he meant what he said—he would never become an office quill-driver. But for all this young

Adolf could not help coming out top of the class always in the three subjects which did happen to interest him, in drawing, in geography, and above all, in history.

He seems to have had a teacher in the latter subject with a singular and original gift for lifting it right out of the dreary atmosphere of the schoolroom. At this time Austrian boys were trained to take an interest in dynastic history by way of stimulating their allegiance to the Habsburg idea. Hitler writes, many years afterwards, in *Mein Kampf*, of his history master with the greatest possible appreciation and gratitude. This Professor, Dr. Leopold Pötsch, seems to have taken much the view of this subject that Mr. H. G. Wells has always claimed for it in any modern scheme of education.

History for Adolf Hitler was by no means a story of the past, of very dead and gone people, and of happenings long since finished. History was made for him the very basis of the present, with living relationships reaching forward to the future. Adolf's school history began that fundamental and far-reaching preparation in his mind which was to issue later in no less portentous a guise than the " Weltanschauung," upon which the structure of his State is to be built up. He was, demonstrably, a very thoughtful boy. And here again at this point in his development we find the beginnings of that militant nationalism which latterly has so astounded our post-war world.

He has already been cracking his brains over obstructions which are merely territorial and not racial, as between Austrian Germans and German Germans, and now we find him distinguishing between the national feeling of an entire people and a mere dynastic patriotism. As has been already remarked, Austria was never at any time a " nation," merely the happy hunting-ground of a dynasty reaching back to the seventh century.

Austria existed only for the Habsburgs, as Vienna existed for the Court. All this clarified itself in the boy's mind very sharply and distinctly. He saw plainly enough that there could be no question of an Austrian nationality to become enthusiastic about in a great sprawling country inhabited by Czechs, Slavs, Ruthenians, Serbs, Croatians, Rumanians, Poles, Magyars, Italians and Gypsies, all in various stages of culture and civilisation some way behind that of the fortieth part of this numerical whole, the German Austrians just across the borders of the Reich.

It belongs to the history of the period to show how the Hungarians and the non-German races in the unwieldy Dual Monarchy were restive under the administratively Germanising tendencies of the Government. While the idea of nationality and any inclusion in the German Reich was obnoxious to the Austrian Government, which itself did not repose upon a national basis, nevertheless, under the " Bach " system every effort was made to Germanise the Croats and Hungarians most unacceptably to themselves.

The steady opposing growth of non-German feeling and tendency waxed ever stronger and stronger until, indeed, it was this which, together with the growing pan-Slavistic propaganda of Romanoff Russia, set the spark to the gunpowder in Europe in 1914. The heir-apparent to the throne of Austria, the Archduke Francis Ferdinand, a nephew of the childless old Emperor, was hated by dominant cliques in Government circles on account of his alleged pro-Czech and pro-Croatian sympathies, and his suspected intention of admitting Slavs to a greater share of political power when he should attain the throne.

All this, of course, is common property and past history, but to recall it here and now serves to show what were the formative influences brought to bear upon the mind of that singularly receptive boy, young Adolf Hitler. He brought the test of his history lessons under Dr. Pötsch to bear upon the everyday events and current talk of his own world, and unconsciously laid the groundwork for future activities in the political sphere as yet undreamed of.

The thing, of course, only came home to him then in concrete example.

First of all in the village school, when it came to singing the Austrian National Anthem, this Waldgebiet youngster and other intrepid spirits of like mind would substitute a German hymn. Whereupon, instant castigation followed, with the inevitable result of toughening their youthful defiance. And then again in Linz in the Realschule : were a boy to dare to turn up with a cornflower stuck behind his ear—the symbol of Germanic sympathies—the Herr Direktor was down upon him at once like a cartload of bricks, and he was sure of a couple of hours' detention.

If on the occasion of some local junketings a few poor German acrobats from across the border were to make a bid for popular favour, the schoolboys had to use every precaution not to get found out if they hobnobbed with them. If anybody " peached " the delinquents incurred the disgrace of having a mark made against their names for " bad behaviour." The bad behaviour, young Hitler soon realised well enough, was neither here nor there : what mattered was his " Deutschtum." Here, then, and thus early was one point of departure for his universal *Kampf*.

Adolf's keen study of the Franco-Prussian War and his intelligent interest in history made him even at this age thoroughly conversant with the politics of Middle Europe throughout the preceding century. This fact must be well realised if we are to understand the schoolboy's heat on this question of " Deutschtum," and his ardour about " nationality." Otherwise he comes before us a prig, as a somewhat doctrinaire and precocious youngster. He was not that, in the least, but a boy of flaming enthusiasms and all-devouring intelligence.

It may not be beside the point briefly to refresh the English reader's memory of an involved period of continental politics.

The question of the inclusion of Austria with Germany had been a more or less burning subject of mid-European debate from the time of the German Federation in 1815, (when the Austrian Ambassador occupied the chair of the great Assembly in Frankfurt), down to the present day. This loose German Federation of Central European States centred more and more upon Prussia, especially after the Prussian-Austrian War of 1866, ending in victory for Prussia. This and the outcome of the Franco-Prussian War altered the position and the outlook of affairs. In 1879 Austria and Prussia pledged themselves to build up a common future, much after the type foreshadowed by Naumann in his classic work *Mitteleuropa*, written in 1916.

How strange it is, in the light of to-day, to read such a passage as the following. " For centuries the

Empire of the Carolingians . . . has been non-existent.
Neither Imperial Austria nor Royal Prussia, when
separated from each other, were quite in a position
to carry on the imperial tradition because each only
possessed a part of the original power. This will be
so until it (the Empire) is born again out of the union
of the Habsburgs and the Hohenzollerns " (!)

In 1916 the old Emperor Francis Joseph died, and
the succession devolved upon an unfortunate man
who himself died miserably in exile only two years
later, execrated for his efforts to desert Germany,
and to make a separate peace with the Allied Powers
on behalf of a demoralised and exhausted Austria.
These pitiable royalties, and the musty old concepts
they stood for, constituted the political world in
which a boy, and then a young man, was growing up
who was to sweep them into such limbo of the forgotten as has never yet been known. Nothing at
first but a schoolboy at Linz, and then yet but an
individual bit of cannon fodder, fighting shoulder to
shoulder in the trenches with comrades as indistinguishable as himself, Adolf Hitler was as yet—to
come !

No one foresaw Hitler. If anyone had told Francis
Joseph in 1916 that the Habsburgs were even then
petering out and that it did not matter in the
least ; if anyone had told the Kaiser William hesitat-
ing at Spa in November, 1918, whether or not to
flee, that the destinies of the Vaterland were to pass
from his incapable hands to those infinitely stronger
of one of his soldiers of the line of whom nobody more
important than his company officer had as yet ever
heard ; if anyone so recently as eighteen months ago
had told the venerated President of the German
Republic that the ex-service man from Munich who

had founded such a tiresome and noisy Party, was to be the last hope of a country tottering to its final collapse—Emperor, Kaiser, and President alike would have exploded with incredulous and aristocratic scorn.

If anyone, indeed, in 1903 had told the Herr Direktor of the Realschule in Linz that the boy who had just incurred reproof and punishment for appearing in school with a cornflower stuck in his hair—that this boy was to rule the German world, leader and saviour, he too could not have believed. . . .

But so it was to be. And in consequence of all this historical reading and cogitating came the Austrian " Schulbub " by his concept of the value and dignity of strong national roots and ardent pride. Adolf felt himself German through and through : German to the core. He felt about that cornflower as a British youngster would feel about the Union Jack.

It is a very remarkable thing, in view of the more recent developments in Austria, that the proclamation made at three o'clock on the afternoon of the fateful November 18th, 1918, when the Austro-German National Assembly met in the Herrenhaus on the Franzenring in Vienna, should have confirmed to the letter all this passionate nationalistic feeling on the part of the youthful Hitler. " At this hour," said Dr. Renner (the man who drew up a Constitution for Austria after the collapse of the Habsburgs), " the German race throughout the world shall know that we are a single race with a single destiny." No answer was given in Berlin.

The German Government there was grappling with the hydra of immediate internal problems. Since then the European kaleidoscope has taken on another pattern, but all this brings out for foreigners the force of the impressions and convictions which went to the making of Hitler's mind as a boy and youth, and latterly as a young ex-service man.

In order to obtain a little first-hand information about Hitler's school days, the writer took a trip in June, 1934, to Linz, where he attended the Real-schule,[1] and had a chat with some of his former school comrades. It was no easy matter hunting these up, for most of them are by now scattered to the four corners of the earth.

For reasons easily to be understood, it were unwise just now to offer names. Suffice it to say that these following interesting particulars are as authentic as anything else in these pages. In Austria at present, i.e. to the authorities, it is looked upon as a crime to speak favourably of Adolf Hitler, and indeed, it was highly risky for every one of the writer's informants to talk to him about Hitler at all.

" I met him," said Herr A., " in 1901, here in the Realschule. We were thirty-two boys all told, all from the same class of life. There was no private school in Linz at that time.

" Hitler didn't live right in Linz, but just outside, at a place called Leonding. He ate his midday meal somewhere roundabouts, and was generally off home in the afternoon as soon as school was over. That's how it happened we didn't see so very much of him, except during school hours, and playing Indians, when he was always on hand.

" We all liked him, at desk and at play. He was no more hefty than the rest of us, but an enterprising little chap. He had ' guts.' He wasn't a hot-head, but really more amenable than a good many. He

---

[1] In the " Realschule," chief stress is laid on living languages and sciences.

exhibited two extremes of character which are not often seen in unison, he was a *quiet* fanatic. The whole class acknowledged this boy as the leader.

" His favourite lessons were history, geography and German. The history master was often astonished at Hitler's aptitude for this study.—Herr Dr. Huemer was our teacher for German. He always picked on Hitler for Repeater, that is, something would be read aloud to us and then one of the boys had to get up and tell it again in his own words. As a rule Hitler made the Repeat a jolly sight more interesting than the original.

" He was good at gym, too. He topped the gym class as long as he was at school.

" Hitler didn't bother very much about what he'd *got* to learn, only over what he wanted to learn ! When things were taught which did not interest him he read Cooper's *Leather Stocking* or something of that sort ; subjects which he liked such as history, however, he followed with close attention.

" The accounts of battles we played out for ourselves, in our ' Indians ' games, down by the Danube meadows. Hitler loved this sort of thing. He gloried in a scrum, and always made for the most redoubtable enemy, when the two would have a first-class wrestle. Hitler got ' all het up ' over this.

" He was very hot, too, like most of us youngsters, about being German. The stricter the measures taken by the Government to suppress this feeling about nationality the more dogged we became. Bismarck was for us a national hero. The Austrian authorities, of course, held his memory in the utmost detestation. The Bismarck song, and lots more German hymns and songs of the same character, were forbidden to be sung. It was a crime even to possess a sketch of Bismarck. Although, privately, our teachers felt well enough that we boys were in the right of it, they had to punish us severely for singing these songs and brandishing our German loyalties.

" Hitler attended our Realschule here for four years, when he suddenly fell ill. Oddly enough I never heard any more of him until I chanced on his name in the paper one day years and years afterwards. It said he was busying himself with politics in Munich.

" I saw him again in 1926. I went to his lodging there. He was awfully pleased to hear of old Linz again, and told me not to fail to look him up now and again. So, I've done so a few times, and always found him friendly, always the old ' Schul-Kamerad.' "

Herr X. was kind enough to introduce me to another " old boy " of the Linz Realschule, Herr Y., who had pretty much the same account to give of Adolf Hitler. One particular stands out.

" Once," said Herr Y., " during his school days Hitler stayed for a little time with an old lady in Linz. This old lady herself told the tale of how the boy was always buying candles, and she couldn't make out what it was he did always to be needing a light at night. She surprised him on one occasion, and found him doubled up over maps, very busy doing something to them with coloured pencils. She asked : ' Why, Adolf, what on earth do you suppose you are doing ? ' and he looked up and smiled and said : ' Studying maps.' "

Herr Y. showed me quite a treasure, a little water-colour he himself had once begun, as a boy at school, and which Hitler had finished for him. The subject was a picturesque little mill among the mountains. It was quite obvious where one artist had left off and the other had taken on. " Hitler was the best boy in the drawing class," said Herr Y., " he used shades in painting which never occurred to us, and painted things so lifelike we were all astonished."

I went on to Leonding in company with these two friends of Hitler's boyhood. We traversed the same road that he had trudged to and fro for four years, a green " Rucksack " on his back containing his books and pencils. For the most part it was steeply hilly, for Linz lies on the Danube plain. Then we came to fields and meadows set here and there with low but massy towers, relics of a Napoleonic day when watch was kept from these over the river below. The Kürnberg towers aloft on the right, crowned by the famous Kürnberg (Castle) in which the *Nibelungen- lied* is said to have been composed.

We had been walking about an hour when we came upon the outlying houses of Leonding. It is a typical little highland village, only to be found in Bavaria and Upper Austria. In the middle stands the village church, and a few steps further along, just across the street, lies the grass-grown cemetery. Here one dis- covers the grave of Hitler's parents.

In the immediate neighbourhood stands the peasant house in which the Hitler family lived. It has often changed hands since, hence the present occupant could tell me nothing of the former owners. Here, however, I came across yet a third school com- panion of young Adolf. Herr Z. had not much to add. " Sometimes we went after apples together," he said, " like the rest of the kids hereabouts," but Hitler never began munching his before everybody else had got one. Otherwise he tossed his over.

GRAVE OF HITLER'S PARENTS AT LEONDING
The plate is not symmetrically fixed on the headstone.

HOUSE OF HITLER'S PARENTS AT LEONDING. NEAR LINZ

Sometimes he'd sit on the churchyard wall, staring up at the stars. No one bothered about the boy staring up into the Austrian night. . . .

But to revert.

The tension at home over the question of Adolf's future was to resolve itself with tragic suddenness. Returning home one afternoon after a visit to a neighbour the father was seized in the street with a heart attack and died in the arms of a passer-by. This was on January 5th, 1903 ; Adolf was thirteen years old.

The shock had a characteristic reaction on Frau Clara Hitler. She felt herself bound to further her husband's design for the boy, and so he continued going to school for another three years with official-dom as the goal still before his eyes.

Then Adolf fell ill and was confined to bed for some considerable time with lung trouble. After that the doctor persuaded Frau Hitler that a sedentary life in an office was not going to be the best thing for the boy : in fact, he must not even go back to school for a year. The poor mother had another characteristic reaction, and now promised he should be taught draw-ing and painting instead.

But even now his hopes were to be frustrated. After a protracted illness Frau Hitler herself died on December 21st, 1908 ; not before the modest savings amassed by the husband had been exhausted. Nothing remained for Adolf but a negligible " orphan-pension," insufficient to keep body and soul toegther. The home was sold up, and at eighteen, Adolf Hitler came face to face with the problem of earning his livelihood.

He does not seem to have been in any two minds about what he meant to do.

He was going to Vienna to study art—to join the

picturesque and adventurous ranks of those who have
been content in every age and centre to live on a crust
in a garret, upborne by flowering genius and the
glorious comradeship of fellow-students, miserable
and enthusiastic as himself.

That he turned his steps to Vienna instead of to
Munich, the art capital of Germany, can be
accounted for in two ways. During the latter half
of the nineteenth century there had been a great
flowering of painting and architecture in Vienna. All
sorts of princely palaces had recently been erected in
that city. It abounded in art galleries and in
magnificent collections of pictures from the master-
pieces of almost every school in the world, to the
works of contemporary men. Vienna was a much
bigger capital than Munich, and Hitler had gathered
every bit of information he could about the great
academy schools there on the Schillerplatz, a stone's
throw from the wonderful Hofgarten and the
Opernring.

He could go by steamboat, which would take him
about nine hours, or third class on a slow train and be
there in seven. It was simpler, and a little nearer
than Munich. . . . Germans living in foreign states
along the frontier wanted at that time rather to form
a German colony, and so lead to German expansion,
than to return to the Reich itself. Young Hitler,
for all his militant " Deutschtums," saw nothing
inconsistent in going to imperial Vienna for art,
rather than to Munich.

CHAPTER II

VIENNA

THE Reichskanzler has often been acclaimed as an artist. In him we have that very unusual combination, an artist and a keen man of practical affairs. His passion for music is well known, especially for Wagner. But, indeed, his highest and most persistent aspiration as a young man was for painting. He had, as a matter of fact, the architect's eye. Grandiose building, imposing vistas, grandly planned elevations, the fine light and shade of dome, architrave, column, lintel, inspired him, as landscape or portraiture inspires others.

It does not appear that young Adolf had ever been in Vienna before the fateful day, when with fifteen gulden in a bag slung round his neck, his sketches clipped under his arm, and all his worldly goods in a small case in his hand, he arrived at the Westbahnhof full of the highest boyish hopes and purpose. Undismayed by the magnificence of one of the most beautiful cities of Europe—perhaps intoxicated by it—or by the stir and traffic in the streets, he made a bee line down the Mariahilfer-strasse to the Schillerplatz and the heart of imperial Vienna.

His idea was to apply for entrance to the schools of the Academy of Art.

As he entered the beautiful square, dominated by one of those public statues than which nothing more

fittingly artistic is to be seen in any other city, and
confronted the imposing academy at last, the young
man's spirits could not but sink a trifle. Heavens !
here were tens—scores—perhaps hundreds of aspirants like himself swarming up the steps between the
two great bronze Centaurs which flanked the entrance
to the vestibule. How would his work stand comparison or competition with so many others ? . . .
Everybody else seemed full of confidence and
energy.

Bracing himself for more of an ordeal than he had
quite expected, Adolf joined the throng and presently
found himself but a unit of the long queue of candi-
dates awaiting admission to the schools. Everything
depended on his sketches now ! He thought of them
with a fresh access of hope and confidence, and
clipped the humble portfolio containing them more
closely to his side. With the pride of utter inexperi-
ence he could not but reassure himself the examiners
would be suitably impressed.

.   .   .   .   .

The writer of these pages has been very kindly
favoured by the present Director of the Viennese Art
Academy with the names of the professors who
directed its various activities about this time. It
might have been Herr Professor Christian Gripenkerl,
Franz Rumpler, Julius Schmidt or another who at
length ruffled over the young Hitler's sketches with
rapid and none too readily arrested hand. The youth
himself was not necessarily aware of the gentleman's
identity—who cares on these critical occasions for
who the examiner may be ? All Adolf knew was that
the hand summarily clapped his portfolio to, and
pushed it back to him.

" No, my boy," came the verdict crisply, " you're not cut out for a painter. You've come to the wrong place here."

Hitler could hardly believe his ears. But this was incredible—!

" Your aptitude," added the professor, softening the blow, " appears to be for architecture. I should advise you to apply to the School of Building. The porter will show you the way."

Speechless, Adolf had no option but to make way for the next candidate for summary extinction. Not quite extinguished, though ; bewildered, incredulous, unbelievably quenched. Was there really no promise in his work ? Hadn't it been worth the pains and hopes and all the fond delight he had taken over it ? Had there been any pause, the blow might have sent him stunned and irresolute away, but then and there Adolf found himself being ushered elsewhere down a long, imposing corridor lined with Greek statuary, only to be brought forwith into the presence of another Herr Professor.

Again the portfolio was lugged forth, and Professor Wagner or Professor Oliman, (whichever it might have been), claimed possession.

This time there was less haste ; less prompt decision. In fact, one or two of Adolf's drawings rather seemed to take the master's fancy.

" H'm, not bad ! Not at all bad ! "

A scrutiny, a pause—more sketches turned over, —then came a sharp bespectacled glance into the candidate's anxious and eager face.

" Where have you studied architecture ? "

" Nowhere," Adolf was obliged to own, " I've not had any lessons——"

The examiner seemed loath to credit it. Turning

over yet more sketches with an approving eye, he insisted :

" You mean to tell me you were never in a School of Building ? Not even at a School of Art Industry ? "

" No," repeated Adolf, " never."

The professor shrugged his shoulders disappointedly. " That's unfortunate," he said, " I'm afraid there's nothing to be done, then, here. This is no place for beginners. You must try elsewhere—get some groundwork in first."

And again the portfolio, clapped to, came back to him rejected.

Adolf realised, dully, there was nothing for it but to go. Presumably he suffered all the agonies characteristic of the beginner's experience. The way had failed to open. His pictures had proved no Open Sesame to the career for which he had put up so strenuous a fight at home.

At a total and sudden loss, Adolf came out again into the gay Viennese sunshine, into the proud white and green of the squares and boulevards, nothing now but a stranger, and one at a frightfully loose end. . . .

He made his way, somehow, to the humbler parts of the city and found some sort of a cheap lodging. Then in a few days his money was gone and he came face to face with the fact that to eat he must work and earn.

Adolf wandered about Vienna before he found a job, as indeed he was often to wander about it hungry and workless during the next two years, with nothing but the cold comfort of the city's historicity and beauty upon which to stay his hope and courage. His talent, they said, lay in the direction of architecture—here, indeed, was architecture

enough to stare at all day long, and wonderful
gardens to sit in, and great galleries to visit.

.   .   .   .   .

The Chancellor has written at some length in
Mein Kampf upon art.

It is quite obvious that the Führer adheres in
his taste to the strictly academic in painting. He
has no sympathy whatever for " Bolshevism in art "
by which he designates its modern post-War tendencies. This fact may certainly be ascribed to the
impressions he received at this period in Vienna
from his wanderings at a loose end through the great
collections there. In the Historical Museum of Art
he could follow all that is finest in painting from the
Italian Primitives down to the great Dutch land-
scapists of the seventeenth century, and at last to
Velasquez.

It would require more space than is at the writer's
disposal to offer here any notes on the reaction of
German and Austrian art over the turn of the century
to the influence of the various new schools in Paris
which were already developed far ahead of those in
any other country, and which had already laid the
foundations for those wildest departures from the accepted, (the academic), which only really soared into
complete incomprehensibility after the Great War.

Had Adolf succeeded in passing the august
Renaissance portals of the Art Academy in Vienna, it is
possible he might have viewed some of the expressions
of contemporary art with the insight which only
comes of technical artistic training, and of interest in
technical artistic problems. For although the first
decade of the twentieth century was marked by no
particular " ism " in the art life of Vienna, the

students there were yet quite free to follow the
dictates of their own inspiration, to make their own
incursions into the unknown and as yet unattempted.

As it was, Adolf Hitler remained outside, as the
Führer may remain a " groundling." The problems
of art are not exercising the credulity of the public
and the ingenuity of the critics to-day as they exercised both perhaps a decade ago. The Führer in
Mein Kampf has delivered himself of an indictment
of extravagance, decadence and insanity in painting,
not so much as an artist as a moralist. He does not
like the type of mentality expressed by that art
which has thrown overboard all the aspiration and
the technique of the painting he saw as a boy in
Vienna. He hopes little from modernism in art as
an educative factor in the life of the sound nation.
There will be hundreds of people who can endorse
his forceful pages on painting, who cannot, perhaps,
see eye to eye with him on all other matters.

As we shall have occasion to relate later on,
Adolf by no means abandoned his drawing after the
rebuff he received on his arrival in Vienna. He
persevered with his pencil, confining himself almost
exclusively to architectural subjects, and attained
sufficient proficiency to fall back upon this sort
of work for a living when all else failed. During the
War he has done some sketching in the trenches.
Some of his things are likely to be seen in the Brown
House at Munich to-day.

The late Professor Troost designed the Brown
House after a rough design and plan of the Führer.
It was to the Studio of this artist that Adolf Hitler
always betook himself in later years when affairs of
State permitted. Hitler personally drew the plans
for the various alterations which became necessary

at Haus Wachenfeld (his country place near Munich)
after his assumption of office. He is still keen about
architecture and building, notwithstanding the immense press of affairs which otherwise occupy his
time and attention. His artistic talent lies chiefly
in this direction. Instead of becoming an architect
in bricks and mortar, however, he has become the
architect of rebuilt Germany.

.   .   .   .   .

Wandering about Vienna, wondering what on
earth he was to do, penniless and alone, Adolf
noticed that everywhere building seemed to be going
on. Enormous palaces were in course of construction
all over the city. It occurred to him one day in
some such busy spot to beard the foreman and ask
to be taken on, brick-layer, mortar mixer, hod
carrier—anything—for a daily wage. The foreman
eyed him over, bethought himself a moment, then
with a nod assented.

There could not have been much unemployment in
Vienna at that date. Adolf, at any rate, was fixed
up for a while. They took him on as a day labourer,
liable any time to dismissal, and paid him scarcely
enough to keep body and soul together. It was a
mere pittance. He found a lodging, but a pretty
wretched one, in a dim, damp, sunless hovel, shared
with a work-mate at the back of a cellar used as a
dwelling-place. The work was hard, and for five
solid years Hitler never knew what it was not to go
hungry, daily.

The story of these years in Vienna has been more
fully and more biographically recounted in the *Kampf*
than anything preceding them. To many students
of Hitler's life they are the most significant of all.

It was in Vienna, in constant need and poverty,
losing a job as soon as finding it, rubbing shoulders
with want and vice and misery in every form,
having endless political wrangles with fellow-workmen, none too friendly disposed towards one, somewhat hard of persuasion, tramping the streets,
observant of all who passed—that Adolf Hitler
sensibly or insensibly laid the foundations for all his
future thinking, study, and activity.

Still a lad in his teens, he had these hard times
to pass in the school of adversity. As a result he
laid it down afterwards in one of the stressed passages
in his book that the Social Problem must be tackled
from below and not from above. That is the dictum
of the man who has been through the mill, not of the
theoretical economist.

His mind was acutely busy, taking in every
problem that presented itself, from the problem of the
despairing woman who on pay day fails to wring a
coin from the still more despairing and therefore
drunken father of her starving children, to the most
philosophical problems of impossible political
expediencies. The Vienna of that time furnished
an extraordinarily strong and analytical young
mind with an amazing human phantasmagoria
upon which to exercise itself. Hitler confronted,
as a boy of sixteen and seventeen, the Gordian
knots which as Chancellor he cuts without further
ado. But it was as that boy under twenty that his
decisions were reached how these things were each
and severally to be dealt with.

He came face to face with Communism, Marxism,
Jewdom, with Capital and Labour, with problems
of race deterioration, immorality and disease, and
instead of accepting the proffered panacea of any

already existing theories of betterment, he smashed, as it were, every one of these hard stones to powder in the powerful machine of his own thought, and began afresh, from the very beginning and with very far-reaching vision to build up in his own mind the entire State afresh as a State fit for decent human beings to live in.

He tells of a discussion, one day, on a scaffolding high up on one of the palaces of Vienna, between himself and some Communist fellow-workmen. The young Hitler had not yet made up his mind as to his own political creed. The Communists were impatient and offered him the alternative of joining their lot or of being summarily stood off the job. It was in the midday pause : they had been arguing and munching bread on the scaffolding.

When the hour struck for turning to again young Hitler found he wasn't wanted any more. The foreman dismissed him. . . . He could not persuade himself that these Marxist mates of his were in the right of it. Merely, so far, from observation, it seemed to him that the Marxist theory offered a paradise quite impractical in reality ; he had no sympathy with its anti-religious side, and no faith in its message to the working man.

So things went from worse to worse. Presently he could no longer afford to share the hovel behind the cellar. He crept at night into some more or less sheltered corner of a courtyard or alley in any one of the narrow streets in the older quarter of the city, if any such spot could be called sheltered in notoriously " windy Vienna." His sleep, there, on the cold hard ground, was broken by the noises of the town and by the sound of distant military music in the cafés and the parks.

By day the gorgeous panorama of the gay and polished life of the great Viennese thoroughfares of pleasure offered itself to his moody contemplation. He contrasted not only his own wretched lot and hopeless outlook with that of the bespangled men and women of the Graben, the Kaerntnerstrasse, the Ringstrasse, but the lot of the hundreds, nay, thousands of others in like case with himself. Instead of driving Hitler into the ranks of the Reds, the spectacle had the opposite effect upon him. He believed that the hideous contrast he saw between rich and poor in Vienna was due to " Marxismus "— a radical, (and later on he came to believe it was a purposeful), misdirecting of the proletariat.

From time to time he got a job. But sooner or later the question was sure to crop up whether he would join a Workers' Union. It speaks volumes for the young man's conscientiousness, that in spite of the inevitable consequence of refusal, he was immensely chary of committing himself. He always got involved in the lunch hour in hot political discussion with his mates. He braced himself to refute such postulates as that the " Nation " was nothing but a concept invented for the advantage of the ruling classes, that the " Law " was only a means of oppressing the poor, that the " School " was a system of punishment, and that " Religion," and " Morality" only amounted to an opiate for the common folk.

It was all new and strange to him, since hitherto he had heard nothing of Karl Marx and his theories, or of the system of Trade Unions. These debates helped him to hammer out his own ideas on the hard anvil of theses utterly repugnant to his personal sense and feeling. He began now to distinguish between the different party programmes of the time, but viewed them each and every one with reserve and criticism. For one thing, he distrusted the universal vote of the Social Democrats to better the state of things just as profoundly as he distrusted Communism.

We get the impression of a fearfully serious and responsible-minded young man debating these things as youths of his age in England might debate the chances of the cup-tie. Undernourished and wretchedly clothed, there was nothing he could afford by way of interest in life except these wordy arguments—no fun, no recreation, no friendships,— no girls. As soon as it appeared to him demonstrable that the Trade Unions were nothing but the tools of " Marxismus," he decided absolutely against them. It was no use bothering him to join any such thing.

" All right, then," his mates would greet him as he turned up at work next day, " you won't join the class-conscious Workers' Front ?—you're a traitor. We've only short shrift for the likes of you. You can clear——"

Once an older man, sorry for the youth, mumbled in his ear as he turned to go :

" What's the use ? It's no good holding out against 'em. They're in the majority, they are—— You've got your grub to earn."

Out on the streets again, Adolf found a queer shelter in the lamp-room of a sort of labourers' barracks. He could roll up here among a collection of indescribable lumber, and, sleepless in the dirt and fetid air breathed over and over again by a number of wretched companions in the night, cudgel his brains as to the outlook. Not the least of his misery came from neighbouring sounds of children crying and of a wife being beaten by her drunken husband.

Everything around him, especially this screaming and these blows, convinced him that these were the consequences and the victims of a teaching criminally false in essence. In the reek and dirt of that place Hitler's youthful resolution hardened to fight " Marxismus " tooth and nail.

But, meanwhile, for himself something else must be tried. Two years of these experiences had sufficed to make it clear that there was no place for him as an unskilled workman and a political free thinker in the ranks of Viennese labour.

He harked back to his old love—drawing. In spite of the death blow to his artistic ambitions with which he had been greeted on arrival in the capital, Adolf felt that this after all offered the only way out of his difficulties. He scraped together somehow or other the few groschen necessary to buy the most essential tools of the poor painter's trade, and hit on a fourth-story attic in a third-class lodging house by way of a studio.

For the next three struggling, saving, starving, working years Adolf Hitler's life took on a strange complexion. His was not the picturesque and har-rowing story of the garret artist living on the flame of his own unrecognised genius with which we are so familiar. What sketches he made, he sold, and so managed to live, but neither his talent nor his market led to much. His interest in politics, so rudely awakened, really coloured all this period. Now that he had time to read, he read, he studied ! He laid hands on every pamphlet, paper, book or manifesto going which might throw light for him on the theories and principles by which the working lives of his former associates were determined, and to whose ruthlessness his own experience bore witness.

Hitler's serious political study began in this studio of his in a Viennese attic.

And then something else attracted his attention, infinitely far-reaching in its consequences.

Prior to his arrival in Vienna Adolf Hitler had never seen a Jew. In Vienna at that time, however, out of a population of some 1,364,500 inhabitants, 118,000 were Jews. One of their synagogues, a brick building in Moorish style, stood in the Tempelgasse, not far from the great Praterstrasse, and in the same Bezirk or quarter of the city, Leopoldstadt, was to be found the synagogue of the Turkish Jews.

It was the odd appearance of a passer-by in his gaberdine caftan which arrested the country youth's eye. He was standing looking in a bookshop window at the moment. Was this tall black figure with the sharp black eyes and queer locks pendant on either side of the face a Jew ? Well, then, what was a Jew ? Was a Jew a German ?

In Linz there had been but few, and these so indistinguishable from the rest of the townsfolk that Adolf knew no other distinction than that they professed a different religion. That they had often been oppressed and persecuted on account of this was also within his knowledge, and the fact was capable of calling up his sympathies. He thought such a thing as Jew-baiting was barbarous. The sudden encounter with this Rabbi gave a new turn to his all-devouring political curiosity, and he determined, next, to study some of the anti-Jewish literature disseminated by the anti-Semite Party.

At the time it hardly satisfied him. He saw in it

mere propaganda. Only later when the " Juden-frage " came to be identified in his mind with the " Marxismus " about which it was already fully made up, did he develop that attitude towards the Jews which it has been so particularly hard for English people to understand.

Those who have had no occasion to study the long-standing question of Anti-Semitism in Europe, and to whom the Jewish question as it may present itself in England presents no particularly urgent or dangerous features, must turn to the pages of *Mein Kampf*, or to General Goering's recent book *Germany Re-born*, to learn the reasons for Hitler's hatred of the machinations of the Jews in Germany. As a youth he had opportunity enough for observations on this head in Vienna.

The first unpleasant discovery he made was that most of the pornography to be observed in the book shops, photo-shops, films, etc. etc. (and Vienna could rival Paris in this respect), in nine cases out of ten issued from Jewish sources. He turned his attention to the Viennese press, and from respect and admiration passed to contempt for the venality and partisanship. He pursued his solitary and brooding studies and enquiries, as the questions arising out of these observations assumed ever more and more importance for his comprehension of the Social-Democratic system which appeared to be responsible for much that struck him as politically iniquitous. He traced everything ultimately to Marxismus, and Marxismus itself to Jewish support and sponsorship.

The National-Socialist case against the Jews has been set forth lucidly enough over and over again. It has received much attention abroad at the hands of friendly or unfriendly exponents of the Third

Reich. It would serve little purpose to cover the ground again here, especially as we have only to do with those interests of the young Hitler in Vienna, which had so great a share in the formation of his political ideas. It was in these years of bitterness and poverty he came to hate the Jew for his financial strangle-hold on all classes of the population, and for the cosmopolitan and materialistic influence he exercised, fatal to the existence of a healthy national growth and sentiment.

Even after the drastic steps recently taken to reduce the number of Jews in Germany and to curtail their disproportionate activity in every sphere of German life, ninety-five per cent of the Jewish population of the Reich still remain.

" I am an ex-Service man," a Jew in Munich recently told the writer, " and a strictly orthodox Hebrew. But I have all the rights of a German because I fought in the War. Hitler is against us but he is as just as anybody can be." This ex-soldier is in fact actually living in a house once occupied by the Führer for eight years. He showed the writer Hitler's room, and spoke of him with extraordinary appreciation. " He did more for my people than many a man has done," he observed, " in making a favourable exception for all of us ex-Service Jews. We have nothing to fear, even to-day."[1]

The idea of the present book is far more to offer a human picture of the Führer, than to make any further contributions (from the Nazi standpoint or any other), on matters which are looked upon outside the Reich as highly contentious. But should the reader, especially the English reader, desire to arrive

[1] Law-abiding Jews living in Germany to-day, go about their business much as usual.

at some real understanding of the grounds upon which
Adolf Hitler as a young open-minded man, new to the
" Judenfrage " in all its aspects, conceived so deep
a hatred of the Jewish race, he cannot do better than
spend the inside of five minutes over a statement of
the case against the Jews in Austria and in Vienna
which precedes Nazi sources altogether.

It was written, in fact, just about the very time
Hitler first turned his attention to the question. In
The Modern Jew, by Arnold White (Heinemann, 1899),
two works are quoted which put the matter in a
nutshell, and put it beyond dispute, the *Antisemiten
Katechismus* of Theodor Fritsch, and *Die Judenfrage
in Oesterreich*, by Crémieux.

It was not Hitler who discovered that " the Jews
. . . form in reality a political and commercial
company . . . which aims at the subjugation and
exploitation of non-Jewish peoples. . . . By the
practice of usury they have completely ruined many
. . . and by dishonourable means and secret co-
operation have so undermined established trades and
industries, and have got so many branches of business
into their own hands that honest non-Jewish trades-
men can scarcely remain in them any longer."

Hitler discovered, and with truth, " that they have
obtained possession of the public press and use it for
their own purposes." Even his observations about
pornography and prostitution were not wrongfully
ascribed. The contemporary indictment continues :
" One would scarcely assert too much if one said that
the majority of unfortunate girls who form the prosti-
tutes of the larger towns have fallen through Jewish
depravity : also that the notorious ' girl-commerce '
will soon be carried on exclusively by the Jews."

" The trouble," commented the English author,

" grows as the years roll by, and the time is not far distant when Jewish ascendency in Austria will bring new forces of resistance into being."

.   .   .   .   .

On the right-hand side of the Franzenring in Vienna, facing the Volksgarten, itself part of the gardens of the Imperial Palace, stands the Reichsrats-Gebäude, or Austrian Houses of Parliament. The curving sweep of a broad approach leads to a fine Greek portico, with fluted columns and majestic tympanum above. The Chamber of Deputies on the left and the Upper House on the right form two independent buildings adorned with marble statuary and bas-reliefs and great bronze quadrigæ.

Adolf Hitler, out of a job, came here, pencil in hand, to distract his thoughts with the problem of these classic and dignified perspectives. It was a great change of subject from the wonderful Gothic of St. Stephen's or the cheerful baroque of the Pigtail[1] Period represented in the old Rathhaus in the Wipplingerstrasse. But as the young man's preoccupation with political ideas came to account for more and more of his time, he found himself rather concerned with what might be going on within the Parliament House than with its exterior attractions.

One day, in fact, he essayed to enter the peristyle. A functionary enquired his business.

" I would like to hear a debate," replied Hitler, " that's all."

" You can't go in without a ticket," the man replied, indicating a notice to this effect, " you must obtain one the day before."

So that was that ! Hitler departed, bought his

---

[1] Zopfzeit, *Anglicé Georgian.*

D

ticket, and turned up promptly on the morrow, full of
interest, respect and anticipation. This was a
tremendous occasion for him, actually to be going to
witness something of history in the making.

" You'll find a seat in the Second Gallery," he was
told, and up he found his way. Along a corridor with
endless doors, on the one side he went. Opening one
of these with noiseless care, he peeped within. Yes,
this seemed to be it, all right—this was the Second
Gallery. Hitler went down a steep little gangway
and insinuated himself into the first vacant seat
which offered itself without inconvenience to anybody. . . .

But, after all, *was* this the right place ? Things
seemed rather odd. Down there in the Chamber
people were jostling each other in the most unruly
sort of groups, shouting, laughing, joking, gesticulat-
ing like an excited mob on 'Change. All was inatten-
tion and confusion. It took the astonished young
man quite a few moments before he was able to
distinguish that somebody actually seemed to be
addressing the House ! A Member occupied the
Rostrum and was short-sightedly reading from a
paper held close to his face, while his right arm made
sundry gestures by way of emphasis and accompaniment. Only by this token, however, could it possibly
be supposed that he was speaking ! No one took the
remotest notice.

The universal uproar around suggested nothing so
much as an annual fair. Then suddenly the Member
finished : stuck his speech in a case, and came down
the few steps which led from the Präsidium to the
floor. A few of his partisans, apparently, chancing
to notice the fact, applauded perfunctorily. Whereupon an extraordinary individual, half-hidden behind

stacks of books and papers, rose up behind the Rostrum and rang a delirious little bell for silence.

For the space of a moment the universal cachinnation died down ; a few heads were turned in the direction whence the new noise came. A second Member sprang up the steps, two at a time, and burst into a flood of extempore speech. Hitler could not understand a word of it. Then it suddenly occurred to him—this wasn't German. This was some Slavonic tongue ! " What the deuce is it all about ? " he wondered, " and however many of them follow him ? "

Hitler had scarcely been sitting in the Second Gallery an hour before he discovered that here in the Austrian Parliament were represented four or five nationalities, no Member of which understood a word of what the others in turn might chance to orate about. Now it was a Czech speaking, now a Ruthenian, now a Serb, now a Crotian, and none but the Czechs, Ruthenians, Serbs or Crotians in the House understood each orator in turn.

The speeches were punctuated by wild outcries of approval or disapproval as the case might be from the parties concerned. Not infrequently a hand-to-hand fight seemed imminent, when the piercing clamour of the little bell did what it could to call the House to order. Whereupon the speaker would resume, and again work himself up to oratorical frenzy, when the chance passing of a German Member across the floor would provide an opportune diversion.

Incited to fury, every member of the speaker's party would precipitate himself upon the offender, and the next instant the whole Chamber would be involved in a ding-dong fight. A bundle of papers,

accurately flung, landed bang in the honourable and
gallant Member's face, whereupon he immediately
collapsed. The German delegates got together and
hung together, and made common cause against the
rest of the heterogeneous assembly. Whatever could
be seized and used as a weapon was snatched up and
flung or banged or whacked or transformed into some
wildly launched projectile.

The din waxed indescribable. One couldn't hear
oneself speak. One couldn't even hear the frenzied
bell however desperately it was plied by the man
behind the Rostrum. This individual suddenly gave
up—grabbed his portfolio—and shot off out of a side
door. Next thing the astonisher onlooked knew was
that the various international scrums going on all
over the floor of the House seemed to come unstuck,
and a general rush ensued towards the exits.

Horrified and amazed Hitler turned to a neighbour
in the gallery and ventured to enquire if this was the
conclusion of the sitting.

" Oh, no," the other answered indifferently, " it's
only an interval." He seemed to consider things
quite in order.

Presently, to be sure, the Members came trooping
back, heralded by the President who himself, this
time, was busy with the bell, very self-assured and
bland. A few of the Deputies came down into the
Chamber and duly seated themselves. Then one of
them, a tall thin man with a dry savant's face, rose
and with dignity ascended the Rostrum. Here and
there the Members prepared to listen, many indi-
viduals dotted about in singular isolation.

The speech had to do with Agriculture—mainly.
As it dragged its length along all pretence was gradually abandoned of paying it any sort of attention.

The Deputies foregathered in knots to talk, or sat reading the newspaper, or scribbled letters. Only the speaker's adherents made the slightest show of supporting him. The majority of the House had departed to the restaurant and was refreshing itself after the previous exciting passage. . . .

Adolf Hitler, up in the second gallery, had had enough !

To the serious-minded young man who had come here, full of respect, for a sort of object lesson at first hand in the working of that grand idea the parliamentary system, the scene he had witnessed was neither laughable nor despicable. It was tragic. Hitler had already read everything upon which he could lay his hands about the English parliamentary system, and he had come to the Reichsrats-Gebäude that day with his head full of fine political theory. What he saw seemed to bear it out in no single jot or tittle.

He couldn't laugh ! Rather he went down into the streets of Vienna once more sick with incredulous disappointment. He retreated to his studious attic and turned to his books again, and wrestled week after week with the tough problem of the wide discrepancy between theory and practice. He took to haunting the Parliament, passing whole hours in the listeners' gallery, loath to credit that the shocking impression he had at first received there was anything but transitory and accidental. Such a conclusion, however, could not be sustained. The Austrian Parliament continually displayed itself to him in the light of an irrational bear garden.

Hitler has said of himself that his impression once strongly recorded, his judgment once clearly formed, he never went back on it. This chaotic and ridiculous

Austrian assembly certainly had a decisive and far-reaching effect upon his earnest and searching mind. It did much at its own date and in its own way to help Hitler to form the idea of the responsible individual as Leader as contrasted with a contradictory, irresponsible and incapable majority.

In such adventures, such hardships and such studies, five years went by for Hitler in Vienna, two years as casual labourer, and three years as starveling painter. They had been years of grinding poverty, but of rich experience. He had come thither as a mere youth. He was to leave the city a grave-minded man. These years in Vienna are looked upon as the formative years in his life, the most significant for all that was to come.

Looking back upon them, later, the Führer has never seen the necessity for changing conclusions arrived at during that time. He left Vienna at last in despair of making good there, and turned his face to Munich instead. A confirmed enemy of Marxism, and of the Jews, he had as yet no idea of politics as a career. He does not seem to have considered himself in such a rôle at all. He was devoted to his pencil and dependent on it. He came to Munich seeking nothing but some sort of a studio, and some fresh opportunity to dispose of his unassuming artistic wares.

CHAPTER III

ONE sunny day, then, in the spring of the year 1912, Adolf Hitler arrived in Munich. He came down the steps of the Central Station with a delighted sense of having left Vienna. Here, rather, was the city of his choice, where everything German in him could expand and flourish ! The speech of the streets sounded familiar to his ear; it was glorious to have got away from the hotch-potch of Vienna and to find himself among the friendly cordial Bavarians. From that day to this, indeed, Munich has been first of all German cities in the Führer's heart.

On that bright morning, twenty-two years ago, the young man turned left at the Karlsplatz and presently came into the Königsplatz. He was enormously impressed at the sight of it. On the one hand stood the column of the Glyptothek and on the other those of the Staatsgalerie, while the Propyläen closed the majestic vista.

After a moment or two of absorbed admiration, he pursued his way up the broad Briennerstrasse, glancing about him right and left taking in every detail of the handsome street. At last, however, he found himself in the Schleissheimerstrasse. At that time this was an unpretentious thoroughfare, somewhat narrow and without much traffic. On either side were rows of long grey lodging-houses with smallish

55

shops on the ground floor. Hitler fetched up in front of one of these little windows on which was stuck a handwritten notice, " Furnished rooms to let to respectable man." ("An soliden Herrn möbliertes Zimmer zu vermieten.") Just the thing, he thought, for him ! He glanced again at the shop window. It was that of a master tailor rejoicing in the name of Popp.

Quickly making up his mind, Hitler opened the door of the house and clambered his way up the dark and narrow staircase until he came to the third floor, where, apparently, was this room to let.

Frau Popp herself loves to tell the tale to this day.

" Yes, I remember it all as if it were yesterday. It was a fine Sunday afternoon in springtime, 1912, when somebody knocked and I went to open the door. A young man stood there and said he'd like to see the room we had to let. So I showed it to him. It wasn't quite so well furnished then as it is now. There was only the bed in it, a table, a sofa and a chair. But those two oleographs still hanging on the wall were there then. The young man and I soon came to terms. He said it would do him all right, and paid a deposit.

" I remember I went back into the kitchen and told our Peppi and our Liesel—they were only eleven and seven then—not to make so much noise, we'd got a new lodger.

" Then later I went in again to ask the young man to fill up his registration particulars. In small some-what cramped handwriting he scribbled : ' Adolf Hitler, Architekturmaler aus Wien ' (Architectural painter from Vienna).

" Next morning my Herr Hitler went out and came back again in no time with an easel he had picked up somewhere. He began his painting straight away and stuck to his work for hours. In a couple of days I saw two lovely pictures finished and lying on the table, one of the Cathedral, and the other of the Theatinerkirche. After that my lodger used to go out early of a morning with his portfolio under his arm in search of customers. He generally visited the same set of people who got interested in his work and sometimes purchased his sketches.

" But he spent a tremendous lot of time, too, in the State Library. He was always getting new books from there. After he'd spent the livelong day at his painting and drawing and what all, he'd often and often sit up all night over these books. I had a look, too, what sort they were—all political stuff and that, and how to go on in Parliament ! I couldn't make it out a bit what he had to do with such things, and why he bothered his head over them.

" At the beginning he used to go out to eat in some restaurant or other. Then, after a week or two, he began bringing home a bit of sausage for dinner or a *Nuss-Zopf* (small white loaf). I supposed he had a bit of money put by somewhere. I know he must have pinched and scraped all that first year he was with us, and often got up hungry from table. He was very well behaved, and never thought of coming into my kitchen when he wanted a drop of water for his tea without knocking. I'd holler, ' Come in ! ' and he'd open the door and say, ' Do you mind ? ' polite as anything.

" Of course, we said he was to come right in and sit down. Then he'd ask permission to make his tea. We said he didn't need to make any fuss, he was welcome any time, but he was always like that. I never in all my life knew such a good-mannered young man !

" My husband was sorry for him having to stint
himself so hard, and more than once asked him to
sit down and have a bite with us. But he never
would, he never did. I liked that in him very much.

" Then whole weeks would go by without Hitler so
much as budging out of the house. He just camped
in his room like a hermit with his nose stuck in those
thick, heavy books and worked and studied from
morning to night.

" During the whole of the two years he was with
us I can't call to mind that he ever had a visitor.
Only once in a while did he ever get a letter—from
his sister who was married and lived in Vienna. Any
how I imagined that was who it was from. He never
spoke of having any relatives.

" We often asked him to come in the little kitchen
of an evening and be with us a bit. But he always
excused himself very nicely and said he'd got to work.
Once, I remember, I said right out : ' Herr Hitler,
don't take it amiss, but you'll make yourself ill with
those books and keeping on reading and reading as
you do ! What's all that reading got to do with your
painting ? ' Hitler got up and smiled and took me
by the arm, ' Dear Frau Popp,' he said, ' does anyone
know what is and what isn't likely to be of use to him
in life ? '

" Well—that's just how he lived here with us those
two years. He never changed his ways, painting all
day, and studying, studying, studying all evening
and night. Things seemed to look up a bit for him
as time went on ; he found a better market for his
pictures.

" And then came August, 1914, and the War ! I can
see him now, that young Hitler, standing showing me
the card he got from the Kabinettskanzlei letting

COAT OF ARMS, SHOWING THE SWASTIKA IN THE BENEDICTINE MONASTERY AT LAMBACH

BENEDICTINE MONASTERY AT LAMBACH-AM-TRAUN, AUSTRIA; THE SCHOOL WHERE HITLER AS A CHILD BECAME FAMILIAR WITH THE SYMBOL OF THE SWASTIKA

him join the German Army." (Hitler as an Austrian
subject had to obtain his Government's permission
to enlist in a Bavarian regiment.)

" When he was in training he used to come along
and see us sometimes, glad of a rest from drill and
exercises. My husband used to send young Peppi
out to get him a glass of beer (Münchner Löwenbräu,
possibly, the best in existence, and a ' Stein,' less
elegant than a ' Glas '). Hitler'd drink it, just to
please the youngster and us, though I know well he
didn't hold with alcoholic drink even then. Only he
was that obstinate—he *would* pay for it himself !
We didn't want him to, but if we hadn't let him he'd
say, ' All right, Frau Popp, then I don't blow in
again ! You haven't any too much to spend.'

" He came the day before the regiment left
Munich to say good-bye. He gripped my husband by
the hand and said, ' If I go west, Herr Popp, you'll
write my sister, won't you, in case she'd like to have
my bits of things ? Otherwise—keep 'em yourself.
Sorry to give you the trouble.' He shook hands with
me, too, while I stood there and cried—we were all
that fond of him ! He hugged Peppi and Liesel,
they'd always been such favourites of his, and turned
tail and ran.

" Then he wrote to us from the Front. Once,
though, when we sent him a little parcel at Christmas
he was downright angry. He wrote back he had quite
enough to eat, and we weren't to deprive ourselves
on his account. He was very strong on the point,
was Hitler.

" Yes, well then, when the War was over he turned
up in our street again and would have come back to
us, but that the boy and girl were growing up now
and we no longer had that room to let. Otherwise

we'd have been as glad as glad to have him. So he bundled his things together and hunted round for somewhere else to go. He left his easel and gave it to Peppi, ' Peppi shall paint pictures on it, eh ? '

" He often came to see us, though, after that, and my husband went on making his clothes until 1928 when we gave up the shop. Yes, indeed—the Herr Hitler—he was the sort one don't come across in a hurry ! "

So much for Frau Popp. What a picture she draws, in her own homely fashion, of this lonely ascetic young lodger, engrossed in his painting and in great big dry and dusty books from the State Library ! There is no suggestion in the naïve recital of any recreations, any youthful gaieties or follies. But a very pleasant impression is derived from it of the sober-minded quiet young fellow's appreciation of the good-hearted folk in the hospitable little kitchen, and of his affection for the—doubtless—*radau*[1] children.

. . . . .

I thanked Frau Popp for all she had been so good as to tell me, and asked her if she had ever seen her lodger again since he had become Chancellor of Germany.

" Yes, indeed," she answered, beaming, " I saw him last year on the 11th of September. I heard, one day, that he was in Munich on a visit to his architect, Professor Troost, so I put on my Sunday best and went there to see him. Only two S.S. men (Picked Guards) stood in the doorway of the house and wouldn't let me pass. I said I only wanted a minute with the Herr Reichskanzler—I had known him so long. They asked how long, and when I said twenty-

[1] Tomboy.

two years, they changed their tune at once. They took me into the court-yard of the house and asked me to wait a couple of minutes. I did so, standing near his automobile. Then Hitler came, accompanied by two other tall gentlemen. He caught sight of me and strode towards me, both hands outstretched, his face alight with pleasure, ' My dear Frau Popp,' he exclaimed, ' it is jolly to see you again ! How good of you to come along ! ' I was all of a flutter like and half forgot all I'd been planning to say to him. I managed to stammer out some congratulations about the great success he had achieved, calling him, of course, Herr Reichskanzler, but he cut me short at that.

" ' Oh, no, the old way's best, please, Frau Popp —I'm still Herr Hitler to you.' And waiving the rest, ' Now tell me all about Liesel and Peppi. How are they ? '

" He was putting me at my ease asking about the children so, just because I was all of a dither.

" I told him as the two of them was married by now—Peppi was in Hamburg and Liesel at The Hague in Holland.

" ' Dear me ! ' he said, ' they're both a pretty long way off, aren't they ? So you're all alone now with your husband ? How are you two getting along ? '

" Nothing would do but I must tell him all about it, and all about the time in between since he left us. At last he declared once more how delighted he'd been to see me, and made me promise I'd come again. He sent no end of messages to my husband, but especially to Liesel and Peppi."

.   .   .   .   .

In Munich, of course, the art centre of Germany,

the young man had greatly extended facilities for the study of painting. In the innumerable Bier-hallen, too, he had opportunities for forgathering with many a discursive chance acquaintance only too ready to argue with him upon politics. In *Mein Kampf* the Führer records a number of these sittings. Overhearing a remark made one day of that pre-War time to the effect that Germany had nothing to fear so long as she could count on the friendship of Austria and Italy, the new-comer from Wien was obliged to throw his newspaper aside, and give the speaker the benefit of his first-hand better knowledge of the subject. " Just get this," he made it plain, " it's only the German part of the Habsburg conglomeration we can reckon on : the other element is dead against us everywhere ! As for Italy, she has never yet forgotten or forgiven the Austrian domination."

The Bierhallen in Munich are by no means mere drinking resorts. They serve a variety of public purposes, and offer spacious accommodation for every sort of festivity or gathering. They are fre-quented by all classes. Everyone has its own particular patrons, and every table serves as a nucleus for one of a dozen informal clubs and groups of like-minded acquaintances. Hitler brought the same powers of observation to bear upon the Müncheners as he had brought to bear upon the people in Vienna.

In the course of a month or two it amazed him to discover how blind or how indifferent many of them appeared to be to the signs of the times, the menace of Marxismus, for instance, and the need for another sort of national expansion than that merely brought about by trade. He had many an oppor-tunity of sharpening his dialectic in the various

Volks Cafés or in the Hofbräuhaus, and every such discussion spurred him on to further and protracted study in the public libraries. Hence Frau Popp's concern over the amount of midnight oil he consumed up in the third story of the Schleissheimerstrasse.

The two years that elapsed between Hitler's arrival in Munich and the outbreak of the Great War saw him making strides, indeed, both as an artist and as a student. His mind, fed by such a persevering course of solid reading, was inwardly shaping itself for the work of the future. It is possible that his self-education owes as much to this period as to that of his preceding precarious existence in Vienna. One thing is certain, Adolf Hitler was happier and more comfortably circumstanced under Frau Popp's kindly roof than he had been since he left his home.

CHAPTER IV

WITH HITLER IN THE WAR

HERR IGNAZ WESTENKIRCHNER, ex-Service man, and war-time comrade of the Führer, received the writer in the waiting-room of the offices of the *Völkischer Beobachter* in Munich. But we repaired immediately to a quieter room where we could talk in comfort.

" Dear me, yes," said he, " the Führer remains ever the good comrade that he was ! They published that story of how he brought me home from America at his own expense, but I'll tell it in full to you. Then you shall have the whole account of our doings on the Western Front. . . ."

A somewhat small-built man, this Ignaz Westenkirchner, thin, with a clean-shaven face much lined and worn, and, of course, somewhere about the Führer's own age. He wore a simple blue suit and had a regular galaxy of various coloured pencils sticking out of the pocket in his jacket. He has a job in the dispatching department of the paper, hence the multi-coloured pencils. His hair is light brown.

" After that hideous night in Flanders in 1918 when he got gassed," said Westenkirchner, " I never bumped up against Hitler again until we ran across each other here in Munich, in the Sterneckerbräu. That was in the beginning of 1920. I belonged to the Green Police just then—I'd enrolled just after

the great bust-up of the Revolution. We old comrades of the List Regiment forgathered at the
Sterneckerbräu : Hitler used the place regularly.

"But in the March of that year I left the police and
went home to my own town not far from Munich.
Hitler was against it. He did all he could to persuade
me to stop where I was. He said he was dead certain
he would himself succeed over his own plans and
political ideas, and that if I'd only hang on, he would
give an eye to me as well. But I wasn't to be turned
aside. After a year or two I got into difficulties—
couldn't make a go of it—and found myself among
the workless and the unemployed.

"I decided to clear out, family and all, to the
U.S.A. At first it wasn't too bad, but things were
none too cheerful even over there, and by the beginning of '33 I was as poorly fixed as ever, and out of
a job.

"Anyhow I'd kept up with some of the old List
comrades and in the autumn of that year one of them
sent me word that Hitler'd like a line from me from
time to time. I wrote straightaway to him in Berlin,
but got no answer. So I had another shot at it and
wrote to his sister at Obersalzburg. And she sent
him my news. Not particularly good news—mine !

"Then, suddenly, one day at Reading in Penn-
sylvania, where I happened to be living, I got a tele-
gram from a German shipping office informing me
that the Herr Reichskanzler, Adolf Hitler himself, had
defrayed all the expenses of my return with my family
to Germany, and that I could set out to come home
just as soon as I liked.

"Overjoyed, the whole lot of us set sail early in
December. We reached Hamburg and went on
straight to Berlin. I just longed to see my old

E

comrade again—Reichskanzler though he be—and thank him from the bottom of my grateful heart for having come so splendidly to our rescue.

" I got to the Chancellery and found him just the same as ever. His greeting was as warm as man could wish. He spoke, too, in our local dialect, ' Jolly glad to see you back, Westenkirchner ! Suppose you just sit yourself down and tell me all the yarn.'

" That was all right, of course, but I had to show him my kids ! Hitler was always fond of the kiddies. We had a good old talk, as you may imagine, and he wound up by saying he'd got a job for me on the party paper here in Munich. Wouldn't hear a word of thanks. I just tried to tell him what I felt and what I thought of him, but laughingly he waived it all aside, ' Take it as read ! Take it as read,'[1] he said, and so I had to."

Here, then, we have the full text of the Westenkirchner story which everyone so liked.

The Führer himself has written of his War experiences in *Mein Kampf*, but it is a contribution to the rapidly growing Hitler literature to have Herr Westenkirchner's verbatim story.

In the few pages in which Hitler describes the atmosphere of Europe just prior to the outbreak of the Great War, using the oncoming of thunderstorm as his metaphor, he attains great impressive dignity. One feels the oppression, the fulminating dread. . . .

Hitler went through the War, on the Western Front.

His contrast between the morale of the German troops in 1914 and their utter brokenness at the end is as telling as anything in the banned Remarque.

[1] A rather free translation for " Schon gut, schon gut," perhaps, but the sense is there.

" Umsonst alle Opfer " heads one of his pages—all sacrifice is vain. He was wounded in October, 1916, went into hospital near Berlin and was returned later to his battalion at Munich. Then, two years afterwards, in the same month, he was gassed at Ypres and blinded.

It was in hospital at Pasewalk, in Pomerania, that Adolf Hitler heard of the Revolution, the flight of the Kaiser, and the collapse of the Fatherland. He writes that he had not wept since he stood by his mother's graveside. Now, however, with the gas still " ravening " on his eyes, and threatening him with their total loss, he weeps again. He stumbles away, falls down on his hospital cot, and cries out in anguish all the sacrifice had been in vain ! " Would not the graves open of all the hundreds and thousands of those who had left the Fatherland full of high belief and hope, never to return. . . ."

It was at this moment, at this heart-breaking crisis, Adolf Hitler made his great decision. He would devote himself to the rehabilitation of his country.

.   .   .   .   .

" Yes, yes," says Herr Ignaz Westenkirchner, " Hitler was always the one to buck us up when we got downhearted : he kept us going when things were at their worst—but he couldn't cook ! That was the one thing he couldn't do.

" One thing we couldn't understand—the rest of us—Hitler he'd always attend church parade, even towards the end, when most of us had given all that up."

Another comrade, Herr Max Amann, formerly regimental clerk, adds that Hitler never wanted a commission. He'd joined up in the ranks, and in the ranks he wanted to remain. " Often," he says, " Hitler'd take another man's place, if he could,— preferably a family man's—and volunteer for the extra dangerous job in his stead."

On September 17th, 1917, they gave him the Military Service Cross with swords ; on May 9th, 1918, he got the regimental diploma for signal bravery in attack ; and on August 4th, 1918, he received the Iron Cross, first class.

It was in his lodgings at Frau Popp's that the young student painter first heard of the shot at Sarajevo. There was a tremendous babble going on suddenly outside ; in the street below people came running together ; a word floated up to his ears, and on his going down presently to find out what the commotion was all about . . . .

Thus Frau Popp, breathless with excitement, " Der Osterreichische Thronfolger Erzherzog Franz Ferdinand ist ermordet worden ! " (The Austrian heir, Archduke Franz Ferdinand, has been assassinated !)

Hitler pushed past her into the street. Thrusting his way into a press of people, staring open-mouthed at a placard, he read the announcement of the crime for himself. The perpetrators, it seemed, had already been arrested.

The whole world gasped at the news. No one in Munich required to be particularly well posted as to the political situation just then to realise that this must mean an explosion in the Balkans. The Bavarian royalties themselves, to whom the unfortunate Archduke and his wife had paid a visit only so recently as the previous March, certainly foresaw great political consequences in Austria and Russia, but never dreamed of an imminent World War. The city seethed with indignation.

In Vienna, too, the populace were furious : mobs threatened the Serbian Legation. This murder was understood there as the overt act of a conspiracy which Austria-Hungary suspected to have its origin in Serbia. The bomb throwers at Sarajevo, and Princip, the man who shot the Archduke, were the emissaries of certain secret societies whose aim was a dissolution of the Dual Monarchy and the setting up of a Pan-Serb State with the assistance of France and England.[1]

A well-posted man like Hitler could grasp the fearful impending consequences better than most people. There followed a few days of high tension, then, on August 1st, in view of the Russian mobilisation, came the reluctant Imperial order for the mobilisation of Germany's great war machine. Bavaria, of course, contributed her Army. Munich got marching orders from Berlin. The aged prince-regent, Ludwig, remained at the Residenz ; his son, Crown Prince Rupprecht, however, departed for the Front, Prince Ludwig Ferdinand at once presented himself for a military surgeon, and his sister, Princess Pilar, became a nurse.

Munich was filled with field-grey uniforms, and an immense military activity. Youth everywhere was sanguine and high-spirited. The sense of war flew to everybody's head like wine. There were processions and great cheering. If peasants called to the colours from the Bayerischer Wald, the mountains and the Franconian plains scarcely knew what it was all about, they only needed to learn that the Fatherland was threatened, to become as conspicuous for their

[1] Amazing details about the background of Pan-Serb conspiracies may be found in the interesting novel *Apis and Este* (by Bruno Brehm), published in England by Geoffrey Blès, under the title *They call it Patriotism.*

enthusiasm at this moment as later they were to become conspicuous for bravery.

Every day troops were moving off. There were enormous parades. The companies massed in great open spaces swore their oath of allegiance anew ; the priests and bishops of the Protestant and Catholic churches blessed their departure ; the trumpeters sounded the Zum Gebet ; and to the accompaniment of blood-stirring martial music, and the tumultuous leave-taking of the townsfolk, masses of men entrained for the Front.

Day after day crowds assembled in dense thousands before the Feldherrnhalle on the Odeonsplatz and b arst into " Die Wacht am Rhein." The quiet-seem ng student painter from Vienna sang with them as lv stily as the rest. No sooner had the war bomb burst than he rushed upstairs to his " Studio " in the Popp *appartement* and dashed off an application to the Kabinettskanzlei of the King for permission to enlist in a Bavarian Regiment and to fight with the German Army.[1]

Immensely to his astonishment and jubilation the very next day brought the answer ! The Herr Kabinettschef of the Prince-Regent Ludwig accepted the young Austrian's proffer of service, and directed him to report himself immediately at the nearest barracks. Hitler fell on his knees . . . and thanked God . . . typical, this, of the passionate enthusiasm of those first few weeks of the War ; typical of high-spirited, patriotic, untried youth debouching on every Front.

---

[1] One of the gibes levelled by his opponents at the Führer is that he was a " deserter " from the Austrian Army, otherwise how came it that he volunteered in Bavaria ? The sufficient answer to this calumny is contained in a document issuing from Austria itself. It states that Adolf Hitler duly reported himself to the military authorities at Salzburg, on February 5th, 1914, but was found to be " unfit " (*zu schwach*) for military service.

He joined up on the instant as " Kriegsfrei-williger " (volunteer), and found himself enrolled as Number 148 in the 1st Company of the 16th Bavarian Infantry Regiment, called for short the " List " after its original Commander.

On the Exerzierplatz of Munich he went through a period of intensive training, of drilling, forming fours, evolutions, then route marching and bayonet practice, such as was claiming the energies of young men all over the world, to fall upon his cot night after night drunk with fatigue.

Not for long, however, was he to remain in the Munich Barracks. The regiment was to put in a few weeks at Lechfeld, a spot at the confluence of the Lech and the Danube about seventy miles west, for further training. The men were all glad of the change, and left the city, after a tremendous send-off from the populace, only eager to come to grips with the enemy before the War should be over !

They had not long to fret on the leash at Lechfeld.

On the 21st of October the Regiment List entrained for the Front.

It is at this point Private Westenkirchner, Hitler's trench comrade, takes up the tale.

" We were all in topping spirits that day," he says, " our heads stuffed with no end of war nonsense, sure as eggs is eggs the glorious fighting would be all over by Christmas or the New Year at latest. We reached the Rhine that night. Lots of us south Bavarian chaps had never seen the Rhine before, and then in the dawn, I remember as if it were yesterday, how it just struck us all to see the sun drawing up the mist from the river and unveiling before our dazzled eyes that splendid statue of Germania which looks down from the Niederwald. How we yelled the ' Wacht

am Rhein '—the whole lot of us for the first time
going out to war !

"It took us two days to reach Lille as our train
only crawled from that point onward. Across war-
ravaged Belgium we poured reinforcements for the
6th Bavarian Division of the Army of the Crown
Prince Rupprecht. The great battles of the Marne
and the Aisne were over by this time ; Antwerp had
fallen ; the first phase of the battle of Ypres in which
the Allied enemy had made every effort to effect a
great turning movement round our right flank,
clearing the Belgian coast line, and forcing us out
of Bruges and Ghent, had failed. We had established
a line to the sea, and we Bavarians amongst the rest
coming up in time for the great offensive of the 31st of
October and the 1st of November, when for forty-eight
hours two and a half German Army Corps stormed
the Wytschaete Messines Ridge, saw the beginning
of the second phase of that enormous struggle.

"From Lille where we put in perhaps half a day
we proceeded by train again to a place called Ledeghem, but after that it was all marching. Now we
were within earshot of the guns : the thunder on
the Front became even nearer. The country seemed
awfully flat and monotonous; the only villages we
passed were nothing but heaps of gaping ruins. Dead
horses blown up like balloons lay in the ditches. We
got the stench of them. We went through places
called Dadizeele and Terhan, and approached Becelaere,[1] a half-demolished village, the centre of the

---

[1] This was on November 11th, 1914, when the Sixth Army, under
the Crown Prince Rupprecht of Bavaria, and the new Fourth Army,
under Duke Allbrecht of Wurttemberg, rallied their forces for a
third great attempt upon Ypres. It was recorded by Headquarters
how the young reinforcements from home had hurled themselves
into the enemy's lines singing "Deutschland, Deutschland über
Alles."

SKETCH BY HITLER AT THE FRONT
Ruins of a church near Fromelles.

SKETCH BY HITLER AT THE FRONT, 1915
His Rest Billet near Fournes, called " Zur schwarzen Marie."

enemy's First Division. Here the fire was intensely hot. We advanced in the face of a bombardment. It was already night, cold and wet. We came well within range, scrambling over the muddy broken ground, taking whatever shelter we could behind hedges, in ditches and in shell-holes, our way lit by the glare of houses burning like torches in the lurid blackness,—and fell at last upon the enemy, in a hand-to-hand fight, man to man, fiercely thrusting with our bayonets and blindly stumbling over fallen friend and foe alike. It was our baptism of fire. Four days we had of this at Becelaere and Polygon Wood and Gheluvelt, four days and nights—sheer hell! Of the three thousand men of the Regiment List, only five hundred came safely out of it. The rest were killed, or wounded, or had vanished. We had gone into battle as youngsters, we came out of it worn, scarred, exhausted men. No longer recruits, we were soldiers of the fighting line.

" We went into rest billets for a couple of days at a place called Werwick ; then found ourselves in the thick of it again at Wytschaete. We broke through the enemy line north of Messines and turned the left flank of the trenches held by the London Scottish. But what ground or advantage we gained at one moment was lost the next. The enemy was forced to retire ; but he came on again a few hours later. The List withdrew, decimated and exhausted, to Commines.

" The weather got ever colder and colder. As the winter set in the line hereabouts established itself and the fighting was no longer so fierce until the turn of the year. When I say this I mean it wasn't so fierce in comparison with what was to come later ! Looking back now, all that business at Becelaere and

Wytschaete was child's play to the fighting still ahead. For the most part all that first winter we occupied trenches between Messines and Wulverghem. Our line was consolidated by then and it held like steel for four years.

" I was a Meldegänger,[1] like Adolf Hitler. There were eight or ten of us altogether. We were very pally and made a mob by ourselves. There were even times when things couldn't be said to be too bad —when we got parcels from home and letters. We shared out, of course. Sometimes, even, we had a game with ' Tommy.' We stuck a helmet on the point of a bayonet and shoved it above the parapet, when it would be sure to draw immediate fire. Even Hitler, who was usually so serious, saw the fun of this. He used to double himself up with laughter.

" For the most part he was always on about politics. Two things seemed to get his goat—what the papers were saying at home about the War and all, and the way the Government, and particularly the Kaiser, were hampered by the Marxists and the Jews.

" ' It was pretty plain,' he said, ' what the working-classes thought about " Socialism " when the War broke out. They just chucked it clean overboard, and joined up to a man. Then, again, it didn't need all that shouting in the papers whenever we gained a victory : it stood to reason that the German Army was equal to its job. Nor did the folk at home need to have their courage damped when things didn't look so well. Going on like that would sooner or later only lead to public indifference about the War altogether. As for the Kaiser encouraging the

---

[1] Messenger, trench runner, whose duty was to keep up communication between Company and Regimental Headquarters.

Marxists, they'd only take advantage of that, to stab the Army in the back.' "

.   .   .   .   .

It was that first winter of the War " that soon after daylight on Christmas morning," writes the English Field-Marshal French, " the Germans took a very bold initiative at several points along our Front in trying to establish some form of fraternisation. It began by individual unarmed men running from the German trenches across to ours holding Xmas trees above their heads. These overtures were in some places favourably received and fraternisation of a limited kind took place during the day. It appeared that a little feasting went on, and junior officers, non-coms, and men on either side conversed together in ' No Man's Land.'

" When this was reported to me I issued immediate orders to prevent any recurrence of such conduct...."

In England, however, the public liked this, and credited the Christian gesture, to the " gentler Bavarians " in the German Army.

.   .   .   .   .

" After a time," continues Private Westenkirchner, " the regiment found itself in Tourcoing, and then, in the spring, when the British Offensive hurled itself against Neuve Chapelle, we moved up in that direction, and occupied trenches in the neighbourhood of Fromelles. Here we remained, more or less, until the following autumn.

" As I said, Hitler and I were Meldegänger. We carried no arms except a small revolver, for the sake of mobility. Our despatch wallets were attached to our belts. Generally two of us were sent out together, each bearing the same despatches, in case anything happened to the one or the other. The despatches were always sealed and marked with one, two or three crosses, according as they required time, haste, or express speed. It was no joke this despatch bearing, especially as Fromelles stood on a bit of a height, and to reach it from the troops in the plains and valleys below we had to toil up slopes raked by the enemy's machine-gun fire every inch of the way. I can see Hitler before my eyes now, as he used to tumble down back into the dug-out after just such a race with death. He'd squat down in a corner just as if nothing'd happened, but he looked a sketch— thin as a rake, hollow-eyed and waxy white.

" It was pretty beastly in those dug-outs all that summer. I shall never forget it. Nothing got on a man's nerves more than to have the ground blow up right under his feet. You never knew whether or not you were sitting bang on top of a powder magazine. Suddenly there'd come the most sickening sensation as a mine was sprung, and the next thing you'd know was that ten or twenty of your pals and comrades, chaps who'd been at your elbow only a minute before, were flying around in ten thousand bloody bits. That wanted some sticking, I can tell you !

" By September (1915) the English were pressing the attack all along our Front harder and harder. On the night of the 25th our position was pretty precarious ; it seemed as if something decisive one way or the other must at last come off. The air was full of the screaming of shells and of the hideous hissing and crashing of the whizz-bangs. Suddenly our Company Officer discovered that telephonic communication with the next section had broken down,

and Hitler and another man got the order to go and
find out what was wrong. They made it somehow,
but only got back by the skin of their teeth utterly
done in. The wire had been cut : an attack in force
was imminent. Warnings must be sent further
afield. Hitler received the order a second time. It
was nothing less than a miracle how he escaped
with his life as he came out on the road between
Fromelles and Aubers. It was literally raining
shells.

" The attack, however, failed. How we withstood
it I can't tell. I only thought to myself at the time
how lucky our English and Indian prisoners ought to
think themselves to be out of such a hell.

" The second winter came along, and whatever
trouble the enemy gave us, the water and the mud
gave us a rare sight more. It's a marvel we weren't
all drowned. We lived waterlogged. Whole sections
of the trenches had to be evacuated altogether. The
pumps couldn't make any impression on the water.
It just gained all the time. When we weren't carrying messages, Hitler and the rest and I, we were slop-
ping about on the duck boards baling with buckets.
He'd carry on with the job long after everyone else
was fed up with it, and had given it up in despair.
There was no snow, but ceaseless rain filled all the
shell-holes around with water so that the whole
expanse of No Man's Land was pitted with hideous
lakes and looked like anything on earth rather than
a battlefield.

" One of our fellows had been hoping against hope
for a spell of leave. In December that year things
were a bit quiet on our sector, so he put in for his
pass. They said he could go on leave for a fortnight
if he could get anyone to work double tides and take

his place. He didn't need to think that over twice. He knew as Adolf Hitler'd do it for him. . . .

" Christmas came round again without any of us yet knowing how soon the War'd be over, or how much more of it we'd got to face. It was pretty miserable, but they'd concocted some punch in the canteen, and at least every man had got letters or parcels from home. Everyone, that is, except Hitler. Somehow Hitler never got a letter even ! It wasn't a thing that called for remark exactly. But we all felt sorry, inside, and wanted him to share and share alike with us. But he never would ! Never accepted so much as a *Kuchen !* (cake). It was no use to keep all on at him. Not that he wasn't free-handed enough when he had anything of his own to share, a cigarette or bit of sausage. The measly pay we got he'd spend on jam. It was jam first and butter after-wards, that is whenever the two things did happen both to be within reach at the same time. It was bread and scrape anyhow, but Hitler he was a rare one for jam !

" He owned up to me sometimes how stony broke he was. Poor chap, he never had a cent ! I blurted it right out once : ' Haven't you got anyone back home ? Isn't there anyone to send you things ? ' ' No,' he answered, ' at least, no one but a sister, and goodness only knows where she is by this time.'

" It was in the summer of 1915 that the enemy began to drop bundles of leaflets into our trenches and behind our lines. This was their idea of making propaganda, sowing seeds of discontent and doubt in our minds as to what the fighting was about and how the Kaiser and not the German people was respons-ible for the War. At first we didn't pay much atten-tion to them, but as time went on we'd read them just for something to do. Mostly we chucked them away. They dropped leaflets against the Prussians on us Bavarian chaps. . . . Hitler knew what they meant by that. He read the things seriously and thought a lot about it all. He seemed to think the English understood propaganda better than we did, and this leaflet dropping certainly did have its effect. Arguments got up. Grousing increased all along the line. The wet and the mud and the weariness, the filth, and the wretched grub were all bad enough, without the men forever scrapping about what the enemy thought fit to tell them. Hitler seemed to expect H.Q. would contradict it. But H.Q. never did. Nothing was done to counteract the bad effect among us of those enemy leaflets.

" Another thing where we found we'd gone wrong —the humorous papers had always given us to understand there wasn't such a dolt on God's earth as the French or British soldier. Now we had to meet them, face to face, we knew a jolly sight better. They were men, and tremendous fighters. We knew, too, how it was all the other way about in France and England. The War propaganda there, making out we Germans were ' Huns ' and savages, capable of every sort of crime, just stiffened the people up to go on. Hitler was bitter over this. The enemy was much cleverer than we were about propaganda. He only wished he could have a say himself! But Hitler then was a nobody like the rest of us, nothing but a man in the trenches.

" The year wore on towards spring. The poor bits and stumps of trees left sticking up here and there like splintered posts in the mud actually began to put out leaves : sometimes a gleam of sun dried the morass a bit. Then the fighting renewed itself : new

and terrific offensives developed all along the line.
This was when the gas attacks began. The battle of
the Somme went on right through July without the
enemy breaking our line anywhere. I shall never
forget the night of the 15th or the 16th as long as I
live. It was an inferno of fire. All our field telephones were out of action and we ' Meldegänger '
were on the go incessantly, our lives at stake every
moment. At one time we were opposed to Aus-
tralians. They came on over and over again only
to be mowed down by our machine-gun fire.

" News came that the enemy were breaking
through the line held by the 21st Infantry Regiment :
word had to be sent along to the 17th and then on to
the threatened sector. Hitler and another trench
runner got the order. They set off in the face of
almost certain death, peppered with shot and shell
every yard of the way. Half the time they were
cowering for shelter in shell-holes and ditches. They
were wet through and half-frozen. Hitler's companion gave out. Buckled right up, unable to stick it
another step ! Hitler hoisted him along somehow,
rather than leave him to his fate, and the two of them
came at last, God only knows how, back to the dug-
out.

" On the 20th we delivered a counter-attack and
wrested back again the few yards of trenches gained
previously by the enemy. There came a bit of a lull
after that and we runners did what we could to repair
damage to our dug-out. Presently with over one
hundred dead we marched into rest billets at Fournes.

" There were letters and parcels awaiting us there
—all except for Hitler. He just looked the other way
and busied himself knocking the mud off his boots and
doing what he could to clean his shirt.

" That Somme Battle, a witches' cauldron of horror and fire and death, went on for weeks. Some time before we'd all been issued with fresh equipment. Now, on the 25th of September, we were marched off to Haubourdin, there to entrain next day for Longwy. From there we marched endlessly it seemed to us through Cambrai to Frémicourt, where we set to work at top speed to dig ourselves in, constructing trenches, traverses and dug-outs day and night. We took part in the battle on the 2nd of October and found ourselves in the sector between Bapaume and La Barque. It was all new ground to us, and we messengers were lost half the time.

" We relieved the 21st Regiment. The men came straggling back scarcely recognisable in their mud, blood and rags.

" Once a shell dropped plump into the middle of our dug-out. For the moment the lot of us were too stunned to know what had happened. Then four of us lay dead, and seven others lay hideously wounded spouting blood on the ground. That was the first time Hitler caught one. A splinter had gashed him in the face. . . .

" On the night of the 5th and 6th of October he was on the go with messages between our lot and the 17th the whole time. For the most part he and his comrade were dodging high explosive in the open, just waiting between earthquakes and volcanoes to make the next bit there and back. The enemy was doing his utmost to smash the German line, but in spite of unprecedented ferocity, the attack was completely foiled. We didn't give way an inch. By day we lay as close underground as we could. Otherwise, the slightest sign of life on our part brought the enemy aeroplanes into play and bombs were dropped right

F

from overhead. Of an evening, as a rule, Hitler
was despatched to Brigade Headquarters at Bapaume.
To get there he ran such a gauntlet between exploding
mines and burning houses, that for the most part his
own clothes singed on his back. Over and over again
the company was only saved by our artillery from
the English onslaughts.

"From the 7th of October for five days and nights
it isn't too much to say that we trench runners got no
sleep and nothing but snatch grub to eat. Our
numbers grew ever fewer and fewer. The stunning
din in the air never let up for one moment. All was
the wildest uproar of death by shot and shell and
cannonade. The thing grew unendurable, not to be
believed. It took six runners now to get a message
through, three pairs of them set out on the off chance
that one man, perhaps, might succeed. Our Lieu-
tenant called for volunteers—only Hitler responded,
and a chap named Ernst Schmidt. The thing was
rank suicide. This time only Schmidt got back.
Hitler had been hit in the left leg. Later on the
regimental stretcher-bearers brought him in. . . .

"They took us out of the line on the 13th of
October. Only a handful of us, apathetic with
shock and exhaustion, stumbled off, making our way
as best we could over the corpses of our comrades."

The Battle of the Somme, as Meldegänger Westenkirchner says, was a long-drawn-out affair. It lasted,
in fact, some three and a half months, from July well
on into the autumn. The Allied offensive was planned
on a single front of about twenty-five miles and was
preceded by immense preparations and reinforcements in men and material. It failed to break our
line, in any sense that the enemy, public or military,
hoped to break it, and this for the reason that our

line was an entire belt of territory scored with lines
behind lines, every one of which must be taken and
cleared and held before the enemy could be said to
have broken through. They failed most signally
and at frightful cost. Over two months were spent
in trying to secure objectives marked down for the
first day or two of the battle : it took weeks upon
weeks to decide the possession of a single patch of
woodland ; prolonged struggles waged backwards
and forwards over a few metres of contested ground.
Verdun was balanced by Bapaume.

" The companies," pursues Private Westenkirchner, " got smaller and smaller ; hardly thirty
men went to a company now. And in this shape we
awaited new onslaughts. The bombardment was
incessant. At length, however, we went into rest
billets at Sancourt.

" Hitler's wound was not too serious, but it would
incapacitate him for some months. He was sent to
the rear to the ' Sammellazarett ' Hermies. For
two long years he had been at the Front : here, for
the first time in all that while, he heard a German
woman's voice again. It was that of the Sister at
the Base Hospital. It gave him quite a shock. But
he went on in the Ambulance Train, through Belgium,
back home to Germany—after two years ! It was
amazing at last to find himself, clean, and lying in a
soft white bed in hospital at Beelitz near Berlin.
He had become so unused to all this refinement !
It took him quite a while to get accustomed to these
new surroundings.

" The thing, though, that struck him most, back
there at home in hospital, was the demoralisation that
seemed to have got hold of the men. There were
chaps there making a boast of how they'd purposely

maimed themselves to get out of the fighting line,
and, what was a jolly sight worse, no one in authority
took notice of it, no one seemed to think the less of
them for it.   What they said was ' Better to play
the coward for a minute than to be dead for eternity.'
Everybody was grousing over the beastliness of the
Front, and the uselessness of the war in general.
Hitler could hardly believe his ears.   It might have
been true, but it was unworthy and unsoldierly.

" Then one day, when he was fairly convalescent,
he got leave to go to Berlin.   Everything there looked
baddish, he thought ; poverty and hunger and anxiety
were stamped on every face.   He went into one or
two of the Soldiers' Homes, but found the chaps
there much in the same frame of mind as in the
hospital, only worse.   The grousers seemed to have
it all their own way.   Hitler felt pretty sick I can
tell you. . . ."

Lance-Corporal Adolf Hitler (as he was now) had,
indeed, come back from the Front (as he was to
emerge from the War at the end), with all his ideals
and loyalties intact.   He had gone from the high
untried courage of the beginning through shock and
horror and exhaustion to admitted cowardice and
fear, but this in turn he had conquered and steeled to
dogged endurance.   It had never yet entered his
head to start malingering ; or to question the obvious
rightness of the War.   He was utterly disgusted by
all this, back in Berlin.

When he was fit for discharge, the " iron train,"
which carried men on leave, took him to his Reserve
Battalion in Munich.   Here things were no better
than in Berlin.   Glowering faces, grumbling speech,
and incessant invective against Prussians and
militarism were to be noted on every hand.   Hitler

couldn't make it out how all this seemed to have got up, and got up so suddenly. He found out, however, that a lot of newspaper men having gone to the Front, their places had been taken by Jews, and that these men were using their opportunity to foment discouragement and disunion. Everything tracked to a nicety with the enemy propaganda in the trenches. If the Bavarians and the Prussians could be brought to loggerheads, so much the better for those who would like to see both go under. The upshot of it all was Hitler put in to return to the Front. Anything to escape the state of affairs at home : to be still fighting for Germany !

" We chaps in the line were glad to have him back, I can tell you. He was one of the best comrades we ever had. The company cook excelled himself that night and turned out an extra special mess in his honour, Kartoffelpuffer, bread and jam and tea. Hitler was cheery, too. Long after the rest of us had turned in, he was still fooling about with a flashlight in the dark spitting the rats on his bayonet. Then somebody chucked a boot at his head, and we got a little peace.

" On March 4th we left and entrained, via Douai, for Hantay on the La Bassée Canal. Things were gingering up and we were preparing for the big spring offensive at Arras. By April 28th we were in position at Biache. There was nothing to see but a waste of water-logged shell-holes. On May 3rd we were in action at Roeux ; and five days later we relieved the 20th, in the middle of a gas attack from the English. The effect of it was appalling. We messengers had a severe time of it, continually under fire, rain in our faces cutting like knives, mud up to our knees. The earth was going up in cascades all about us; we continually fell headlong into shell-holes old and new. The company got scattered anyhow; many of them never turned up again. Hitler and the rest were kept hard at it all night. At one time they were within an inch of capture by the English.

" But Ypres was the worst experience of all. Fifteen hundred strong the List Regiment was moved up into the salient on July 13th. We had come by night from Roulers to Ledeghem; from there we marched via Terhand to Gheluveld. All this was covering old ground for us, but it was no longer recognisable. We saw nothing but ruined villages, whole towns lying in masses of rubble, the very configuration of the streets all gone, here and there a gaunt and jagged gable still gaped to the sky. Then for ten days and nights on end we were bombarded without pause or slackening. There was the sound underground of mining and boring, and fleets of war planes rained bombs from overhead. For twenty-four hours at a stretch we suffocated in our gas masks.

" Then three days of rest billets in Dadizeele. Then in the line again between Gheluveld and Becelaire.

" On July 31st the English brought their monsters of tanks into action over a frontage miles long. They were accompanied overhead by planes, and heralded by intense machine-gun fire. Our artillery checked their advance. The rain foiled them still worse. It came down the whole time as if the heavens had opened. The field of battle was turned into one vast flooded area in which the enemy tanks were useless, and men and horses on either side were in as much danger of being drowned as shot. It went on, like a second deluge, for four days and nights, and was succeeded by weather black as winter.

" Anyhow, Regiment List was sent southward for a spell, to Hochstadt, near Mühlhausen in Alsace. After Flanders this was a foretaste of paradise ! We only had a couple of months' rest there, however, and then went up into the line again near Lizy on the Aisne. The fighting here was dogged and obstinate and lasted practically all that winter. Only at the end of January, 1918, were we withdrawn to Commines for another spell of rest.

" Hitler's interest in things in general never dwindled away to just concern for nothing more than what the day brought forth. That winter the Russian Front buckled up, which was an immense thing for us, and so did the Italian ; but them came the munitions strike at home. For three long years we'd held the Russian hordes at bay on the east. Endless columns of Russian prisoners swarmed over the high roads in Germany and yet there seemed to be illimitable numbers yet to come. It seemed almost laughable to us that the German Army, strung out on half a dozen fronts, should hope to resist this perennial flood. It held out successfully until the events of this winter allowed us to concentrate on the west.

" For the first time it almost looked as though we could change over from a war of defence to one of attack. The spirits of the men went up, and one even heard snatches of song again in the trenches. We got the idea that the enemy was losing heart : it could only now be a matter of one last terrific effort, before they, too, collapsed like Russia. As the spring advanced it was pretty plain they were jumpy and uneasy in those opposite trenches.

" Then came the munitions strike at home, the
most incredible bit of treachery and knavery the
world has ever seen. The German Army was knifed
in the back. The lives of hundreds and thousands
of our men yet to be slaughtered were to lie at the
doors of those who fomented and engineered this
monstrous treason. Although the strike was called
off too soon for the effects of it, as far as armaments
were concerned, to be much felt at the Front, the
consequences on our morale were deadly. Everyone
began to ask what was the good of our carrying on
out here if the people at home had thrown up the
sponge ? The Army began to be divided against
itself. The enemy wasn't slow to take advantage of
all this. They peppered our lines again with propaganda leaflets : ' Germany in the throes of a general
strike,' ' Give it up : we've won.' Nevertheless,
somehow, we fought on.

" In March, 1918, we List fellows evacuated our
old position on the Oise-Aisne sector, and pushed
forward on a four-days' march which I shall never
forget. Forty miles we covered, every day of it, and
this over roads you couldn't call roads any longer,
they were so ploughed and shot to pieces. We had
to make way all along the march for endless trains
of munition waggons, and the incessant struggling
forward of heavy artillery.

" Every now and again the whole advance would
be held up by some heavy trench mortar having
got stuck in a shell-hole. Horses had to be
taken from the limbers of the other guns to try
and haul it out, and masses of men turned to
to lend a hand. A dozen or so gunners hauling on
long ropes, a grey coil of exhausted men, would bow
forward at the word of command, ' Heave,' and

HITLER IN WAR HOSPITAL AT BEELITZ NEAR BERLIN
Second figure from the right in back row is Hitler.   The left one lying on the
ground is Bachmann.

HITLER AS FRONT SOLDIER—WITH THE LITTLE DOG WHO LEFT THE
BRITISH TRENCHES AND WENT OVER TO "FRITZ"
Hitler first figure on the left in front row.   Ernst Schmidt behind him standing.

strain till the sweat poured down their powder-
blackened faces, while the horses floundered up to
their bellies in the mud. If at last the monster at
which they pulled reared itself by degrees out of the
hole, there might be some chance of getting forward
again. In silence and haste we struggled forward,
our wide coats flapping and waving, with the belts
unfastened, the covers of our helmets all in rags.

" By evening, one day, we reached Fourdrain. We
camped three nights at Ferien and then did fifty
miles at a stretch. The horses of the batteries ahead
went down literally in dozens, and had to be summarily put out of their misery.

" We marched on through heaps of unrecognisable
ruins, once villages, past La Fere, Vouel and Noyen,
themselves nothing but burnt and shattered shells.
On the third day we came to Lassigny and Amy.
The further ahead we pushed the more cumbered
grew the way with the corpses of shot horses and the
wreckage of heavy ordinance.

" The French made terrific efforts to hold Mont-
didier ; they hurled their coloured troops into the battle
here. After indescribable struggles on March 28th
we reached Fontaine, about five kilometres west
of that place. Here we went into the line again for
about three weeks. The whole Front was in an
unceasing uproar day and night. It blazed and
roared and quivered with incessant explosions.

" The air was for ever filled with the screaming and
the whistling of the shells, the flash and thunder of
explosives and their sickly smell. If this wasn't
enough, we were on starvation rations now, and
suffered agonies from thirst. The baggage waggons
and the field kitchens got held up and hopelessly
stuck in the wrecked roads to the rear, or came

within range of the enemy guns, so that we were cut
off even from such supplies as there were. One
whole week we got practically nothing. I remember
how Hitler and I sometimes, on an extra black night,
would crawl out of the trench to scrounge round for
something to eat. He'd have an empty petrol can,
and I'd have a knife. We hunted round where they'd
been slaughtering the horses, and if we could hit on
some poor shot beast which didn't stink too badly
as yet, we'd slice a bit off his quarter. Hitler'd
fill the can with shell-hole water, and, stumbling back
again to the dug-out, we'd deliver this booty to the
cook !

" We were a crew of scarecrows, I can tell you,
when at last we were relieved, half-starved and with
the sore, red eyes of men who haven't had what you
could call one decent sleep for nearly a fortnight !
We were nothing but a handful of tramps, mud from
top to toe, not a whole tunic amongst us. We came
out of the line over twelve hundred fewer than we
went in.

" They marched us another two or three days to
rest billets at Chery les Poully. For weeks we'd
never had our clothes off—now, first to sleep, and
then to eat ! After that we had a clean-up, if our
bits of once-upon-a-time shirts, or remnants of
once-upon-a-time boots were yet worth the time and
trouble. In the middle of it, though, the alarm was
sounded ; we were to be rushed to a sector, Anizy-
Lizy. Grousing and swearing we limped off again
towards the trenches.

" The Front was roaring and blazing away in full
blast. We were only a few hundred strong now, and
were sent to hold a line some four miles long, for ten
days and nights. We spent hours sheltering in shell-

holes, battered with flying clods of earth—when not directly hit by shot and shell—which hit like fists and knocked a man's breath out of his bellows.

" Then at last, on May 15th, when the 6th Division was relieved, the strength of the List Regiment had dwindled to that of a single company. Many of the chaps had to be carried on stretchers, or helped along somehow, or they couldn't have made the retreat. Two of us messengers were senseless, and the rest were ghosts rather than men. We filed out of the trenches, as usual, before the greying of the dawn. Muddy and sunken-eyed came the pitiable line of stumbling figures, lots of them with flapping empty sleeves, unbuttoned tunics, and blood-soaked rags bound round head or arm or hand. Others came two by two, leaning on each other, dragging, limping. The stretchers got knocked about over the broken ground. Single figures brought up the rear laden with rifles and equipment, packs, buckets and gear of every indescribable description.

" On May 26th our artillery began a fresh attack on the French trenches. Gas followed. The enemy was completely overborne on the Soissons-Fismes sector. We List found ourselves in Juvigny. Then we marched without pause to Epagny. We remained a good long time in trenches between Vezaponin and Nouvron, and spent the first part of June reconnoitring in that region.

" Then a queer thing happened. It was still day, the 4th, as a matter of fact, and the firing had died down for the nonce. The sun was hot. Men were sitting about, silent, weary, unsociable, sleepy, reading letters or writing home. Hitler had gone off by himself and must have been half a mile away. He had just surmounted a slight rise in the apparently

vacant landscape when suddenly he heard the
whirring of a machine-gun and bullets peppered all
the air about him. He flung himself face downwards
on the ground. The gun ceased fire. Gingerly Hitler
essayed to move. Instantly it spat again, lead and
fire.

" At length, however, he managed to worm his
way to the next hole, ' Evidently a French ambush,'
he thought, ' with a camouflaged gun,' and paused,
and thought things over. ' Quite a number of men,'
he supposed, and rightly. For within the next ten
minutes or so, at least half a dozen of them, fully
armed, appeared climbing over the top of the trench.
' One, two, three—five—eight—*Donnerwetter* ! ' he
thought, ' however many more ? ' Then like a flash,
he leaped to his feet, dragged his revolver from his
belt, and levelling it at the enemy, shouted to them
to surrender. ' Whichever of you budges, he's a
dead man ! ' Whether the Frenchmen understood
what he said or not, they understood what he meant,
and promptly fell into line as ordered. ' You're my
prisoners ! March ! ' Hitler signalled the way. Off
they went, Hitler in the rear. Perhaps they'd covered
a hundred metres this way, perhaps two, when the
whole twelve of them began to wonder where the
rest of the German detail might be which had captured them. Another hundred metres they plodded
silently forward without a single enemy more showing
up than this fellow with the revolver. ' Sacré Nom ! '
—exclaimed one of them—but got no further. He
found himself directly menaced by that shining
barrel. Forwards ! Half a mile further and they
came to the German trenches, when Hitler turned
the lot over to the company, amid roars of laughter.
' Heavens ! if we'd only known ! ' muttered the

prisoners, ' but the blasted blighter carried the thing
off so mighty high handed ! '

" The fighting between the Oise and the Marne
was stubborn and bitter beyond description. Step
by step we were forced back by overwhelming numbers. We made a stand along the line Aisne–Marne,
however, from July 1st to the 14th, from which the
enemy failed to dislodge us.

" On the 15th our big offensive opened in Cham-
pagne and we succeeded in retaking a good slice of
the country from the enemy. The battle was waged
without cessation day or night ; from a huge de-
fensive action between Soissons and Reims it gradually involved the whole Front from the Marne to the
Aisne. The barrage was unintermittent. For fourteen days shot and shell rained on the trenches. We
crouched in a veritable hell of fire and flying iron.

" We were relieved on July 30th. They brought
us out of the line to go through a ten-days' course of
instructions, of which interval we took advantage to
get back somewhat to the semblance of ordinary
mortals. By the middle of August we entrained to a
point whence we could take part in the defence
between Arras and Albert. We stuck fast to our
trenches in a line Monchy–Bapaume, and the most
savage onslaughts failed to dislodge us. We remained
there until the end of August, and then marched east
towards the frontier between Belgium and Holland.
Not far from Bruges we put in a spell of guardwork
on the frontier. Once we touched Ostend. By
September, however, this interlude was over, and we
found ourselves, Hitler and I, in the middle of the
last of the fighting we were to see together.

" For the third time we were back on the old
ground fought over in 1914. Now we had to defend

it, inch by inch, all over again. We were in the neighbourhood of Commines ; dazed and bewildered with the ceaseless flash and thunder of explosives. Fiercer and fiercer grew the firing. On the night of October 13th–14th the crashing and howling and roaring of the guns was accompanied by something still more deadly than usual. Our company lay on a little hill near Werwick, a bit to the south of Ypres. All of a sudden the bombardment slackened off and in place of shells came a queer pungent smell. Word flew through the trenches that the English were attacking with chlorine gas. Hitherto the List hadn't experienced this sort of gas, but now we got a thorough dose of it. As I stuck my head outside the dug-out for a quick look round I found myself confronted by a hideous lot of bogies. In the place of men were creatures with visages of sheer horror.

" At that I shot into my own gas-mask ! For hours we lay there with this foul stuff poisoning every gulp of air outside. Suddenly one of the chaps could stand it no longer. He sprang up, wrenched the mask from his head and face, gasping, only to encounter a waft of the white-green poison. It caught him by the throat and flung him back choking, gurgling, suffocating, dying. The gas left off by morning and the shelling began again, to our unbounded relief. Better the deadliest bombardment than that poisoned drowning stifling. How we tore off those masks, and gulped in the air ! It was still stinking of the stuff, and reeked again of high explosive, but to us it was the very breath of Heaven. Every now and then, the enemy still sent a gas bomb over together with the rest.

" A man would shriek, throw up his arms, and fling them across his eyes. There was nothing for it but to clap the filthy masks over our heads again. The ferocity of the attack increased. Hour after hour of this inferno went by. It seemed as though that paling in the east which heralded the longed-for dawn would never come again. We chaps just hugged the ravaged and shattered ground, lying, indistinguishable lumps of filth and earth ourselves, within the sheltering lip of the water-filled craters torn up by previous shelling. We were practically finished. Only a handful of us yet remained. Most of us lay there, black bundles, never to move again. As for me, I was at my last gasp. I began vomiting into my own face—wrenched the gas-mask off—and knew no more.

" About seven next morning Hitler was despatched with an order to our rear. Dropping with exhaustion, he staggered off. It was useless by now to count up how many days and nights we'd gone without sleep. His eyes were burning, sore, and smarting—gas—he supposed, or dog weariness. Anyhow, they rapidly got worse. The pain was hideous ; presently he could see nothing but a fog. Stumbling, and falling over and over again, he made what feeble progress he could. Every time he went down crash, it was harder and harder to drag himself to his feet again. The last time, all his failing strength was exhausted in freeing himself from the mask . . . he could struggle up no more . . . his eyes were searing coals . . . Hitler collapsed.

" Goodness only knows how long it was before the stretcher bearers found him.

" They brought him in, though, at last, and took him to the dressing-station. This was on the morning of October 14th, 1918—just before the end.

" Two days later Hitler arrived in hospital at Pasewalk, Pomerania."

．　　　．　　　．　　　．　　　．

Among the innumerable libels with which the Führer has no time to concern himself, if he is to get on with the job of governing Germany at all, is that which accuses him of "skulking" during the War. He is supposed to have managed somehow or other to have kept well out of the firing line. A substantial array of well authenticated official military testimony goes to contradict any such supposition. Many of Private Hitler's commanding officers have written with the highest appreciation of his soldierly qualities.

" I cannot remember that Private Hitler ever failed in his duty," writes one of these. " He carried out his dangerous duties, not only with alacrity but with distinction," testified another. Generalmajor Engelhardt gives us this glimpse of him. " Once," he relates, " as I emerged from the wood at Wytschall during a fierce attack, in order to make some observations, Hitler and an orderly from the Regimental Staff, planted themselves bang in front of me to shield me with their own bodies from machine-gun fire." Michael Schlehuber writes, " Politically I am poles apart from Hitler, but I can testify willingly enough to his courage in the War, as I thought highly of him as a comrade in the trenches. I never knew him shirk his duty, or dodge any danger."

CHAPTER V

HITLER RETURNS TO MUNICH AFTER THE WAR : HERR
ERNST SCHMIDT'S STORY

IT would be a superfluous task in this place again
to describe the state of political chaos into which
Germany fell after the revolt of the marines at Kiel,
the flight of the Emperor and the proclamation of
the Republic in Berlin. The tale has often been told.

But if we are to arrive at any idea of the state of
things obtaining at this period in Bavaria, in order
to form some picture of the despair and hopelessness
in Munich during the first months after Adolf
Hitler's return thither from Pasewalk, we must go
to Herr Ernst Schmidt for our history.

It is a highly confusing interlude for the English
reader to grasp. The whole purport of Herr Schmidt's
story is less to elucidate kaleidoscopic affairs in
Bavaria than to show how Adolf Hitler reacted to
the situation. It was a period of internecine violence,
and of acute crisis.

About a hundred and twenty miles east of Munich
lies the little village of Garching, on the Alz, not far
from the Austrian frontier. I took a trip to this spot
to meet a former war comrade of Adolf Hitler's,
a man called Ernst Schmidt, one of his original
intimates. Herr Schmidt, indeed, met me at the
little station, and was delighted to receive me. He is
a man of about the Reichskanzler's own age, thin and
sunburnt, and unmarried ; leads a somewhat lonely

life. He is a painter by trade, and works with two mates in Garching and its neighbourhood.

He rents a room of his own in an inn here, and has furnished it with his own things, very simply but effectively. The most outstanding piece of furniture is a large bookcase well filled with such works as those of Goethe, Schiller and Shakespeare. The classics, too, are represented. Herr Schmidt noticed my interest in all this, and immediately reached down a couple of volumes to show me. One was *Bavaria in the War*, and the other *Mein Kampf*. He showed me an inscription on the flyleaf of the latter : " To my dear and faithful war-time comrade Ernst Schmidt, in remembrance, Adolf Hitler." Of course I recognised the well-known handwriting.

We sat down at a table and Herr Schmidt began his story.

" I took to the painter's trade as a youth," he said, " and after my apprenticeship, began by being a journeyman, and travelled all over France, Switzerland and Italy. When war broke out I returned home, and by the middle of November, 1914, I was already at the Front. That was at Messines. I belonged to the trench runners. And because of that, I came across Hitler. We messengers were a chummy crowd generally, but three of us in particular seemed to hang together, Hitler, Bachmann and I. Personally I was very much attracted to Adolf, and not the less as I had so often occasion to notice how he risked his life for somebody else, and never said a syllable about it. Seemed to think a thing like that was all in the day's work, nothing to go and make a song about, anyhow. They used to call for volunteers when any particularly nasty job was on hand, and Hitler always answered. When

I saw him step forward, I stepped forward, too, and
so did Bachmann. We sort of belonged together,
especially facing death.

"This was how it happened we all three got
wounded at the same time and place, in October,
1916. Hitler and Bachmann made it, somehow, to
the first field dressing-station, whence they got sent
down to Beelitz. But I collapsed on the way, and
was picked up later and shunted to hospital in
Brandenburg.

"In December we all knocked up against each
other again in barracks at Munich, and presently,
one by one rejoined our regiment. Bachmann got
sent to Roumania where he was killed. In October,
1918, I got leave and went home, but by the beginning of November I was on my way back to the Front.
I got no further than Cologne. It was the 6th of the
month and everyone was saying the War was
finished . . . anyhow I got the right-about-face,
and fetched up again in barracks at Munich where I
heard all about what Hitler called the greatest crime
a people ever suffered, the November Revolt.

"I suppose you know what happened in Berlin?
The Revolution began in the fleet at Kiel. The
mutiny reached its climax on the 4th. Next day the
whole town was in the hands of the mutineers, and
the Red Flag was everywhere hoisted aboard the
ships. Very soon Hamburg, Bremen and other ports
were in the hands of the revolutionaries. On the
8th the Social Democrats Ebert and Scheidemann
had an interview in Berlin with the Chancellor,
Prince Max von Baden, the 'Red Prince,' and
persuaded him that the people were behind them,
that there was nothing for it but that the Kaiser
must abdicate. Without consulting Wilhelm II,

who was at Army Headquarters at Spa, Prince Max fell in with this, and Scheidemann declared the Republic from the steps of the Reichstag. 'The German people have won all along the line,' he declared—a glaring lie—' and now it is our duty to see that this glorious victory is not defiled.'

" On the 10th the Kaiser fled to Holland, and the Revolution was an accomplished fact.

" It was on the morning of the 7th that I arrived at the Hauptbahnhof in Munich. I repaired to the Luisenschule where our regiment was quartered, and reported. The place was swarming with young fellows loafing about with their hands in their pockets, anyhow. They had never been at the Front, they were doing nothing but waiting for something to happen. And sure enough something *did* happen !

" As I turned out in the street again I saw a mob of people coming along with placards displayed in front, ' Come to the Meeting on the Teresian Field ! Down with Capitalism ! Up with the Proletariat ! ' It suddenly struck me what this was—the Majority Socialists and the Independent Socialists were making common cause against the Monarchy. I wasn't much inclined to mix myself up in the thing, but went along out of a certain amount of curiosity.

" Thousands of people assembled on the meadow. Kurt Eisner harangued them and worked them up to a tremendous pitch of excitement. Loud speakers were bawling ' Down with the Kaiser,' ' Down with the Crown Prince,' ' Clear out the Wittelsbachs.'[1] The crowd seethed like a cauldron. And the cauldron boiled over. Like an all-devouring stream of molten lava pouring from a volcano, the mass came surging back into Munich ; yelling and exulting it poured

[1] The reigning family in Bavaria.

into the streets and made for the prison. The doors were locked and guarded. But in a trice they were beaten down, keys were torn from the warders, and every murderer and criminal in the place set immediately at large to join the triumphant rioters without. Meantime over a thousand mutineer sailors had come into Munich, and these now swelled the throng. The uproar was terrific. Shops were universally plundered.

" The King, old and grey-headed, abdicated, and fled the city after nightfall that same wild November day. The military had been forbidden to fire on the crowds so that the mutineers could have things all their own way.

" During the night a Workmen's, Peasants' and Soldiers' Council was set up and Bavaria was declared a Free State. Kurt Eisner, an old man and a Jew, an erstwhile journalist and ever a firebrand, was nominated President. All night long there was fighting in the streets as the shopkeepers tried to defend their goods and property from the mob. Hand-grenades were thrown, and the shooting never let up until dawn.

" Eisner proceeded to get some sort of a government together, and in the course of the next few hours the tumult was allayed and comparative order restored. He enjoyed at first a certain prestige and had an undoubted following, but he quickly forfeited the people's trust and favour by introducing Jews everywhere to office, and Jews moreover out of Poland and Galicia who could scarcely speak German. The Bavarians weren't going to stand for too much of that.

" Meantime Hitler had turned up, back from Pasewalk. We met, we two, and cemented our old

friendship. This was the first I heard of his being
gassed and in hospital. He hadn't much to say
about the Revolution, but it was plain enough to see
how bitter he felt. I too saw red over the way
things were going, especially over the demoralisation
in barracks. The laziest and most impudent among
the men were, naturally, those who had never been
anywhere near the trenches. The place was full of
laggards and cowards.

"Then, one day, volunteers were called for as
guards for the prisoners' camp at Traunstein, a little
town not far from the Austrian frontier. Hitler said
to me, ' Say, Schmidt, let's give in our names, you
and me. I can't stick it here much longer.' Nor
could I ! So we came forward. Lots of others did,
too, but they were the sort I've just been speaking
of—make-believe soldiers, no decent stuff in 'em. It
was mid-December when we went to Traunstein.
They were mostly Russian prisoners there, and a few
English. An officer met us at the station and saw us
detrain. When he went to fall us in, the Revolution
men grinned in his face and asked if he didn't know
drill had been done away with ? He made no reply,
but packed them off to barracks. Then he assembled
us men from the Front and instructed us that this
sort of insolence wasn't to be too much regarded, or
all the prisoners would get away. He merely returned the whole company to Munich by the next
train, retaining only we Front soldiers, Hitler among
the rest.

"We hadn't a great deal to do. We mounted guard
at the gate over the outgoings and incomings, for
twenty-four hours at a stretch. The next twenty-
four hours were off duty. At the end of January
they broke up the camp, and sent most of the

prisoners back home. So we, too, returned to barracks at Munich. There, there was absolutely nothing to do. We got perfectly sick of it, especially Hitler. So one day we reported, and asked to be put on a job. We must have work of some kind ! They hunted up something for us to do—old gas-masks to test. There were whole mountains of these things. We had only the mouthpiece to unscrew and examine, and if anything was wrong, to put it on one side. The work was easy, and to our joy, we got three marks a day for it. At this rate we could manage sometimes to go to the Opera. Hitler was a regular Opera ' fan.' We only bought the cheapest seats, but that didn't matter. Hitler was lost in the music to the very last note ; blind and deaf to all else around him.

" Meanwhile Kurt Eisner lost ground day by day. His throne was very soon tottering. Bolshevik ideas were rapidly gaining in every direction, and every day witnessed mass demonstrations in the streets. On February 21st, 1919, the members of the Landtag[1] were assembled in session and awaiting the President. Suddenly the cry was raised, ' Eisner has been shot.' The utmost consternation ensued. As this somewhat subsided and Auer, the Leader of the Majority Socialists, could make his voice heard, he was attempting to address the assembly when the doors were suddenly flung open, a shot rang out, and he instantly collapsed. A panic stampeded the members. More shots added to the terror and confusion, and two other delegates fell bleeding to the ground.

" The news of the assassination of the President flew like wildfire through the city, and, although

[1] Landtag as distinguished from Reichstag. State as distinguished from Central Parliament.

Eisner had practically lost the popular favour, the Communists made capital out of his death and proclaimed a general strike to revenge it. Again masses of excited demonstrators gathered in the streets. Again newspaper offices and shops and warehouses were raided and plundered. The 'Bolshevik' Revolutionaries marched to the spot where young Count Toni von Arco Valley had shot down Kurt Eisner, erected a portrait of him there, and obliged every passer-by to uncover before it. The late President was buried on February 26th, with almost royal pomp on the Munich 'Ost-Friedhof.'

" Followed a period of muddle and confusion with half a dozen so-called Governments all in power at once. A stop-gap ministry was formed to carry on, but the working-classes came forward demanding the arming of the proletariat. They sought to overthrow the Council. The Communist Central Office in Berlin sent the Jew Leviné, a man of their own, to Munich, and on the night of April 17th, 1919, a 'Red' assembly was held in the Wittelsbach Palace which inaugurated the brief 'Red' régime, with yet another Jew, Ernst Toller, at its head.

" Nothing in all this sufficed to allay the unrest in State and city. The peasants in the country were losing all patience, and now threatened to withhold foodstuffs from entering Munich. This menace was so serious that a new Social Democratic régime under Hoffmann was set up. Like all its predecessors, this also was destined quickly to fail. Severe strikes in the Ruhr, inspired by the Communist leader, Karl Liebknecht, the proclamation of a republic in Hungary by the Jew, Bela Kun, and the general unrest everywhere, had their repercussions in Munich.

ABOVE THE DOOR, THE WINDOW OF THE ROOM IN WHICH HITLER LIVED IN MUNICH FROM 1920–1929

Strife of every sort broke out among the various
parties in the city, all led, without exception, by
Jews. By April, 1919, the Hoffmann Government
was obliged to betake itself to Bamberg, from whence
it ruled the northern half of Bavaria, leaving Munich
and the southern half of the country in the hands of
the Bolshevists who sought to link it up with the
Hungary of Bela Kun and Russia of Lenin.

" Then one day armoured cars were to be seen
racing through the streets distributing leaflets in
favour of the Hoffman administration. Those who
opposed such propaganda were at once shot down
by machine-guns. Next came armoured cars adver-
tising the Red régime in the same manner, with
placards demanding the fall of Hoffmann. Those
who failed to comply with this new coercion were
also at once shot down by more machine-guns.
Hardly had both sets of armoured cars disappeared
then a force of Spartakists, three thousand strong,
marched on the principal railway station which was
already held by Hoffmann's troops. Firing broke
out and the Spartakists gave back, only to rally, and
bombard the place in their turn for over half an
hour. The station was captured and its defenders all
shot, to a man. This seemed to break the back of
the resistance to the ' Red ' régime for the moment.
New strikes were immediately organised.

" Hitler and I looked on at all this with the utter-
most repugnance, as you can well suppose. Hitler
had already come up against the Communists, for
disobeying some of their orders. They already had
an eye on him. It seemed better, they thought, to
get him out of the way.

" One morning, very early, three Red Guards
entered the barracks and sought him out in his room.

He was already up and dressed. As they tramped up the stairs Hitler guessed what was afoot, so grasped his revolver and prepared for the encounter. They banged on the door which immediately opened to them :

" ' If you don't instantly clear out,' cried Hitler, brandishing his weapon, ' I'll serve you as we served mutineers at the Front.'

" The Reds turned instantly, and tramped downstairs again. The threat had been far too real to face an instant longer.

" Just think of it ! The City Commissary, and the Commander-in-Chief of the Red Army at this time, was one of the sailor mutineers, a man of no more than twenty-one, who had already served terms of imprisonment, and who in 1917 had been condemned to death—unfortunately the sentence hadn't been carried out !

" It was winter time, and snow lay deep in the streets. Soldiers were streaming back into Munich still, from all the battle-fronts, weary, battered, disorientated men, coming home to a foundered country where neither food nor peace nor work was to be had. There were thirty thousand unemployed hanging about the streets. Food grew ever scarcer and more scarce. The people ate anything they could lay hands upon that was remotely eatable. A fallen horse was a godsend. Such a carcass was immediately pounced upon by the starving populace, and in quicker time than it takes to tell every shred of flesh was stripped from the bones.

" During all this confused and calamitous time Hitler remained with the Army (which endeavoured to take up a neutral position among the warring factions), but I got demobbed, and sought work in

Munich.   I still met Hitler every day, because we used the same ' Stehrestaurant '[1] to have our meals in.   At that time soldiers were not boarded in barracks as formerly, but drew ration money and could lay it out where and how they pleased.   That's how it happened that Hitler and I could feed together. The grub was pretty poor, you may be sure, the place was dirty and crowded, the tables bare, and one had to fetch and carry for oneself.   We paid about thirty pfennige for this.   We used, often, to get through an evening here, too, drinking tea— Hitler seldom drank coffee—and talking over things. Hitler used to get all worked up and hot and angry, and I often thought to myself he'd make short work of the mob at the top just now, if he'd had any sort of a say.   But we were nothing but a pair of nobodies, without a pull anywhere.

" In the middle of April, 1919, the Hoffmann Government decided to call upon Berlin for help against the Bolshevists in Munich.   Berlin sent help and the Reichswehr, men consisting of old Front-line soldiers.   These were glad enough to take up arms against the Reds, not out of any love for the Republic, be sure, but for the sake of the Fatherland.   Independent bodies of men gathered together to the same end, especially the Freikorps Epp which later on put in some particularly good work.   Four groups of these gradually approached Munich.   Each group possessed artillery, cavalry, sappers and armoured cars.   The Red Army numbered some 20,000 men. On April 15th, 1919, 15,000 of these, fully armed, marched through the city to meet the ' White ' invaders.

" The Whites, led by experienced officers, gradually

[1] Emergency restaurant.

closed in round Munich. On April 29th, they were at
Dachau, a small town some ten miles to the north,
which formed a good strategical objective. It was
quickly captured. Meantime the Reds in Munich,
feeling their ascendancy was at an end, gave themselves over to an orgy of destruction. Again the
shops were wrecked, streets were barricaded, machine-
guns mounted, and everything got ready for cramped
and intensive urban fighting. ' For every Red, five
citizens,' was the slogan of the Bolshevists.

" Just as the White Army was drawing nigh, ten
people of the city's upper ten, including the young
Countess von Westarp, were arrested and brutally
shot in the courtyard of the Luitpold Gymnasium.
This barbarity inflamed the Müncheners more than
ever against the Reds, and the news of it served to
quicken the relieving troops. On May 1st, battle was
joined, and once again the streets of Munich were
filled with fighting men. The Whites had a hard task
before them. They were fired upon from every van-
tage point and corner, from every roof and window.
They had, literally, to take every single house on
their way towards the centre of the city. The battle
raged hottest of all in Giesing, the ' Red ' quarter,
where General von Epp was in command.

" Although non-combatants were forbidden to go
out of doors, I couldn't stay quiet within. I had to
get out and see things for myself. Everywhere there
was firing. It reminded me of Flanders ! It was
risking death to attempt certain crossings. Most
of the public buildings had first been stormed by
artillery and then attacked by hand grenades. . . .
The fight went on all night. By dawn the Reds had
entrenched themselves, as it were, in the Matthäser
Bräu situated opposite the place where now the

Hanfstaengl Galleries on the Karlsplatz are located in the centre of the city, from which place it would be difficult to dislodge them. But a severe bombardment did it at last, and their resistance was practically broken. Desultory fighting went on for a day or two yet, but on May 3rd the Whites and the Free Companies entered the city in triumph to the jubilation of the population.

" The new masters of the situation had the leaders of the Reds arrested—those of them who had not already escaped—and imprisoned, or shot on the spot. Order was soon restored. But the wresting of Munich from the Red Terror was a costly business. The Whites lost twenty-eight officers and one hundred and ninety-four men. The Reds lost four hundred and fifty—one hundred and thirty-five of these were shot out of hand.

" This one month of bolshevism had cured Munich once and for all of dalliance with the Reds. Munich had had enough of Communism.

" One day, shortly after all this business was over, I met Hitler in the street. He looked pretty pinched and peaky, but he was glad enough to see me. ' I've just come out of chink, Schmidt,' he explained.

" ' How's that ? " I demanded, astonished. So he told me. The military in Munich had held themselves a bit too much aloof. When the Whites entered a few stray shots seemed to come from the barracks. No one could account for them, but the Whites made short work of the business. They took every man in the place, including Hitler, prisoner, and shut them up in the cellars of the Max Gymnasium. A few days later, however, an officer who had been at the Front, happened to come along and spotted Hitler among the prisoners.

"'Why how's this?' he demanded, 'you're no Communist—' and had him immediately set free.

"With the disruption of the Reds, order was re-established in the Army. Discipline was tightened up. Hitler remained a soldier and was given the job of testing every man's political soundness. It was to be avoided at all costs that former ' Reds ' should now try and re-enlist in the Reichswehr. Hitler was specially fit for this job on account of his political acumen, and because he was considered to be a good judge of men.

" He put the thing through so well that later on they promoted him to Regimental Instructor. Hitler had now to hold regular classes to instruct the men on political matters, and in a true sense of patriotism. He had to eradicate the last traces of the poison which had led to the setting up of ' Soldiers' Councils,' and abortive revolutionary measures of that sort. Hitler did all this extraordinarily well. He discovered his own gift for public speaking and exposition. He rather imagined he had such a talent, but these classes in Barracks were useful enough to exercise and prove it.

" As a matter of fact this military duty gave him the key to his own future. He decided to leave the Army and go in for politics altogether. After a few more months he returned to civilian life. He would have had, perhaps, an easier time had he remained with the Reichswehr, but by now he had conceived his great idea, and was convinced that, whatever it might cost to realise it, he would bring it to fruition in the end. He had already joined the Deutsche Arbeiter-Partei.[1] . . .

" I joined it, too, almost from the start. Hitler

[1] German Workers' Party.

never brought any pressure to bear upon me to do so, but I was ready enough to follow his lead wherever it led.   And that he was filled with the noblest and most unselfish passion was never for one moment to be questioned by any one who really knew Hitler then.

" I often met him during the week, either in the Barracks, and later in his lodging in the Thierschstrasse, or in the now famous Sterneckerbräu, and came to have my share of all the first ups and downs of the Party.   But you know about those—let's stick to Hitler himself.

" There's one thing I must tell you ; he's passionately fond of animals.   One of the Party friends had the lucky idea of us giving him a dog[1] for his birthday in 1920.   He rather thought a Deutscher Schäferhund (German shepherd's dog) would be the thing and we bought one remarkable for size rather than for breed since funds were none too flush—Hitler was awfully pleased with it.   But the dog was ill—we hadn't known that—and it went and died.   So early next year somebody else sent him a young Wolfhound.   Hitler fell in love with him, and they became inseparable companions.   When, later on, he got more dogs, (they are still living at his country place), this one remained his prime favourite.   He kept him some ten years or more and then some enemy managed to poison him—some Communist belike.   He must have known that to kill Hitler's dog would hit him harder than any political revenge.   Shows, doesn't it, how vile this enmity was—to wreak it on that sort of friend !

[1] During the war a little dog deserted from the English lines and came over to us. Hitler adopted him and called him " Foxl." He is seen in the picture.

" I came here to Garching in 1922. But I've often seen Hitler since then—once at Landsberg, when he was in prison in 1924, and afterwards on happier occasions. I saw him last on November 9th, 1933, in the Brown House at Munich. Another old comrade and I looked him up there together——"

" By the way," added Herr Schmidt, as I thought he had concluded, " I might as well say that the War knocked Marxian ideas out of me. It wasn't Hitler. He didn't try to bring any political influence to bear on one at that time. But he certainly did live up to his convictions and the rest of us fellows saw it. He was a walking example of the motto he after- wards gave the Party, ' All for one, one for all.' One doesn't fight like that for vague international generalities. This is the reason why so few old ex-service men went over to the Revolution."

In those first terrible months after Hitler's return to Bavaria, away in Versailles the German delegates to the Peace Conference waited like prisoners behind wire and partitions to be informed as to the terms of a Treaty which they had no option but to sign. The soldiers in Munich and the people in the streets waited, too, for the news from Versailles. Then it came—to such a city, and to such people, at such a time ! Seven million Germans were to be lost to Germany by expatriation, and so inconceivable a sum of money was to be paid by way of war indemnity that it exceeded the total wealth of the Reich. The work of whole generations would not suffice to pay it.

Hitler as Bildungsoffizier (Regimental Instruction Officer) in Munich watched the course of events with closest attention. Of one thing he soon became fully convinced and dangerously aware, so desperate was his anxiety for rational effective creative effort in some promising direction, namely, that the last hour had struck for Germany—was then striking at Versailles—unless this wild political welter could be reduced to order, and a national unity, bigger far than a mere Bavarian unity, powerful, purposeful and enthusiastic could be welded out of it. Something more must come out of this endless talk around the tables in the Bierhallen than mere jeremiads, sighs and theories, and hot air.

Hitler perceived that all political experimentation in Germany was beside the point so long as no voice was raised against the crushing exactions of the Versailles Treaty. No resurrection was even thinkable for the prostrate shattered country, unless apathy could be overcome, despair could be counteracted, violence could be harnessed and national feeling could be awakened to the one supreme creative end of rebutting the exactions and denying the imputations of the Treaty under which, otherwise, Germany was condemned to speedy death. He went everywhere ; noted everything ; measured to a nicety the worth or worthlessness of the speakers and things spoken ; plumbed the people's hopes, fears, aimlessness, incapacity, and—readiness to respond, when and if it should come, to some Trumpet Call to life ! By February, 1920, within a year of Kurt Eisner's death, Hitler himself sounded such a reveillé in Germany that it rang through the entire German world.

He saw the road to take—the straight road, the only road.

But how was he to point it out not only to the Müncheners, not only to Bavaria, but to the nation at large ? How was he to start the march, to lead the way, to form the vanguard, to draw all Germany

along behind him until the goal should be in sight—
the goal that he reached indeed, *for* Germany, in
March, 1933 ?

■   ·   ·   ·   ·

Fate at this moment made use of three little
mice.

Hitler went on frequenting the small clubs and
groups of ineffectual men who met here and there
under that or the other rather high-sounding name
to discuss the political situation. To him they all
seemed tragically laughable. None of them had the
slightest spark of life in it ; no constructive idea ;
no programme ; no policy. The personnel of no
single one seemed to furnish a man of any parts.
They were all alike—mere talkers, ineffectuals.
Hitler's search for a *point d'appui* wearied and
disgusted him. He was actually driven back upon
the question as to whether or not he himself should
found a party. But he asked himself, how could he,
a " Namenloser "—an unknown soldier—without
backing, or any sort of influence, succeed in such a
step ? It would probably be better, willy-nilly, to
associate himself with the least feeble and ridiculous
of the little groups he had already surveyed.

Three little mice, scampering about the barracks
floor, one morning early, kept Adolf Hitler awake.
He found it impossible to drop off again to sleep.
Idly he reached out for something to read—anything that came within grasp. Somebody overnight,
at some little gathering or other, had thrust a
pamphlet into his hand as he went out. He remembered an urgent word or two impressing it upon his
notice. All right then—let's have a look at it now !
In the early hours of the morning while the mice

squeaked and gambolled without let or hindrance, unwashed, unshaven, Hitler lay in a poor tumbled bed—and found what he had sought so long, so vainly, found that of which he had well-nigh despaired. This pamphlet thing, *Mein politisches Erwachen*,[1] seemed to hit things exactly on the dot ! It sort of crystallised ideas of his own—Hitler's— put them in a nutshell, suggested lines to him on which things might be got going. . . .

He read the slight thing from cover to cover, slapped it down with decision, and promptly sprang up.

Hitler had found his starting-point.

It is, to-day, Anton Drexler's proudest remembrance that through the perusal of this little brochure of his, Adolf Hitler came to join the German Workmen's Party, to bring to it those qualities of energy, enthusiasm, vision, to demand from every member of it that spirit of ready sacrifice and unbounded daring, without which neither the still-born movement nor this little writing would ever have been heard of again. Drexler had dreamed of such a man, but it had scarcely ever entered his head to hope that such a one would actually materialise, and in the little Bierkeller where he and his friends forgathered !

Who, then, was Anton Drexler ?

To revert a little. Leading to the principal Bahnhof in Munich is a long street of buildings entirely occupied by the management of the Bavarian Railways. The largest of them is the Reichsbahn Zentralamt. In the spring of 1934 the author of this book found his way inside and

---

[1] *My Political Awakening. From a Workingman's Diary*, by Anton Drexler.

traversed innumerable halls and corridors, passed hundreds of doors with all sorts of names and inscriptions on them, and came at last to room No. 553. Here the legend ran " Anton Drexler, Foreman."

I knocked and was bidden to enter.

I encountered a sharp bespectacled scrutiny from an individual seated behind an enormous desk. I mentioned my name, whereupon he got up and stretched out a cordial hand.

" Oh, yes, I know all about you. Come in and sit down. I'll attend to you in a minute—just let me finish what I am about, and then we'll get going."

I liked the look of Anton Drexler. He is to-day a man in the early fifties ; not a bit the stereotyped official, but the craftsman and the worker.

" Before I begin about Hitler," he said at last, " and how he and I met in 1919, and about the politics of that time, perhaps I'd better say a word or two as to myself. It sort of leads up.

" My father was a working man here in Munich. He belonged to the Social Democrats. I remember how he and my mother used to take me out into the woods on the first Sunday in May and how lovely it was. It was a festival, a springtime festival ; we all looked forward to the first of May so much. Then I went to school, and later joined a Munich Schützen-Verein (Rifle Club). I remember how when strikes came along there was no more wandering in the springtime woods for us. Politics knocked all that sort of thing on the head.

" I took to the locksmith's trade, and when my apprenticeship was over, set out on my journeyman's travels. In 18— I got as far as Berlin in the course of time. I found work there, but soon struck a snag. Berlin's commanding proletarian leader of that time was Adolf Bebel, who was never tired of spreading the unions everywhere. Everybody was after me to join the union. I didn't want to do so straight away, although I knew, of course, one had to join a union sooner or later. The trouble was one got drawn into politics. Not only that—one got involved in communistic scraps. I wasn't having any. So I got the cold shoulder. Found myself out of work. It wasn't any use hanging on in Berlin, so I started off home again, taking what jobs I could on the way. I worked on the farms. There was always something for a handy man in the locksmith line to do about the farms and smithies.

" It chanced, too, that a Jewish cattle dealer took me on for a bit. He was a brute, that man, and turned me against the Jews one and all, for good. Never had no use for them since ! I can't stop to tell you all that he did, how vilely he treated me—but this I can say, he opened my eyes to things I'd never thought of before. I came to realise what a menace he and his kind offered. He wasn't no exception to the rest—the blood-sucker !

" Back in Munich I got a job in the railway works. Even now I wasn't keen about joining a union, but somehow I managed to keep my end up and hold on. I kept on in the works for some years, in fact right up to 1914 when Europe burst into flames after Sarajevo. With the outbreak of war came an enormous demand for railway material of all sorts, and the pressure at the works was terrific. There was no question of my joining up. I'd just got to stay put and fight for the Fatherland, not in the trenches but at my vice.

" But I kept my eyes open, I can tell you, as to how things went, and from now on began to get interested in politics. Why, right from the first those blessed Social Democrats were kicking against spending the money necessary to keep the Army in the field. But there were splits, too, in the camp. Half of them remained where they were (the Majority Socialist Party) and the other lot formed a sort of radical wing called the Independent Socialists. They engineered a strike of 55,000 munition workers as early as May, 1916.[1] After that strikes were always happening. Then things were so jockeyed in Parliament as to bring about the ' Black Red Coalition,' which ultimately was responsible for the Revolution of the 9th of November, 1918, and culpable of signing the Versailles Treaty.

" The Social Democrats owned it themselves that they were out to sabotage the War. They weren't, of course, at one with the enemy, but they went about the way to realise their objects as though they had been. Both aimed at the overthrow of the Monarchy, the destruction of the German Army, and the lasting disarmament of Germany. The Marxists saw in all this the best possible augury for the realisation of their own schemes. Hundreds and thousands of our men at the Front fell, victims of the strife at home and of the rascality and treachery of those who fomented it, far more than victims of the War itself. The whole thing was a hideous tragedy. There was another disastrous strike in the munitions industry in January, 1918. The spirit which animated people and Army alike at the outbreak of War was evapor-

---

[1] And yet we so constantly encounter the objection that Hitler ascribes the collapse of the German Front in 1918 to the wrong causes. The black-red " Stab in the Back " was the main cause, despite a thousand others.

ated. Even[1] the Socialists had marched in 1914 to the defence of Home, Hearth, Family and Fatherland, at one with their fellow countrymen. Had any one dared breathe the word ' Strike ' at that time, he would have been strung up on the nearest lamp-post.

" Where I come in, in all this, is that in January, 1918, the *Münchner Zeitung* published an article of mine in which I had my say, hot and strong, about the munitions strike, and a good lot of other things as well. I was all for carrying the War on till we won it, and dead against profiteering and usury and all that dry-rot at home. So was the somewhat bourgeois ' Vaterlands-Partei ' of Tirpitz.

" As a result I got it in the neck all round ! The men at the works had nothing for me but hatred and scoffing. Some of them went and dug a grave near the place where I worked, and stuck up a post and nailed the top of a box on it, on which they painted in big black letters ' Died of Hunger for the Fatherland. Gentleman 1918.'[2]

". . . There is one thing to be said though. The leaders of the ' Vaterlands-Partei,' decent men enough, had no real idea of the state of common people's feelings, how everything was boiling up to bursting point. Anyhow a tiny group of us workmen got

[1] The use of this word " even " in such a connection serves to show, plainly enough, how deep and bitter was the cleft separating party from party in Germany. Herr Anton Drexler's narrative is given at some slight length here by way of commentary upon what has been said above as to the political condition of things in general, and of Bavaria in particular, by way of setting the stage for the entrance of the dramatic figure of the Führer.

[2] The mere translation of this epitaph entirely fails to convey its scorn and sarcasm. It represents the German equivalent to the English offer of a white feather. It suggests that this self-conceited nobody, a mere workman like themselves, who yet thinks so much of himself and aspires to print (" Gentleman ") might die of hunger for his country (anybody could do that in Germany in 1918) but would manage conveniently to evade the Front.

together somehow, among the workshops, and
founded a sort of forerunner of the German Workmen's Party. I was chairman of the committee. But
we were all poor, powerless, unknown. We didn't
succeed, really, in getting anywhere with our ' Free
Workmen's Committee ' as we called it. We only
made things impossibly difficult for ourselves all
round. Nevertheless we managed to get into touch
with another like-minded little group in Bremen.
We even got so far as to hold a small public meeting
in Munich, in October (1918), but I can't say it had
any results worth mentioning. It ended up with
a row.

" Then next month they went and let that Jew
Kosmanowsky, who called himself Eisner, out of
prison. Whatever induced them to do it passes my
understanding to this day. A friend of mine and I
went to some of the meetings of the Independent
Socialists and did what we could to protest against
the speakers and the speeches. We only got howled
down for it, and often barely escaped. On November
7th there was a big meeting on the Theresienwiese
when they yelled ' Down with the Kaiser, down with
the Crown Prince, and clear out the Wittelsbachs !'
and the whole mob surged into the city and broke
open the gaols and let loose upon Munich all the
criminal riff-raff together with the political prisoners
held in them. The Münchener underworld went
mafficking through the streets with a murderer still
in chains at the head of it ! The riot kept up for days
—there was shooting when the tradespeople
attempted to defend their goods and shops—and in
the middle of everything the King, Ludwig III,
escaped from the city. The only thing which might
have quelled the Revolution would have been if the

THE FAMOUS BÜRGER BRÄU KELLER, MUNICH

FIRST OFFICE OF THE GERMAN WORKERS'
PARTY IN THE STERNECKERGASSE, MUNICH

troops had been called out against the mob—but they weren't—for fear of inciting it to further violence. Anyhow Eisner had got the upper hand. You know the rest. What sort of a government he set up, and what ultimately became of him and it.

" As for me and the Freien Arbeiter-Ausschuss, we had a meeting to protest against the doings of December, 1918, in Berlin and Hamburg. It so happened just when things were at their worst I had to go as the Bavarian representative of our little group to a conference about Bolshevism in Berlin. It was held at a place in the Potsdamerstrasse. I had no sooner put my nose inside the door than I was arrested by a couple of heavily-armed Reds. They clapped me into a dark little room at the back while they proceeded to break up the concern there, an editorial office, where we had proposed to have our meeting. In the end, though, I was allowed to communicate with some relatives living in Berlin, and found myself once more at liberty.

" After that I brought the Freien Arbeiter-Ausschuss into touch with another little group called the Politischer Arbeiter-Zirkel, run by a journalist of the name of Harrer. He had got together all sorts of books and facts about the War, the Russian Revolution—and our own Revolution—which we all set to work to study hard, by way of trying to find some way out of the débâcle. We discussed a new name for our combination, and decided on a new departure. United, we numbered perhaps thirty-five members. We agreed to meet on January 5th in a little eating-house in Munich called the ' Fürstenfelder Hof ' to found the ' Deutsche Arbeiter-Partei.'

" But before the day came the animosity of the Reds was already awakened. Some of our would-be

members were arrested and done to death : I myself
only escaped the same fate, one dark night waiting
for Harrer, by a hair's breadth. These Reds were
Marxists, Jew-inspired. That's another reason why
we hated the Jews.

"Perhaps I ought to say that our Party didn't
really aspire—yet—to be a party. It only consisted
of the committee of six men. But, of course, we
couldn't make any sort of headway. Our meetings
were private because of this Red threat. We seemed
to have got ourselves into a blind alley. We could
do little but discuss and study. I embodied my own
ideas in a slight brochure called *Mein politisches
Erwachen.* From the diary of a workingman."

Here Drexler turns to a drawer in his writing-desk
and brings a copy of it into the light. A little affair,
this, of some forty pages bound in a tattered blue cover.

"Let me read you a bit," says the author eagerly,
"just one or two of the most telling passages——

"Oh no, first I ought to make it clear that this
didn't pretend to lay down lines for a Party exactly.
I only aimed really at setting down the views and
thoughts of a starred man of the street, of the War,
the Front, and the Revolution, and to draw out the
necessary consequences——"

Then he reads, jumping from page to page (the
book is evidently known to him by heart), and I
gather the impression of a hefty invective against
usury, profiteering, cowardice, and class privilege.
. . . The whole thing, I know, merely voiced the
passionate convictions of hundreds and thousands of
inarticulate workers here at home in Germany. It
suggested, however, no solution for the problems so
trenchantly envisaged and presented. How could a
group consisting of merely six men, with no following

worth speaking of, and no representation in the
Landtag, make its voice heard in the political world
at that time ?

No one was more aware of the futility of it all than
Anton Drexler in 1919.

" If only someone would turn up," he breaks off
reading and resumes his story, " I used to think if
only someone would turn up with go and grit in him,
who could make something out of us and this,"
slapping the pamphlet, " and contrive a real driving
force behind us. It would need to be an outstanding
personality, anyhow, who could even attempt to do
such a thing, a man of intense conviction, single-
eyed, and absolutely fearless. I never really hoped
or dreamed that such an individual would ever blow
in at the Sterneckerbräu ! A genius such as we
needed—such as Germany needed—only turns up
once in a century !

" If we carried on, it was only in some unexpressed
sort of dream and hope that our little group might at
least offer a starting point—sooner or later—for
greater and more efficient things.

" A little bit before this I happened to have come
across the writer and poet Dietrich Eckart. He had
read my articles in the Munich paper, and was good
enough to say it was fine that at last a working man
had expressed himself about all the corruption going
on in high places. In fact we became good friends,
Eckart and I, and I asked him to come and speak at
one of our little gatherings. He would have done so,
but that he fell ill. So I got Gottfried Feder[1] instead.

[1] Eckart and Feder. Famous names, to-day, as those of two of
the Führer's first firm friends.   These are names which are household words in Germany.   Eckart was a writer, and Feder an expert
on financial matters.   With the introduction of these two names
into Drexler's narrative the curtain rises on Adolf Hitler.

" My goodness, but it is well known now—that
story of our little meeting at eight o'clock one
evening in the Sterneckerbräu, when Feder got up
to speak ! First there'd been a bit of a clash between
our first speaker—who suggested a union between
Austria and Bavaria and the formation of a Danubian
State—and a newcomer at the back of the room.
Then Feder seemed to grip the audience. He had
something very interesting to say about the difference
between loan (or unproductive) capital, and
industrial capital which feeds productive industry.

" I had been much struck by the objector from
the back. He spoke uncommonly well, and used his
arguments with force as telling as a flail. He seemed
to know his ground, too, better than most. I thought
to myself ' Herr Gott ! here's a chap worth getting
hold of ! ' I kept an eye on him and when the
meeting broke up, made a bee-line for him just as he
was leaving. I gave him a copy of my pamphlet—
asked him to come again—hoped he'd read it——

" AND THAT MAN WAS ADOLF HITLER."

CHAPTER VI

ADOLF HITLER tells the story in *Mein Kampf* better than anyone has told it since. He read Drexler's little pamphlet. Still, curiosity rather than anything as yet quite like decision, led his steps once more in the direction of the Sterneckerbräu, or perhaps it was to the " Alte Lilienbad " in the Herrnstrasse, where the queer folk he had unearthed there a few nights previously, seemed wont to forgather on a Wednesday evening. . . . There was certainly a good lot in what that chap Feder had been saying. . . .

He writes : " I crossed the badly lighted common room where no one at all was to be seen, and sought the door leading to a room at the back. . . . There in the glimmer of a semi-broken gas-lamp four young men were sitting at a table, among whom was the author of the little brochure " (previously given him to read, mark and digest), " who at once came forward and greeted me in the most friendly manner and bade me welcome as a new member of the German Workers' Party."

Hitler was a trifle nonplussed. However, he meant to see the evening through, and bit by bit got hold of the names of those present. They read the minutes of the last meeting, and then went into Party finances—a matter of some 7·50 marks—and read letters from absent members.

---

[1] German Workers' Party.

" Fürchterlich, fürchterlich. Das war ja eine
Vereinsmeierei allerärgster Art und Weise. In
diesen Klub also sollte ich eintreten ? "

(" Dreadful, dreadful ! This was a wretched little
group of the feeblest sort and kind. Was I going to
enrol myself in a Club like this ? ")

Yes, indeed. So it fell out, for want of an alternative. Hitler was not the founder of this party. Those
four poor ineffectuals in the " Alte Lilienbad " at
Munich gave him his opportunity. But it seemed
all too negligible and hopeless. How, in God's name,
Hitler asked himself, was anything to be made of
such a beginning ? How was a miserable little knot
of pale people like this (he was the only soldier among
them), to be welded into any decent sort of a going
concern—club, or whatever it liked to call itself?
How was any kick to be got into it ? How was such a
club to be carried any further, brought to the semblance of some sort of a society ? How was this
society to become a significant movement ? How
would such a movement proceed to the uplifting of a
prostrate, demoralised, humiliated country ? For
that and no less an aim from the first was in Hitler's
mind as he stumbled through the dark of the empty
guest room in the " Alte Lilienbad."

The answer to this riddle comes as one of the most
dramatic things in *Mein Kampf,* a book packed with
passion, drama and inexorable purpose.

The new associate was dutiful enough to attend the
next little meeting of the " Deutsche Arbeiter-
Partei," and the next and the next. Nothing
happened. Numbers did not increase. The all-
devouring question still hammered in the brain that
would not despair. Hitler discovered three radical
reasons why this little association should be so feeble.

First of all it had no faith in itself, its purpose, or the possibility of its ever amounting to anything. Secondly, no remotest likelihood seemed to exist of any increase of its membership. Various efforts to this end, including a hand to hand distribution of hand-written invitations to its meetings, met with no sort of response. Thirdly, it was possessed of no funds. It could not afford the cheapest sort of leaflet publicity.

Hitler felt at once that much was needed here if the " Deutsche Arbeiter-Partei " was to constitute any sort of a starting-point for the energetic political campaign he had in view. Instead of the mere little weekly committee meetings, it must embark on frequent public assemblies, whence it might be hoped (and the event amply justified the aspiration), that money for propaganda might be forthcoming. Also the nucleus demanded fresh young energetic blood! " During the long years of my military life," he writes, " I had come across a lot of sterling comrades, many of whom through my persuasion began now to join the group. . . . They were sound energetic young fellows, well disciplined, and schooled through army life to the axiom that nothing is impossible, everything is attainable by the man of strong will."

The first few of the new series of meetings thus inaugurated were not particularly successful, but at last Hitler's driving and energetic power made itself felt. " Our audiences," he writes, " mounted very, very slowly in number. From eleven hearers we went on to thirteen : presently to sixteen, three and twenty—perhaps even to four and thirty ! "

Something more, obviously, had to be done about it.

Enough marks were scraped together to insert a small advertisement in a Munich newspaper of an ambitious meeting proposed to be held in the Münchener Hofbräukeller, a smallish room capable of seating some hundred and thirty people. This was to be the sort of meeting which, it was hoped, would really attract some public attention. All depended upon Adolf Hitler himself. As he went down to the hall that night his heart was in his mouth. He scarcely dared hope the place would be more than a third, or at very most, half-full. . . .

By seven o'clock a hundred and eleven people had actually turned up, and proceedings began. This was the first occasion (apart from his lectures to soldiers) upon which Hitler was to speak in public. He was allotted twenty minutes. . . . Then it was that both he and the audience made the discovery upon which the future of the German nation was to turn. The moment this ex-service man, this energetic recruit to the flabby little group which called itself the German Workers' Party, got upon his legs to speak was the decisive moment for the Germany we see to-day. His tiny audience was electrified—transported !

Amazed himself, Hitler perceived in an illuminating flash wherein the secret lay,—in oratory, convinced and dynamic ! He had not dreamed that he possessed such a gift. He tried it out that night with staggering success. The message he had to proclaim was not that with the German Workers' Party nothing but a new election cry had been added to the existing political babel, but that the foundation stone had been well and truly laid for the rebuilding of the shattered nation. In the American phrase, Adolf Hitler "got that message across"! The money required[1] poured in. When all was over

---

[1] Hitler seldom appealed directly for funds. He appealed to the audience to support the movement.

the hall emptied to scatter Hitlerism broadcast throughout the city.

From now on big meeting followed big meeting, with ever mounting success until early in 1920 Hitler (who had, naturally, assumed the leadership of the group) determined upon the first great mass meeting, despite the danger, by now grown to appreciable proportions, of its being suppressed by the authorities, or broken up by the opposition. It was held on February 24th, in the famous Festsaal, (not the Keller), of the Hofbräuhaus, and numbered an audience of two thousand. Hitler's business was to lay before it nothing less than the reasoned and detailed programme of the new party.

" As the time went by," he writes, " hostile interruptions gave way to acclamations. As one by one, point for point, I laid down the five and twenty planks in our platform, and submitted them to the judgment of the audience, there gradually arose an ever-swelling jubilation in response, and as my last words made their way to the very heart of the mass, the whole room surged before me unanimous in a new conviction, a new belief, and a new determination."

The " Deutsche Arbeiter-Partei " was now fully in shape to draw upon itself the implacable enmity of the constituted authority, the Communists, the Marxists and other political organisations whom its programme affronted or threatened. It had become a force in Munich. It took to itself a flag and a symbol. Hitler himself, after many attempts, designed this standard. " We National Socialists see our purpose in our flag. The red stands for our social programme, the white for our national, and in the hooked cross we symbolise the struggle for the supremacy of the Aryan race."

In 1920 it had already become dangerous to hold meetings and to flourish this flag, and the worthy Müncheners who frequented Nazi[1] demonstrations did so at increasing risk not only of bodily injury, but to life itself. It was this state of affairs which gave rise to the so-called " Saal-Schutz."[2]

About a year after Hitler's first great successful mass meeting in Munich, he decided upon holding a still greater one, upon which, in fact, the whole future of the young Movement might be held to turn. Were it to prove a fiasco, the " Deutsche Arbeiter-Partei " would disappear in the welter of mushroom parties of that date : were it to succeed it would dominate in Munich and gird itself for a Reich-wide struggle.

Already the local forces of opposition were fully alive to the significance of the new political activity, and the occasion of this unprecedented effort on its part was chosen for a decisive counter-demonstration. The Reds in Munich determined once and for all to smash up the " Deutsche Arbeiter-Partei." Hitler tells us that not only was appeal for police protection futile, but beneath the dignity of the Movement. The Movement must defend itself. Only so could it command the respect of those it would attract, or ensure the safety of its audiences.

A band of hefty and enthusiastic young supporters were specially told off by Hitler himself to keep the doors, and to act as ruthless chuckers-out at the very first sign of disorder. They were to fight with the gloves off and to show no quarter.

The event fully justified these precautions. After an enormous gathering in the Zircus Krone in

---

[1] Nazi, short for " Nazi-onal (National) Socialist," a nickname given the new movement.

[2] Party-body organised with the express purpose of protecting the meetings against red disturbances.

Munich, which had been an unqualified success, another meeting was held well packed with opponents only too eager to snatch the next best opportunity to wreck the whole business once and for all. Hitler was on his legs speaking on " The Future or Collapse " when the signal was given. Thereupon followed such a scene, such a smash up, such an uproar and such a blood shedding, that it actually recalled to the ex-service man moments at the Front !

The " Saal-Schutz " received their baptism of fists and chair legs, but bit by bit, fighting literally like berserkers, they hurled the enemy out, slung him head foremost through the doors, drove him into a corner and pummelled him into a jelly. Hitler stood still and looked on. His threat to rip the brassard from the arm of any one of his troopers who showed the white feather in this scrum, called for no fulfilment. Within appreciable time order was restored— the speaker took up the thread of his speech, and the meeting closed to the echoing strains of a patriotic song.

We have indeed an account of it from one of the eye-witnesses still living in Munich, from an old lady called Frau Magdalena Schweyer.

When Hitler was first demobilised he would have liked to have returned to his old lodgings with Frau Popp, but since she no longer had a room to spare he took up equally modest quarters in a little street called the Thierschstrasse near the Isar.

Immediately opposite the house stood a little shop —it still stands there. One could buy everything in it from matches to a cabbage. The legend over the door ran " Spezerei-Waren, Obst und Gemüse,"[1] with the shopkeeper's name underneath, " Magdalena Schweyer."

---

[1] Spices (i.e. general chandlery), fruit and vegetables.

Frau Schweyer still stands behind the old-fashioned little counter within. She is an aged woman now, short of stature, and with grey hair. She came forward as I entered one day in the spring of 1934, glancing sharply up at me through her spectacles, and briskly smoothing down her apron with her toil-worn hands.

" I want to know something about Herr Hitler in the old days—in the beginnings of it all——"

Her eyes instantly lighted up. No one in Munich to-day is more proud than little old Frau Schweyer of her friendship with the Führer from the first, of the fact that she joined the Party in 1919 when it was utterly obscure.

" How I got to know him ? " she asked, and planked herself down on a little stool, happy to expand on this theme. I leant on the counter and watched her animated expressive face. Here was one of those working women who befriended Hitler through some of the thinnest times he had to experience ; here was one of the people to whom he so urgently and so clearly and so simply aimed to bring his message home, here was one of the women whom he sought to place in positions of least danger at his meetings.

" Ja, ja, ganz richtig," said Frau Schweyer, " it was in November, 1919. A young man came in here to buy some little thing or other—probably some fruit. He was rather poorly dressed : he never seemed to have more than one coat. I shouldn't have taken no more stock of him than of another, most likely, if it hadn't been he struck me as so well spoken. He was that polite. It didn't seem to go with the poor clothes, somehow. I watched him out of the shop, and noticed that he went into the house over the way. So that, I supposed, was where he lived.

" I didn't notice him come in again for a bit, and thought no more about him.

" Then one day—just about the turn of the year it was—a neighbour of mine happened to tell about him. She said his name was Adolf Hitler and he had something to do with a lot called the ' Deutsche Arbeiter-Partei.' By all accounts he was a brilliant speaker—talked something astounding. My neighbour wanted me to go and hear him. She said the very next time there was a meeting on I had to go. She'd take me along with her.

" So we went. She came in one evening and said there was to be a meeting in the Leiberzimmer¹ of the Sterneckerbräu.

" Well, I did go, and I got all worked up. It was wonderful, what he said and all—I could understand every word. He seemed to think there was a way to be found out of all our troubles and miseries. We was all to join his party and help. I joined then and there. They gave me a number—90.

" I went to all Hitler's meetings after that, and got to know him himself. It didn't take much to find out how poor he was. I had more than half a notion that often he wouldn't have had nothing to eat, but for folks giving him a bit now and then. It gave me an idea, that did. I thought I'd be able to help by sending him across a few things now and again—a pot of jam, or a snack of sausage, or a handful of apples. But it was as plain as daylight he hated to take them. He only did it because he was so poor. He never failed once to come across to me, after I'd

¹ Name of a room reserved for the members of the Infantry Life Guards.

sent him something, to thank me for it. Often though, when I was thinking to myself that would pretty well do him till next day, one or another of his pals come in and just let on as Hitler'd given every bite away to them. They was such a hungry crowd, the whole lot of them ! Anyhow he must have kept something for himself once in awhiles or he wouldn't be where he is to-day !

" Then there was a Herr Esser[1] 'd pop in sometimes, one of Herr Hitler's friends, and buy a couple of Rettiche (large white radishes) for the pair of them. That was their idea of a supper.

" Things must have gone on just like that for a twelvemonth—them just living on folks remembering that they hadn't got nothing in their insides. But the Party presently began to grow a bit, and when everyone helped as well as they could things got a little easier for Hitler. Even when I knew he must have a bit coming in like, now, I used to send him them apples now and again. He was that fond of fruit.

" It was wonderful how the Party grew. I know because I hung on all those first hard months, and went to every meeting, and saw how they had to be held in a bigger room every time. We soon outgrew the Sterneckerbräu. We went after that to the Hofbräukeller, then to the Eberlkeller. Then Hitler rented a little sort of office called the ' Deutsches Reich.' Things was really looking up.

" But the meeting I remember best was that big one they held one February, 1920—the 24th to be exact—in the assembly room of the Hofbräuhaus, when they had that terrific dust up with the Communists. A real battle that was ! I shan't ever

---

[1] Herr Herrmann Esser, to-day a Minister in Bavaria.

forget it as long as I live. If I hadn't kept my head low over the table that night and folded my arms above it, like all the rest of us women was told to do, sure as fate it would have been clean knocked off my shoulders. The beer mugs was flying around that night something alarming !

" Not long before this meeting was billed to come off there'd been an attack made on one of the members of the Landtag, Herr Auer. No one seems to have witnessed it. Auer himself seemed to think his own bravery saved him. But the Party he belonged to[1] set it about that it was the new Hitler Party what had done it. They went about all they knew to stir up the people and egg the working folk on to get a blow in at the Nazis. Everyone knew—everyone of us I mean—knew that something would be tried, that night, to bust up our meeting. We didn't take it too serious as we was pretty well used to this sort of threats which so far hadn't gone no further. This time, though, was to be different !

[1] **Auer** belonged to the Social Democratic Party, then officially in power in Munich. Dr. Gustav von Kahr had been appointed as General State Commissioner with dictatorial powers. This régime was inimical to the Republic as represented at Berlin. It favoured the dispossessed Wittelsbachs. Its members took oath to the Bavarian State, not to the Reich. It is necessary to recall these political facts in order that the reader may obtain some idea of what and who the " authorities " were, in Munich, with whom the newly constituted National Socialists (Hitler's Party) were soon to find themselves in conflict. From what has already been written about the bitterness of party warfare in Munich it can be well understood that the danger which threatened the big meeting described by Frau Schweyer was by no means negligible. The break-up of a political gathering in Munich at that time might easily involve fatalities. It may be confusing for the reader to hear that Hitler's Movement was opposed by the *working people* (that it was the *Workers* themselves who proposed to smash up his meetings and his party), since it was the interests of the common folk he had so supremely at heart. When it is remembered, however, that these workers were Marxists and Communists, light is at once shed on this matter. Hitler was all out against Marxism and Communism, for reasons already given in a previous chapter.

" It was to begin sharp at eight o'clock. My neighbour came to fetch me as usual. The first thing we saw as we went in was a group of young men standing about the entrance each with a band round his arms with a hooked cross on it. They were ex-service chaps, friends of Hitler from Traunstein. I heard him come up and tell them to keep order at all costs. He spoke sharp and soldier-like : said he'd rip them bands off their arms if so much as one of them showed the white feather. No one of them was to clear out unless he cleared out dead ! He smiled though, and added he knew well enough as they wouldn't !

" The place was pretty well full. We womenfolk were told to get well up in front : it would be safest there, far from the doors. I was too excited really to be frightened. It was plain there'd be some trouble : half the people in the place belonged to the Reds. I found a table right in front. Then they came and set another near it, and a Herr Esser got up on it to open the meeting. As soon as he jumped down again, Herr Hitler took his place. They greeted him with a few boos and yells, but after a bit he gripped even the enemy, and was speaking without interruption for quite an hour, before things began to look threatening again.

" People were drinking and attending, all ears. Then I noticed that whenever more beer was called for, instead of giving up the empty mugs, fresh ones were brought, and the old ones were piled under the tables. Whole batteries of beer mugs grew up under the tables. . . .

" Hitler had been speaking some time when the sign was given. Someone shouted ' Freiheit,'[1] and

---

[1] The Marxist battle cry, " Liberty."

HERR ANTON DREXLER

a beer pot went crash! That was the signal for things to begin. Three, four, five heavy stone pots flew by within an inch of the speaker's head, and next instant his young guards sprang forward shouting to us women to ' duck down ! '

" We ducked sharp enough ! The row was ear-splitting. Never heard anything like it in your life ! Pandemonium had broken out ; it's no use me trying to describe it. One heard nothing but yells, crashing beer mugs, stamping and struggling, the overturning of heavy oaken tables, and the smashing up of wooden chairs. A regular battle raged in the room.

" Hitler struck to his post. Never got off that table! He made no effort to shield himself at all. He was the target of it all : it's a sheer miracle how he never got hit. Them murderous heavy mugs was flying at his head all the time. I know because I got a sharp look round just between whiles : there he stuck, quiet as a statue waiting for those boys of his to get the tumult under. Goodness only knows how long it went on—twenty minutes perhaps, but it seemed never ending. The Reds was five times as many as we Hitlerites. The boys with the arm-bands were enormously outnumbered. They were in a fine state I can tell you before order was restored, their jackets torn half off their backs, and their faces all patched and dabbled with blood. Anyhow, they *did* get the Reds outside somehow, and then, cool as a cucumber, up gets Herr Esser beside Herr Hitler and calmly announces that the meeting will go on. The speaker was to continue.

" That's famous now. Everyone in Germany remembers them words : ' Die Versammlung geht weiter ' . . . ' The Speaker will proceed.'

" The room was simply wrecked. There was over

four hundred smashed beer mugs lying about everywhere, and piles of broken chairs.

"This, you know, was the first time them Reds got as good as they gave. This was the first time since the Revolution as anyone got up and gave 'em the no to their face—the first time they got roundly trounced and walloped themselves. *I* say it was the real beginning of our Party as a force and power.

"Ever after this Hitler's young men what he told off to keep order were called the Storm Troops. People ought to have seen that fight and that room afterwards to know how necessary they were. We should have gone under, for good, then and there, without the 'Saal-Schutz.' Because from now on the Movement had to fight and fight and fight, and always—at first—at tremendous odds. Up to now the Reds had had it all their own way. It was always them what did the smashing up and the storming of other people : they'd done enough here in Munich ! Now they was to meet a Party what wouldn't take it from them lying down no more. . . ."

.   .   .   .   .

Frau Schweyer had become quite excited as she retailed the story. Something of the light of battle flashed in her eyes again. They were brave women who attended Hitler's first meetings.

"But then," she said, "you see we knew him, what sort of a man he was ! I'll tell you—just one little thing :

"In the middle of December the year after he'd been shut up in Landsburg, we National Socialists in Munich heard that he was to be set free. Just before Christmas, too, on the 20th. We was wild with joy ! We hadn't expected that. We'd been thinking how miserable everything would be this year. Then between us we struck on a bright idea to welcome him. He would come out of the fortress just as desperately poor as he went in. So we arranged to to have a bit of a collection, just in our part of the city, so as he should have a little money to put in his pocket straight away. Altogether we scraped up about fifty marks. But more than that—on the day itself we filled his old room in the house opposite my shop with flowers (although it was winter time), and covered the poor table with good things to eat, and saw that there was fruit and stuff in the cupboard. We even secured a bottle of wine for the occasion, although we knew he never touched it.

" It was December 20th, 1924, a raw, grey, miserable day. The hours dragged by ; I began to be mortal afraid somehow that he wouldn't come after all. I was always running to the door and looking up and down our street. And then, sure enough, about two o'clock in the afternoon a motor drove up to the house opposite. Hitler was in it. I saw him through the window. He got out and was just going in at the door, when he turned round and caught sight of me standing staring across the way. He just came over and shook me by the hand and said : ' Grüss Gott, Frau Schweyer,' as though nothing had happened at all in all that long sad time since we'd seen each other last.

" His hand was icy cold and his grip was like iron. It gives me the creeps to think how cold and how hard it was, to this day. I remember the thought went through my head—how awful to incur the enmity of such a fist as that ! I couldn't say a word. My throat swelled and the tears would come. It was such a joy to see him back again.

" Well, he *had* come, anyway ! I went back into the shop all flustered, thinking of his climbing those stairs opposite and coming into his old room, and finding the flowers and the eatables and our little preparations for his welcome. I could just imagine him sitting down in the middle of it all and starting to think of nothing but how to get the Party going again.

" An hour or two went by and then a neighbour of mine come into the shop asking for a subscription to the organ fund for St. Anne's Church. She had a list with her. I couldn't afford much ; nor could anybody else apparently. All down the list people had only been able to give a few Pfennige each. We were only poor folks round about there. Frau Pfister agreed. We had a little talk together. She said what awful difficult work it was to get anybody to subscribe for the organ, times was that hard. And I suddenly said, ' Well, go over to Herr Hitler, see if he'd give you anything. I know he's got a bit. Tell him what it's for. He's not the one to say no.'

" Frau Pfister got up and crossed the street. I watched her enter the house opposite.

" In a few minutes she came flying back, radiant, and thrust the list under my nose, so that I could see for myself what an incredible lot Herr Hitler had given.

" Fifty marks ! There it was, just under his name, Adolf Hitler.

" I could scarcely believe my eyes. I stared at the figure, stared at Frau Pfister, took off my glasses and looked again—' Adolf Hitler, fifty marks.'

" ' Well, I never ! ' I exclaimed, ' if the Führer hasn't gone and given the whole lot away—— ! '

" Frau Pfister nodded, beaming.

"'He was that kind,' she said, 'do listen! He opened the door to me himself and asked what I wanted. When I told him, he made me come in and sit down. So I did and Herr Hitler catched hold of a glass and filled it with wine and gave it to me, with a cake and said I was to eat and drink. I didn't like to. I tried to excuse myself. I said as how the things on the table was all for him. But he would have it, 'Now you do as I bid,' he said, 'I don't drink wine, but that little drop it won't hurt you.' Then he reaches for my paper, glances at it and scribbles something under his own name. He puts it down and goes over to a little side table, pulls out a drawer and comes back and pushes fifty marks over to me. 'There you are,' he says, 'I'd give you more, but that's all I've got. Some friends of mine have just dotted that up for me.' I gaped and couldn't for the moment find a blessed word to say, but he read my face clear as a book and laughed and added, 'Believe it or not as you like, but I'm jolly glad to have it to give. It's a good object. The priests don't particularly love me, but that's neither here nor there.'

"'I tried to thank him, but he shut me up. He wouldn't hear a word . . .'

"He used," Frau Schweyer concluded, "to come across to the shop as long as he lived in our street, and often afterwards when he had become a very much bigger man. He didn't forget me. When my husband died in 1929 Hitler was in Leipzig. But he sent me a lovely wreath and wrote ever such a nice letter with it.

"People needn't wonder why we love the Führer. He was always for us small folk. He never had no time and no wish to think of himself. He was always out for everybody but himself. . . ."

CHAPTER VII

EARLY STRUGGLES OF THE MOVEMENT: GOTTFRIED SCHMITT'S STORY

G ERMAN people express themselves very differently from English people; moreover, they
are highly metaphysically minded. The everyday
Englishman never talks metaphysics: the German
does little else. The German, and particularly the
young German of to-day, is intensely serious, desperately in earnest. He can't for the life of him see
anything to be funny about in politics. Unlike the
Englishman he does not seek to mask his thinking,
his dearest convictions and strivings, under an
apparent carelessness or a rampant humour. It has
been said that a sense of humour would be fatal to the
make-up of a dictator. It would be fatal to a
revolution, too, and to the revolutionaries.

Gottfried Schmitt tells me his story as only a
German working man would tell it. For the English
reader it needs not merely to be translated, but to be
put into a wholly different vernacular. "To my
idea," diffidently says the Englishman when he can
be got going at all, whereas the German readily speaks
of his "Weltanschauung"[1] and of his "innere
Einstellung."[2]

Gottfried Schmitt remains to-day the same man
that he was twelve years ago. He has not gone up

[1] Cosmic view of things.
[2] Innermost spiritual conviction.

in the world one step. He still lives in one poor crowded room in Giesing, the slum-quarter of Munich (if Munich can rightly be said to have slums), which was at that date a hot-bed of " Red " violence and lawlessness. Hitler's Storm Troops were soon to sweep it out with iron brooms, and sweep it clean for good—but that is to anticipate.

In April, 1934, I made my way hither to this dwelling, and was bidden to enter and welcome. Schmitt lugged a box out from under the table, on which I sat down. It is a narrow little room this, a " Schlauch " as they call it here. A few poor sticks of furniture don't leave much elbow room either. A laundry basket perches on a broken-down sofa with the latest little new-comer in it. Five people live in this room which also serves as a kitchen.

I blurt out : " But good Lord ! Herr Schmitt, how can you stick it in this hole ? Why on earth haven't you got a better place to live in after all the yeoman service you've done for the Cause ? "

He gives me a serious square look. " We National Socialists weren't out to feather our own nests," he implicitly rebukes me, " we weren't out for mere selfish personal material improvement. Our struggle was for Germany ! I was nothing but a working man, and I've never been nothing but a working man since —nor wanted to. We working men wasn't counting the Revolution just to fill our pockets. We wanted to bring about the sort of socialism which had been dangled before our eyes for decades without its never coming to anything at all. What I've got to say for Adolf Hitler is that he, and he alone, ever made a practical reality of it. He kept faith with the working man. He's not only a Workers' Leader, but he himself is a working man. He gave us back our

honour. That's what it amounted to. He put it
short and straight himself, ' There is no patent of
nobility,' he said, ' but that of work.'

" But don't you worry about me. I'm going to get
out of this sure enough, and pretty quick now. All
round Munich there's hundreds of little houses been
going up, each with its own bit of garden, all destined
for the working man of the future. It's the Hitler
State what's building them. Hitler says every man
ought to have enough ground just to dig his spade
into for himself, so as he grows up on and with his
own bit of soil. He's all against these mammoth
block buildings like human rabbit warrens. He says
they drag the people's roots right out of the land.
And so they do !

". . . Well, well," he gives the subject a turn,
" about the beginnings of our *Kampf*—— ? You've
got to know as after the Revolt in 1918 I was a
Communist. I couldn't see any other way to bring
the sort of Socialism about that we wanted. They'd
always been painting the future so rosy what with
their ' Life in beauty and worthiness.'[1] And nothing
has come of it. It wasn't what you could rightly call
a Revolution in 1918, only a lot of places emptied to
be filled up with nincompoops with no idea in their
heads but to fill their own stomachs, and to have a
good time themselves. They forgot all about us
workers. The only people we've got any use for is
those what don't confine themselves to words, but
who go and do something ! That sort of thing turned
me Communist.

" Then in 1921 or thereabouts everyone in Munich
seemed to be talking about some new Party or other
here, what called itself ' Nationalist.' The name

[1] Something like the English " Land fit for heroes to live in."

alone was enough to make us hate it. Not that I worried myself much about it at first. Never give it a thought, until one day some of our chaps turned up in the factory with their heads in bandages. At first they wouldn't let on what had happened, only mumbled something, and turned aside. But it must have been pretty lively, that scrap, the way them chaps seemed to have got it in the neck! It all came out, of course, sooner or later. A hundred or more of them had made it up together to go to one of this new Party's meetings and smash it up. They hadn't succeeded.

" I couldn't rightly believe my ears when I heard as it was only a handful of fellows at the meeting as had chucked them out. But everybody was talking of it. It was a sort of sensation for a day or two in Munich.

" That attracted my attention. I thought I'd go and have a look in at the next meeting of these here Nationalists.

" I stuck myself in a corner and kept my eyes and ears well open. The first thing I seemed to notice was that this wasn't no mere ' bourgeois '[1] gathering, and no ' high-brow ' one neither. The audience was made up of plain folk like myself, working men and petty shopkeepers.

" Then this man Hitler got up to speak. . . .

" I saw at once this wasn't no common or garden tub-thumper, no gasbag like the most of them.

---

[1] The epithet " bourgeois " or " bürgerlich " in Germany means something more opprobrious than its mere equivalent " middle class " in English. The bourgeois and his class in the eyes of his political opponents means the miserably small-minded section of the community which cares for nothing but self-interest and cannot see beyond the end of its nose, a class incapable of high endeavour, long vision or self-sacrifice, hence a drag and a menace upon any Party out for the common good.

K

Everything he said was just common sense and sound. Although I wasn't one to be won over all in a moment, it didn't take me no longer than that first meeting to realise that Hitler was straight as a die, and a safe one to put your shirt on.

" I went to every one of his meetings after that. Bit by bit he won me round. He got in blow after blow at all the ideas I'd been holding on to up to now and laid them out flat. He knocked the Red nonsense out of me—all about the World Revolution to put the world right, and hot air like that. Instead, I seemed to see what he was driving at. Instead of prophecies and far-off Utopias like, in National Socialism, he gave us a good working scheme of things we could get busy on right away.[1]

" The first thing for me to do was to break with the Communists. So I did, and in the spring of 1922 I joined Hitler's Party. They shoved me into the guard straight away, the Storm Troops they were called, whose job it was to keep order at the meetings.

" People were flocking into the Party every day, deserting the Reds and the Democrats and the rest for the National Socialists. Hitler made his aim so clear, any right-thinking man could follow his ideas. We learnt to trust them.

" It was about this time Hitler organised the 'Storm Troops.' The number of us had so greatly increased it was necessary to give us a proper standing. We met one day at the beginning of August in 1922 in the 'Alt-Münchner Saal' in the Bürgerbräukeller, about three hundred of us, and Hitler divided us up into hundreds, and these hundreds again into smaller divisions. I was posted to the third hundred."

These " Storm Troopers " had indeed become of

[1] See the end chapters of this very book.

such vital and ubiquitous necessity in the propaganda campaign of the Party, that the Leader had now to turn his attention to giving them a thorough-going special organisation of their own. In the beginning the Storm Troopers were generally enormously out-numbered at the meetings, but it was seldom, if ever, they encountered defeat.

Hitler was confronted—as time went on—with mortal danger from the State (the Government in Munich at that time envisaged his Movement as Monarchist and reactionary in intent), and from the marshalled might of all those proletarian forces he sums up under the heading of " Marxismus." He was confronted by the terrorist methods of experi-enced opponents. Force and terror, he decided, were only to be countered by a still more active and ready force and terror. It had been an axiom of the Party, laid down from the first, to hold no sort of parley with opposition and obstruction and with the forces of destruction, but to grapple with them on the instant, ferociously enough to down and quash them then and there.

Conviction in the rightness and supreme necessity for Germany of his gigantic undertaking, in its ultimate triumph at all and any temporary or individual cost, underlay the constitution and the morale of the Storm Troops. Hitler made a consid-ered study of the Reds' terrorist methods in order to meet them by something still more decisive and more adequate—thus at the beginning, to obtain a hearing for National Socialist speakers at National Socialist meetings, and to ensure safe conduct for sympathisers and possible converts.

The name " Storm Troops " which sounds so ominous in foreign ears, was all of a piece with the political nomenclature of the moment. All the parties had their organised chuckers'-out, who went under some such name. The " Sturm-Scharen " of the Roman Catholic Centre Party, indeed, were called almost exactly in the same way.

In the beginning, at least, the National Socialist Storm Troops were allowed to have nothing whatever to do with military organisation and military aims. They were, writes Hitler, " purely an instrument for protecting and educating the National Socialist Movement." Here, very briefly, are the lines he laid down for their development :

" The Storm Troops are not to be trained from the military point of view, but from that of how to carry out the principles and objects of the Party. Since the men must be strong and fit, store must be set far more on sport (such things as boxing and jiu-jitsu) than on military drill. . . . When, and if, in the future an army should become necessary to the Nation, here would lie its finest material." (*Mein Kampf*, p. 611 ; or in the abridged English translation, p. 217.) The formation of the Storm battalion was not to be a copy of the old Army either in arms or equipment, but at the same time the Leader most emphatically exacted that every manly hardihood, every highest soldierly excellence of discipline[1] and obedience, should be required of his " Troopers."

" At the end of August," continues Herr Schmitt, " there was to be a big meeting held by some of the societies in the city (the Vaterländischen Verbände) to protest against a new law what had been passed in protection of the Republic. We National Socialists were also invited to take part. Hitler thought it an

---

[1] Every Storm Trooper knew, from the first, that the penalty for treachery would be death—death without trial.

A 1 opportunity to bring his Troopers for the first time into the open, and to give Munich an idea of their strength and discipline. We were six companies[1] strong by then, we had fifteen flags and two bands. We turned out and marched with music at the head of the column into the Königsplatz where the meeting was to come off. At first we encountered little that was unpleasant. They flung a few stones at us from some of the sidestreets, but we was under strict orders to take no notice of such petty manœuvres, so we kept straight on. But then things got a bit livelier. Just before we reached the square Hitler right about faced and gave the signal to clear the streets. We flung ourselves upon our attackers, and with two shakes of a lamb's tail there wasn't a man of them left to be seen. And in the Königsplatz itself we got a downright ovation. The people hadn't seen anything like us with our formation, flags and bands, for ages. A crowd of forty thousand greeted our appearance.

" Hitler addressed it. He said we weren't there to protest against any law about the Republic, but to protest against time-servers and swindlers in high places. It was because of them that the Republic wanted protection. He carried the crowd with him. Munich was downright impressed that day with Hitler's sheer ability and with the solidity of us Troopers.

" By now the Movement was really making headway in Munich itself and the time was ripe for us beginning to spread ourselves a bit. We began to look further afield.

" In the September (1922) we Storm Troops had

---

[1] A company consisted officially of one hundred men, but not all of these were as yet up to strength.

our first propaganda outing. We was loaded into
two lorries, and drove out to Tölz,[1] where our coming
had already been billed and placarded. Hitler rode
in front, as usual in his old trench coat and black
velours hat. In fact I don't suppose he had any other.
Not that he would have worn another if he'd owned
it. For years he clung to that old hat. Why, right
down to a year or so ago he was still going about that
shabby it was all his friends could do to persuade him
to rig himself out a bit more decent. Even my wife,
who often darned his socks said as how some of us
ought to see as he looked after himself a bit better !

" Well, as I was saying, we got to Tölz. It wasn't
to be a big affair, only a small meeting in a little inn.
Anyhow the room was full when we arrived so that
things could start straight away. I took a place near
where the Führer was to stand and to speak. He
turned round to me, and said softly, ' Look out,
Comrade, it's pretty sultry in here. If anyone starts
a racket you scrag him by the collar, and you—to
my mate—shove him along behind. Get the door
open, slick, and chuck him out. Only don't start
unless I give you the tip.'

" We didn't have long to wait. A heckler soon
bobbed up. My mate and I exchanged looks but
Hitler put up with the yelling and the nuisance for
a bit. When the fellow showed no sign of shutting
up, he at last signalled with his hand to me. In a
trice we'd nabbed the chap and run him to the door.
A good one on the backside sent him flying down the
steps. . . . We didn't have to repeat the lesson,
Hitler finished what he had to say to the good folks
of Tölz without further interruption.

" That, of course, was what we was for.

---

[1] A town about forty miles south of Munich.

" But the affair at Koburg was on a much bigger scale. There was to be a ' German day ' held there, a sort of whooshing up of patriotic feeling. Hitler was invited to attend it and to ' bring a few friends.' He wasn't slow to seize the opportunity. It was a rare joke about those ' few friends.'[1] The order came as the whole lot of the Storm Troops was to turn out. We was about six hundred strong ! It was a Saturday, in the middle of October. We were to assemble early at the Central Station and bring along rations for two days. The band was to march in our van. Hitler turned up well beforehand and we found a special train awaiting us. The music rang out gaily in the early morning air, and the people had hung out flags to make a sort of festival of the occasion. We stopped once or twice during the journey to pick up a few more of our comrades from the more outlying places, and arrived at last eight hundred strong.

" There was a deputation of the big-wigs in Koburg awaiting us at the station, all very solemn and proper in frock coats and top hats. But they got the shock of their lives, I can tell you, when they saw what sort of ' accompaniment ' Herr Hitler had brought along. I was close up to them, there on the platform, and heard what they said to him.

" ' We must earnestly beg you to control your following ! The city of Koburg explicitly forbids these men to march through the streets in rank and file with flags flying. It would be highly provocative of disorder.'

" Our Leader was a bit astonished at this and asked for explanations. What sort of trouble, then, did they expect ? They said there'd been a bit of a misunderstanding in the City over the organisation

[1] " Etwas Begleitung erwartet."

of the festival and its promoters had had to give a
strict guarantee that nothing would be done in the
least likely to provoke the Communists.

" Hitler received this with undisguised scorn.
What kind of a ' patriotic ' day did they suppose
could be held if the Communists were to have it all
their own way ! ' Good Lord ! ' he said, ' aren't we
in Bavaria ? Haven't we the right to move about
as we like ? '

" Whereupon he turned sharp round, much to the
discomfiture of the deputation, and gave us the word
to move off.

" We of the 3rd Company marched two by two
into the town on both sides of the band, and sure
enough soon encountered storms of abuse from the
crowds *en route*. Hitler led and we followed. At the
fire station they were ready to turn the hoses on to us,
but just didn't—at the critical moment. Stones,
however, began to fly around. Then things got hotter.
The Reds set upon us with iron rods and cudgels.
That was going a bit too far. Hitler swung round,
flourished his walking-stick (that was the signal), and
we flung ourselves upon our assailants. We were
unarmed save for our fists, but we put up so good a
fight that within fifteen minutes not a Red was left
to be seen. So we arrived finally at the place in the
centre of the city where the meeting was to be held.

" When it was over we formed up to betake ourselves to the Schützenhalle, a big hall on the outskirts
of Koburg where we were to spend the night. On the
way the former racket got up again. Hitler decided
once and for all to lay this Red menace here, and
gave us the word of command. We counter-attacked
for all we knew. It was jolly hard work, I can tell
you ! They rained tiles on us from the roof and

windows and tore up the cobble stones for missiles. I got a thundering blow on the head which had to be attended to before I could carry on. I only found out afterwards how serious the wound was.

" We reached the Schützenhalle and dossed down, without undressing, on a thin spreading of straw. Hitler turned in amongst us, on the floor like the rest. But first he set the watches, and arranged for patrols. He came in quite the old soldier over this, anxious to provide against possible surprise.

" I was detailed, with another man, for patrol work. Our watch begun at 2 a.m. We cast around a bit at some distance from the hall and found ourselves creeping through a spinney in its neighbourhood. We caught a glitter—made cautiously in that direction. Detected two of the enemy with their party-masks off. One of them had a revolver in his belt, the other carried hand-grenades.

" ' So they'd try that dirty trick,' I thought, and rage seized me at the thought of that whole barnful of sleeping men being suddenly blown sky-high into the night. At a concerted signal my comrade and I flung ourselves upon the pair, and for the next few seconds there was a berserker struggle in the underbush. We got them under, and unarmed them. We tied them up good and tight and went through their pockets. There were a few ' egg bombs ' to be sequestered in the latter. Then we marched them into quarters. I could hardly stand, myself ; the blood was pouring from the wound in my head, and blinding my eyes. I turned the precious pair over to Hitler and showed him the bombs.

" He looked ugly at that, but made no further sign. Quietly he ordered the captives to be taken to a room at the back, beckoned to a hefty couple of our chaps,

furnished them with a stout stick apiece, and signed
to them to get busy within. Some time afterwards
the two would-be bomb throwers were seen to leave
our camp, very much sadder and very much wiser
men. It is to be doubted if they'll forget the whallop-
ing and basting they got that night to the last day
of their lives.

" On the Sunday morning we all took an oath of
fidelity to the Cause, and then marched off to have
a look at the Castle Koburg.

" Meanwhile it came to Hitler's ears that a mass
meeting in protest was to be staged in the market-
place that afternoon. The Reds were calling in
supports from the outlying villages, and these men
were rolling up by the lorryful. There might be ten
thousand of them, altogether, by two o'clock.

" Undeterred by the news Hitler at once decided
to face the issue. The decisive blow it seemed had
not yet been struck by which the Red domination
here was to be broken. At twelve we were again on
the move, marching back to the market-place. But
the upshot was ludicrous. Instead of the crowd we
had been led to expect, we encountered no more than
a hundred people at the most, and these, too, melted
away into doorways and down convenient turnings
at our approach. Here and there a knot of fellows
who had come into Koburg from the country, and
had not so far had a taste of our mettle, put up a bit
of a fight, but we soon scattered them. We betook
ourselves to the meeting-hall of the previous day,
and stayed there until the time came to leave the
town.

" Then a queer thing happened. We was all
sitting about, quiet and waiting, when what should
show up in the entrance but a trickle of chaps coming

in, by ones and twos, or perhaps a little group at a
time, most of 'em with their heads or arms tied up
and bandaged. They were our erstwhile enemies. At
first they hesitated about putting their noses inside
the door, but then one of them came forward and
said, ' Look here, you fellows—-what's all the trouble
about ? You're workmen like us. Why are we at
each other's throats ? '

" Someone said, ' Why didn't you think of that
before, mate ? '

" ' Well, they told us as your Leader was against
the working man ; as you belonged to the bourgeosie
and had got to be resisted regardless.'

" It turned out that not long before our column
entered Koburg, Schnaps had been circulated to
such purpose among our opponents that few of them
knew well what they were doing. Money had been
spent, too, and word had gone round that if anyone
defaulted he was to be done in on the spot.

" Anyhow we got talking. More and more of them
turned up. We laid ourselves out to explain things
and make them see what we were standing for. Lots
of them felt like joining us. By evening, when we
were to march off again to the station, quite a few
came along too. It was a bit of a triumph, that.
The whole town seemed to breathe more freely ;
people cheered us, and flowers was thrown.

" But at the station, although the train stood
ready, there seemed to be nothing doing. There
wasn't an engine-driver on hand. This was another
snag. So Hitler threatened the officials that his
men would capture every Red in the place. If the
worst came to the worst, one of his troopers could
drive the train to Munich, but in every coach one of
the prisoners must travel with it. If the whole thing

went smash, at least these would be involved in the catastrophe. He would have been as good as his word, too, if just then an engine-driver hadn't come forward and volunteered !

" That was the Koburg affair.

" As the time went on we used to have ever bigger and bigger meetings in Munich. Sometimes Hitler would turn up with some of his Troopers at the House of call used by us men from the East Station quarter. I remember once I put him a question about the Unions. ' What are we going to do, Herr Hitler, about these here Trade Unions ? ' I asked, ' wouldn't it be a good thing if they was all to be united ? '

" But he said no, there was no point in that. ' Such a combine,' he said, ' would perforce be, *par excellence*, an international organisation ; what we want is to form a united Front of German labour. We don't propose to destroy the Unions or their Executives, but we must control the latter.'

" Then, on January 28th, 1923, we celebrated the first Party Day of the Movement. About one thousand Troopers assembled on the Marsfeld, together with at least four thousand members of the Party.

" It was always becoming necessary to do something about the ever-growing numbers of the Storm Troops, so that now again the units were reorganised. Hitler designed and gave us our standards ; Munich got two of these, Landshut got a third, and Nuremberg the fourth. A month or two later, in the spring, the famous war-time ace, Captain Goering, was appointed to the leadership of the whole body.

" In the September of that year, Sedan Day was celebrated in Nuremberg. We National Socialist Troopers found ourselves there in company with three or four other similar organisations, the ' Reichs-kriegsflagge,' and the ' Bund Oberland ' and the ' Waffenring,' destined to play a momentous part in the events of the following winter.[1] We got a splendid welcome in Nuremberg ; better than any we'd experienced as yet at home. The celebrations were to take place in the Herkules Saal. There were over eight thousand Müncheners there who one and all acclaimed Hitler with enthusiasm. Nuremberg hadn't expected anything like it. The Leader was enormously heartened by the whole thing. The Nurembergers have stuck to him through thick and thin ever since, so much so that when this same anniversary came round again last year (1933) the Führer ordained that in future, as a sign of his gratitude and recognition, the Party Day should always be held in Nuremberg."

[1] More will be said about these bodies later. The " Reichs-kriegsflagge " was an informal army composed of ex-service men. Then there were the " Young German Order " ; the " Oberland," commanded by Dr. Friedrich Weber, the " Black Reichswehr " and others. All were destined to side with (and be merged in) or against the National Socialists in the course of the next few dramatic months.

CHAPTER VIII

HERR DREXLER CONTINUES HIS STORY

FROM the date of Adolf Hitler's joining the 'Deutsche Arbeiter-Partei," to that of the apparent ruin of all their hopes, in November, 1923, an enormous amount of spade work had been accomplished. Adolf Hitler, without home and ties of any sort, gave himself body and soul to the nascent movement. He lived for it alone : had no other thought. It was quickly perceived by Anton Drexler and his five original companions that Hitler was the only man among them with the force and drive and will to bring this thing into the open and to make of it a nation-wide affair. The whole direction of the infant Party was soon to be confided, with the utmost enthusiasm and unanimity, to his hands alone.

Hitler's colleagues perceived just what his audiences were soon to comprehend, that with him this Movement meant action and not merely talk. This man, with his gift of apt and ready political speech, could conceivably have won for himself a sufficient position with one or other of the big established factions ; as it was he devoted all his time and strength and powers to the promotion of one of the obscurest efforts to find a way out of the despair and confusion of the time. From the date of his first taking over entire conduct of the propaganda, January 5th, 1920, the Party took to itself a more comprehensive name. Since Germany owed the sad plight in which she found herself to the un-Socialistic Nationalists, and to the anti-National Socialists, so it must be through the programme of a properly conceived National Socialism that she must be rehabilitated.

It has been the endeavour of a great many writers to make these distinctions intelligible and significant to foreign students of German politics. Whether or not they have succeeded may be open to question. It is no part of the present writer's intention to essay the attempt again. Suffice it in this place and in this connection to say that the revolution of thought and programme indicated by this new juxtaposition of old political labels, was abundantly plain to the man-in-the-street in Germany in 1920. It was not only plain to him, but the combination was, through Hitler's exposition, so peculiarly apt, that none other would have captured public attention so sharply.

The programme of the party was epitomised under some twenty-five headings, the very first of which, of course, pledged it to loud and insistent repudiation of the terms of the Versailles Treaty. But to recapitulate this " platform " here, would be to postulate some adequate explanation of it, and an adequate explanation would entail a book in itself at least as long as the Leader's own, *Mein Kampf*. The writer rather proposes to confine himself to the story of how Drexler and Hitler put their heads together to draw up this momentous document, and how it was received by the public in the great gathering of February 24th, 1920, in the Hofbräuhaussaal.

" Hitler and I had been hammering hard for a real big meeting for some time," continues Herr Drexler, " but Herr Harrer feared the risk of failure was too great."

It was Herr Harrer who had doubted, at first, if this new associate, Hitler, could really address and hold an audience. At this point he retires from the chairmanship. Hitler and Drexler were all for bold measures. " We had all along decided," the founder goes on, " that if we could attract five hundred people we might hope to attract double the number. Events seemed to have proved that our audiences were steadily augmenting.

" We used to meet, he and I, three or four times at least every week, and we'd sit up to one o'clock in the morning working out our plans and ideas. Hitler would have come even oftener, but I lived some way out of the city at that time, and he couldn't always afford the tram fare. We'd get to work the moment he turned up, and grind right on until my wife called us to table for supper. She had to call more than once, too, I can tell you ! We'd shove our writing aside then and fall on the potatoes. My little girl used to climb on Hitler's knee ; she knew as she was always welcome, and as he'd share all he'd got with her. He was ' Uncle Hitler ' to her—she was only three then—and always a prime favourite.

" I had already written a pamphlet called *Whence comes the ' Deutsche Arbeiter-Partei ! What are its aims ?'* and had read it at one of our meetings. A lady had been so struck with it that she volunteered three hundred marks, then and there, to have it printed. *Herr Gott !* What a joy that was ! We sold copies at ten Pfennig[1] each, so that more cash might be raised for more pamphlets and more printing. We got what we could out of our members for the same purpose.

" It was about this time Hitler came to know our

---

[1] Roughly 1d.

never-to-be-forgotten Dietrich Eckart. Eckart and Hitler both spoke at the last meeting we held in the Deutschen Reich, when the people were packed like herrings in a box.

" Up till now the Press had taken little notice of us, unless it were to hold us up to ridicule. This made Hitler all the more keen about coming right out into the open and doing something spectacular. The Hofbräuhaus Saal could seat two thousand people. There were at least a couple of hundred tables in it. That was the sort of hall we wanted. And next—a well-known man to speak. A Dr. Johannes Ding-felder had written a striking article lately, in the *Münchener Zeitung*, called ' Was uns not tut ' (what we need). He had quite good things to say about usury and profiteering and all that, and people had been struck by it. So we invited this man on to our platform for that night, to open the proceedings.

" Beforehand, Hitler and I had worked hard to draw up our official Party programme. He turned up at my place one evening armed with a sheaf of manuscript in which he'd roughly sketched it out. For hours we worked at it, boiling it down, and condensing it, and making it as short and pithy as we could. We knew it mustn't be long-winded, and yet it was all-important to get every point clear and comprehensive and exact. We cracked our brains over it, I can tell you ! It was all hours in the morning before we got the thing into final shape. It consisted then of twenty-five headings. Adolf Hitler sprang up, when we'd really done, and banged his fist on the table under my nose.

" ' Old boy ! these points of ours are going to rival Luther's placard on the doors of Wittenberg ! '

" Well—indeed it looked like it ! When the great

L

evening came, and Dr. Dingfelder had finished his address, Hitler got up to speak. So far all had been quiet. No one had been rubbed up the wrong way, and the Communists in the audience had made no sign.

" Hitler began quite simply, without particular emphasis. He just outlined the history of the past ten years or so, came to the War, and then got into his stride over the Revolution. His manner altered ; passion crept into voice, look, gesture. And now opposition awoke. Cries came from all parts of the hall. The story of what happened is well known. The yells waxed to a storm. The beer mugs began to fly. There was soon a ding-dong battle in full swing. When at length our *Saal-Schutz* managed to restore order, Hitler just went on as if no interruption had occurred. At last he came to the outlining of our Party objects.

" Point for point he went through the programme, explaining and illustrating as he went along. He never passed from one head to another without demanding of the audience if they fully understood and if they fully agreed. And every time a storm of assent replied : two thousand throats cried ' Yes,' and two thousand hands showed high. Enthusiasm waxed from minute to minute. The great hall was half-wild with joy. People who had suffered so much and so long felt that at last they could lift their heads again and draw breath, and trust that the unbelievable had come to pass, a man had arrived who *could* and *would* lead them out of the Swamp of Despair !

" As for Adolf Hitler himself, it was here in the Hofbräuhaus Saal this night that he received his Mandate. . . .

" Four hours long that meeting lasted. When it was over two thousand propagandists were let loose on Munich. The seed had fallen on good ground. Never had Hitler been so happy in his life !

" From this point on we held meetings and meetings, and then more meetings ; meetings galore ! The opposition in Republican Germany had never dared so much before. Every week one or two meetings were held in this, that or the other of the bigger halls in Munich. People swarmed into the Party.[1] The time came when its headquarters could be moved into three decently furnished rooms in the Corneliusstrasse, but far more significantly and far more importantly, the time came when the Movement could begin publishing a newspaper.

" There was a paper going called the *Völkische Beobachter* (*People's Observer*), which was for sale. It represented the affairs and interests of the man in the street, and had hitherto been supported by various popular societies and clubs. In December, 1921, Dietrich Eckart and I busied ourselves to see if we couldn't buy the thing up. It would mean an enormous pull for the Party to have its own press. We brought off the deal, and the *Beobachter*, as our paper, began with a bi-weekly appearance. But by the turn of the year we were in a position to make a daily of it, and it has been of the greatest service to us all along, right down to the present day.

" Hitler next designed the Party flag. A whole lot of considerations had to be brought to bear upon that. We wanted something red enough to out-

---

[1] In Germany to belong to the National Socialist Party did not merely mean that this party represented one's own political opinions and therefore attracted one's allegiance, but that one was actually registered with a number as an active working member of the Party, at death grips with all others.

Herod Herod, i.e. to challenge and outdo the Reds on their own red ground, and get something quite different. A black-white-red flag still existed which denoted little but the vain hope of re-establishing the pre-War German Monarchy. Our flag was to embody not a reactionary aspiration, but a counter-revolutionary one. Hitler was well used to designing posters for us : at last he achieved our flag. He kept the colours black-white-red, because Germany had fought under the black, white and red in the War. The red ground stood for Socialism, the white inset for Nationalism, and the swastika[1] for racial purity and creative work.

" The Party was delighted with the flag, but it didn't at all please the Reds."

As time went on Adolf Hitler's work increased by leaps and bounds. By the year 1922 the Party had made such great progress in Munich, and indeed, throughout Bavaria, that it began to be heard of in Germany at large. The Leader was kept incessantly busy addressing mass meetings in one city after another. Everywhere he became immensely popular. Important men in foreign countries turned their eyes upon him. The National Socialist Party, however, still ranked merely as one of a perfect legion of political groups.

From the date of the French Occupation of the Ruhr in January, 1923, onwards, Germany may be said to have touched bottom. Perhaps it has never been fully and vividly enough realised in England how this Occupation, apart from Reparations and every other crushing thing in the Versailles Treaty, really broke the German people. What the invasion of Belgium was to the Belgians in 1914 was the

[1] Nordic Sign of the Sun.

invasion of the Ruhr to Germany—and the latter took place in " peace time."

The Hitler Movement was not yet far flung enough or powerful enough to cope with this national shame and misery, but a small body of desperate men, already inspired by the Munich idea, gave themselves up to acts of " passive resistance " (derailing the trains transporting coal to France), in the Ruhr-gebiet, which sooner or later cost them their lives. An outstanding name in this connection is that of Schlageter—the man to whom an undying flame burns now on the Rhine. " These Ruhr fighters," says an English writer, Mr. Geoffrey Moss (*I look to the Stars*), " kept the soul of Germany alive when all seemed lost."

It was at this time that " the great delirium called ' Inflation '—a new word in human history— reached its apex." This, continues another very fair-minded Englishman, Sir Philip Gibbs (in *The Cross of Peace*, p. 137), was " when the greatest industrial nation in Europe lurched into bankruptcy and lived through a nightmare in which many went mad. Money meant nothing but astronomical figures printed on a bit of paper. Trade came to a standstill in great cities. The wheels of industry ceased to turn. Armies of unemployed men stood outside deserted factories where no chimneys smoked. . . . There was an epidemic of suicide among young people on the threshold of life. Despair crept into the soul of the nation."

As we have shown, the Great War cannot be said to have ended for Germany when it ceased for the Allies, in November, 1918. The very vitals of the nation were being internally torn and ravaged for years after that. There was an effort made to tear

away the Rhineland. . . . War veterans back from
the Front had to arm afresh and fight again in the
streets of their own German cities. Every centrifugal
force in a country only welded together after 1870–
71, reasserted itself, and threatened to break up
Bismarck's Imperial creation.

"The winter of 1921," continues Herr Drexler,
"was a severe one. Food riots were breaking out
everywhere ; tragedy was piled on tragedy. Pressure was being put upon Germany from Paris and
from London to pay her impossible reparations.

"Daring more than he had ever dared before,
Hitler chose the Zirkus Krone in Munich for a gigantic
protest meeting. This place could accommodate an
audience of six thousand. At first it looked as if the
thing would be a spectacular fiasco. The weather was
inclement to the last degree. People would never
turn out *en masse* through so much sleet and snow !
Owing, however, wholly to the vigour of Hitler's last
moment publicity campaign, the opposite result was
achieved. The Zirkus Krone was filled to the doors.
Hitler spoke for two and a half hours and was received
with tumultuous acclaim.

"It was in the July and August of this year that
Hitler thoroughly reorganised the Party. As now its
sole responsible Leader we had got rid of the slow and
clumsy method of submitting our decisions to the
consideration of a voting Committee. It was ever
so much more practical to turn affairs over to departmental chiefs directly responsible to the Leader. We
found we could get on in this way far more quickly,
and do better work. You never could quite reckon
on a majority in Committee, and altogether the new
system was vastly superior to the old. Hitler was
always anxious to make individuality tell. He had

long ago studied the parliamentary way of conducting affairs, and was now glad to throw it overboard in the Movement.[1]

" In the spring of 1923 I, personally, met with a serious disaster. Some of the men at the works made up their minds to take it out of me pretty thoroughly. They were Marxists—inveterate haters of us National Socialists. One day one of them attacked me in the shops with a shovel. I was knocked senseless and all but killed. I was in hospital for weeks after that, and then spent from May to July in a sanatorium on the Obersalzberg, near Berchtesgaden. Hitler often came to see me there. This, really, is how he got to know the Obersalzberg. He loved it from the first, and when things developed still further he rented and later on bought a little house[2] near there, in the Bavarian Alps, as a sort of refuge and rest-place.

" Things in Germany were at a desperate pass in the autumn of 1923. They'd shot Schlageter in Düsseldorf, and the French were still in the Ruhr. The inflation was at its height. People were facing ruin everywhere, and those who couldn't face it

---

[1] That Hitler builds all on personal (and national) individuality may strike the reader as an extraordinary assertion. People outside Germany appear to imagine that " individuality " is the one thing above all others likely to disappear in the completely " Nazified " State. They suppose the average German under the Hitler régime to be cut strictly to pattern, soul, mind, clothes and body. But this is not the case. By individuality Hitler means something the reverse of mass. He does not want things done by committees, by majorities, by groups of people no single one of whom can be held personally responsible for what is done. He wants the capable individual, and the individual alone, to emerge in factory, workshop, office, institution, as the Führer, the Leader. He holds the opposite method, the parliamentary method, to be the antithesis of individualism. He wants the Nation itself to produce the one responsible individual at its head. He wants the individual home rather than the block tenement ; he wants the individual shop rather than the departmental store. Under a Dictatorship, perhaps, individuality is impossible. But Hitler is a Leader, not a Dictator.

[2] Now the famous Haus Wachenfeld, to be described later.

were putting their heads into the gas oven every day.
Adolf Hitler, with practically over a third of Munich
behind him, could stand it no longer.   There was talk
of cutting Germany in two, so as to have an agricultural South and an industrial North—the knell
had struck for the National Socialist Party to make
a bid for power and to stem this tide of national
suicide and despair ! "

" Had it succeeded," added Frau Schweyer as she,
too, came to the story of the *Putsch* of November 9th,
1923, when relating her own version of these events,
" had it succeeded not only Bavaria, but all Germany
would have been saved ; as it was we had another
ten years to wait."

CHAPTER IX

" UND IHR HABT DOCH GESIEGT[1] "

STURM Abteilung Oberführer[2] Joseph Berchtold, Editor of the *Völkischen Beobachter*, is a man of many activities. At one minute he is to be found in his office, at the next in the City Council, (he is a Councillor of Munich) ; every Ministry knows him ; he is to be met with in every hole and corner of the city. But he never has a moment to waste. One is supposed to catch him in his own office between 11 a.m. and 12 noon, but so many people are awaiting him then, only the half of them can expect a hasty interview.

He was good enough indeed to receive me at eleven o'clock at night at the printing works, Schelling-strasse 39, where all was in full blast turning out the paper's daily edition of about 300,000 copies.

I sent in my name, and was requested to wait a moment or two. I glanced through the window across a yard at the printing house where gigantic machines could be seen stamping and pounding at top speed setting the whole place humming. Everything over here, too, was in a perfect fever of work, messengers rushing hither and thither, people coming and going without an instant's pause. Telephones were ringing, type machines clacking, . . . a messenger

---

[1] " You have conquered after all." The inscription of the Monument on the Odeonsplatz, Munich, marking the spot where sixteen of Hitler's followers fell on November 9th, 1923.

[2] Colonel of Storm Troops.

169

appeared : " Herr Berchtold will see you," and my turn had come.

I found myself ushered into a fair-sized room in the middle of which was planted an enormous writing-table. There were others round about. Huge fireproof cupboards lined the walls. Herr Berchtold was bending over a paper as I entered, doing busy things with a big blue pencil, but he looked up at once, extended his hand, and indicated a seat.

I got this impression instantly—no sedentary individual, Herr Berchtold, and no one bound down by red tape. A practical man ; agile and decisive both in mind and body. Full of temperament, but no neuropath.

" Lots of people," he began, " look upon that so-called *Putsch*[1] of November 9th, 1923, as a bolt from the blue which split up the Movement. But it wasn't really anything of the sort. It was a perfectly logical and necessary outcome of all that had gone before. We National Socialists knew well enough that some such gesture was bound to come : what we didn't know, and what we weren't prepared for in the least was the betrayal of the whole thing by sheer reactionary cowardice.

" I will mostly confine myself to telling you what I know about it at first hand and content myself with a mere sketch of what happened when I wasn't, myself, actually present. I had been attracted to the ' Deutsche Arbeiter-Partei ' so far back as 1919, not so much for itself as on account of this Adolf Hitler. To hear him was to be convinced that he had got hold of the right end of the stick. But for all that, there weren't many who believed then any use could be made of the fact. What exactly was Hitler's

[1] Revolt, uprising.

" UND IHR HABT DOCH GESEIGT." THE FELDHERRNHALLE MONU-
MENT IN MUNICH, TO THOSE WHO FELL NOV. 9, 1923

THE FELDHERRNHALLE IN MUNICH—THE MONUMENT IS ON THE
LEFT WALL IN THE RESIDENZSTRASSE

message ? He appealed to reason when nobody else had hope of things being reasonable any more. He took his stand on re-establishing order in Germany, since without it the whole country trembled on the brink of final collapse and ruin.

" I felt that no Party could achieve such an end. It was not the job so much for a political Party as for a sort of superman. Only he could set himself to such a task who possessed a strong hand, great decisive power and an incorruptible purpose. The last quality seemed to be remarkable for its absence in all parties at that time.

" As for me, I no sooner heard Hitler in the Sterneckerbräu than I became a convinced adherent. I resolved to follow this man no matter whither he led. I ' joined up ' with the Party in January, 1920. As an active sort of man I didn't want to be merely a passive member, but an energising one. From this it follows I was pretty well mixed up with all the frays and conflicts in the beer halls and the streets which marked the rise of National Socialism—particularly did I lend a hand on the famous occasion of the Battle of the Hofbräuhaus. I was one of the Guards that night. We laid about us as we did, simply because our opponents left us no choice. It may seem pretty brutal to have to defend ideas with beer mugs and broken chair legs, but necessity knows no law. We weren't pummelling people out of an irresponsible love of fighting, but to gain a hearing for our Leader.

" The S.A.[1] took its rise, as you know, from all this. By the spring of 1923 it already amounted to a respectable number of men. Among these, however, were many who, despite all the goodwill in the world, were not fitted for the rougher work for which the

[1] Sturm Abteilung—Storm Troops.

Abteilung was constantly called upon. So it gradually became necessary to form a small body of specially picked men on whom the most absolute dependence could be placed. They had to be ready to deal with the worst elements of the underworld under all and instant circumstances. Such a detachment was organised in May, 1923. It went by the name of ' Stosstrupp Hitler '[1] and came under the Leader's immediate orders. Later these men were commanded by Captain Goering. One of the units was placed under me. In a few weeks' time my detail reached full company strength of 120 men. For the most part they were all old Front-line soldiers, thoroughly dependable men.

" The Storm Troops at that time wore grey waterproof, and grey cloth caps, like the former Austrian Infantry. The uniform of the Shock Troops was the old field grey uniform of the War ; with the addition of high black boots or gaiters, and a black cloth cap with a silver death's head on a red ground. Our shoulder straps exhibited the initials ' St. Tr. H.'[2] We had arm-bands with the hooked cross in red. On special occasions of danger we exchanged our cap for a helmet with death's head and swastika upon it.

" The Shock Troops were designed for specially dangerous work at specially dangerous places. Whenever the S.A. went on the march we led the van, or followed up the rear. We were put through continuous courses of training especially with a view to street fighting and fighting in assembly rooms. When, on our National Socialist expeditions, the spitting or stone-throwing of the onlookers, (the Reds), waxed beyond a joke I blew my whistle, and in no time at all

---

[1] Hitler—Shock Troops.
[2] *Stoss-Trupp Hitler.*

the Shock Troops had cleared the streets. Their efficiency and discipline soon won the admiration of the populace. After a while the enemy learnt to let us alone : only those who had not yet had a taste of our quality still ventured to dispute our passage.

" Hitler had his own method of attaching each and every man to himself. He would appear unannounced in our quarters, here in these offices in the Schellingstrasse, on a drill night, and after a word or two with me, he would address the men in the most comradely way possible. Then he'd inspect the Company, but not so much like an officer as like a friend. He would shake each man's hand, and look him squarely in the eyes. It was this glance, more than anything, which made every trooper Hitler's man to the death !

" By the first week in November, 1923, it was abundantly plain that things could not go on as they were ; something was bound to happen. Dr. von Kahr, the head of the Bavarian Government, himself declared, ' The critical moment is at hand.' Even he knew that something decisive, something spectacular, had to be done. And yet he hum'd and ha'd and hesitated. Hitler saw plainly enough that the people's hopes were all destined to be dashed, and wasted, if things were to be allowed to drag on indefinitely to no purpose and no end."

It would be as well, perhaps, at this point to interrupt Herr Berchtold's narrative briefly to epitomise the state of affairs in Bavaria and in Munich at this crisis.

The National Socialists under Adolf Hitler in Munich—and by now in many other cities of Bavaria —were not alone in their distrust of President Ebert, Chancellor Stresemann, and the other Republican authorities in Berlin, under whom the whole country had come to so deplorable a pass. Many other patriotic associations were raising the cry : " Down with Ebert ! Down with Berlin ! " Bavaria, indeed, cut herself clean away from the Republic, and showed herself generally ready for some decisive action should the word be spoken.

After the celebrations in Nuremberg on " Sedan Day," in September, both organisations known as the " Reichskriegsflagge " and the " Bund Ober-land " amalgamated under Hitler's political leader-ship with the National Socialist Party. The whole body was then called the " Deutscher Kampfbund," and was commanded by Lieut.-Colonel Kriebel.

The Presiding Bavarian Minister, von Knilling, looked with distrust upon this very considerable augmentation of the Party's forces, and appointed Herr von Kahr, an out and out Monarchist, as General State Commissary to watch over and control events. This was on the 26th of September. Herr von Kahr had more than once been obliged to give way to the feeling of the people which was ever veering more and more towards National Socialism. And ever more and more was he drifting towards an open rift with Berlin where Communism was getting the upper hand.

On the 29th of September von Kahr withdrew the State of Bavaria from the control and from the pro-tection of Berlin. The step met with general approval in Bavaria and also with that of the National Socialist Party. Dr. von Kahr, indeed, hated the Republic, and would like to have seen the Wittelsbachs, the Bavarian royal house, restored. He had been given dictatorial powers, and at once took steps and gave orders in Munich which meant open revolt against the Central Berlin Government. The Bavarian rail-

ways were withdrawn from central control, and the
Bavarian Reichswehr under General von Lossow took
oath of allegiance to the Bavarian State rather than
to the Republic.

This last step was occasioned by the following
sequence of events :

In the middle of October an article appeared in the
National Socialist organ, the *Völkischer Beobachter*,
criticising certain matters concerning the Reichswehr. Whereupon the publication was suppressed
throughout Germany. It continued, however, to
appear in Bavaria without let or hindrance. Presently, however, von Lossow received orders to
bring Bavaria to heel. He laid them before von
Kahr, who set them aside, declaring that it was his
firm determination to weld all national aspirations
into one firm body of political opinion.

Berlin insisted : von Lossow replied it was impossible to carry out the order. He gave his chiefs to
understand that the Bavarian temper was so exas-
perated against Berlin, that the least injudicious
move at this moment might precipitate a crisis.
Von Seeckt, the Commander-in-Chief of the Reichswehr in Berlin, was not to be moved ; Lossow
would have been court-martialled for insubordination
but that he was stoutly supported by von Kahr and
Knilling. The Minister for War retorted by cashier-
ing him.

Whereupon von Kahr took a decisive step. As
already related, he appointed von Lossow Commander
of the Bavarian Reichswehr, and so withdrew the
Bavarian forces from the control of the Republic.
Orders came to re-establish constitutional[1] authority
over this body, but they were ignored.

[1] The Republic of 1918 was established by the Constitution of
Weimar.

President Ebert in Berlin foresaw a rising. The Reichswehr were furnished with extraordinary powers to counteract it when it came, although the President was in the dark as to how the Reichswehr itself might react to the Movement in Bavaria.

Dr. von Kahr had, meanwhile, came closely into contact with Hitler. The latter understood that the Commissary was fully prepared to take upon himself the consequences of a break with Berlin. The two men were fully agreed that this was a necessary step to take. The public tension was waxing even greater and greater. Expectation of a crisis was on tiptoe. Everyone was talking of a " March on Berlin." Hitler, von Kahr, von Lossow and Seisser were all persuaded that the Government there must be overturned.

All waited for von Kahr to appoint the exact moment for action.

He hesitated. Failed to decide. Whereupon Hitler determined to force his hand. Hitler felt sure Kahr would follow if the lead were given, however incapable he were himself of giving it.

On the evening of November 8th, 1923, the fifth anniversary of the " Stab in the Back " which put the German Army out of action at the end of the War, the State Commissary convened an enormous meeting in the Bürgerbräukeller, representative of every patriotic association in Bavaria. All the officials of the Bavarian Government were present, including Colonel Seisser, the Chief of Police and General von Lossow, the Chief of the Bavarian Reichswehr. Herr von Kahr was to address the Bavarian people. . . .

This, then, Hitler decided, was to be his great, his unique and psychological opportunity ! With the utmost expedition he prepared his plan.

Now to revert to Herr Berchtold's story:

" Adolf Hitler chose the day of von Kahr's great meeting for his attempt. About eleven o'clock on the morning of the 8th of November I got the order to stand ready for the National Revolution.

" My men took a last oath, to serve true to death if needs be, and we got our final instructions from Captain Goering. I busied myself all day with preparations, and then at six in the evening assembled the troops, in instant readiness for action in the Torbräu, opposite the Sterneckerbräu. I harangued my fellows, ' Any one of you,' I said, ' who isn't going into this thing heart and soul had better get out right now.' As no one budged by so much as an inch, I pursued, ' It's our job, as Shock Troops, to bear the brunt of what's coming. We're going to run the Government out. Hitler and Kahr are united over this, they are going to set up another one.' Everyone of us gripped hands, and we were ready.

" We marched off and took up a position in the neighbourhood of the place where von Kahr's great gathering was to be held. It was already crammed to bursting ; a group of police near us could find no standing room within, so hung about outside.

" I glanced at my watch. Now for it !

" Shouting orders to the Troop I sprang forward brandishing my revolver.

" ' Out of the way—you there ! ' I yelled to the police, who incontinently fell back amazed and unprepared, and burst our way into the entrance. I ordered my men to cover every window and exit, but pressed on myself with the rest into the hall.

" Hitler was already there. Catching sight of us, he at once placed himself at our head, and led us quickly and quietly right down the main gangway

M

until we reached the platform. The audience numbered several thousand. It was listening to von Kahr
who was addressing them on the subject of ' The
People and the Nation.' The State Commissary was
supported by the Minister President von Knilling,
by General von Lossow, by Chief of Police Seisser,
Advocate Pöhner and other notabilities.

" Our sudden appearance in their midst caused
consternation. Von Kahr was struck dumb. People
began shouting to know what was the matter.
Women fainted ; here and there panic was imminent.
Meantime we had mounted the platform, and Hitler
made an attempt to speak. But the excitement was
so great he could neither make himself heard nor
understood. So he drew his revolver and a loud
report rang out. He had pointed it upwards, to the
ceiling. An instant silence fell in which his voice
could be heard proclaiming the end of the Red
régime.

" Immediately thereupon he left the platform in
urgent speech with Dr. von Kahr. This personage,
together with von Lossow and Seisser all disappeared
with Hitler into a room at the back.

" No one in the hall knew what this might
portend. . . .

" So Captain Goering sprang into the gap. He
made a timely bid for attention and came forward
and soon managed to dominate the uproar in the
assembly.

" ' This is a new start altogether,' he shouted,
' we're going to found the State afresh. No harm is
meant to Dr. von Kahr. We all respect him. We're
not fighting the military or the police—they're on
our side—we are only fighting the Jew régime in
Berlin.'

" The announcement provoked a storm of applause, which broke out afresh, as the speaker managed to add :

" ' We've taken this step because we're convinced that the men who stand at the head of us here in Bavaria will help us wrench free from Berlin and the Jews. The new Government will form itself round Hitler, Ludendorff, Pöhner and von Kahr ! '

" In the meantime General Ludendorff had been urgently summoned by telephone. On arrival he declared himself fully in sympathy with Hitler's action. The two betook themselves to the three others in the room to the rear, convinced that the decisive hour had struck. Only Lossow hesitated for an instant. Ludendorff, however, scattered his scruples to the winds. ' Throw in your lot with us, man, give me your hand upon it,' he urged, and the other complied. All four men vowed themselves then and there to further this business to the utmost of their power.

" Then, hastening back to the platform, Hitler became spokesman. In very few words he related what had passed and declared for the new Government. His announcement, and the reappearance of his supporters, together with the presence of General Ludendorff, aroused the utmost enthusiasm. Enormous jubilation broke out ; everything that had been done was unanimously carried by von Kahr's great meeting.

" The Commissary declared himself willing to take over the Regency of Bavaria. . . . ' I will take,' he said, ' the destinies of Bavaria into my own hands, let us hope to the universal betterment of our beloved country and of Germany at large.'

" ' To-morrow,' rang out Hitler's voice at last,

' finds either a National Government established in
Germany, or the lot of us dead ! ' ''

.   .   .   .   .

Although Hitler had grounds, as has been shown,
for believing that Munich and Bavaria in general
would support his *coup d'état*, the men at the head of
the Munich administration in 1923 were not of heroic
cast. They were only to be depended upon in the
event of success. Hitler browbeat them, in that
private room behind the scenes of the Bürgerbräukeller, for Germany's and their own good, and
sugared the potion with important Cabinet posts
under the new régime. All might yet have gone
according to plan but for the " General with the
Unlucky Fist ! " When the meeting broke up and
Hitler himself had to get busy over a thousand last-
moment arrangements all over the city, three men,
von Kahr, von Lossow and Seisser, were left, practically as prisoners, under Ludendorff's eye.

As Herr Berchtold explains :

" Hitler again invited the three of them into that
room at the back until he himself should return
thither. The General was on no account to let them
go.

" The Storm Troops had withdrawn meanwhile
into the garden of the Bürgerbräu, and presently we
got orders to go and clear out the offices of the
Munich Post, a much-detested Social Democratic
paper, often styled the ' Munich Pest.' We forced
the doors of this place, ransacked the building, and
flung all the printed stuff we could lay hands upon out
into the street where it was promptly burnt. This
was about eleven o'clock at night.

" Then came a Sergeant of Police to request that

we abstained from doing any damage to the building
and its fittings, to which I was quite ready to accede.
The officer cared, probably, no whit for the destruction of the Press ; he might even have been privately
delighted. I reassembled my men before the main
doors of the premises and ordered them to wait there
until I should return, with a convoy of perhaps
twenty men, from a visit I intended to pay to the
house of the notorious Social-democrat Auer. We
drove off thither in an armoured car, but Auer was
not at home, and there was nothing for it but to
return to the *Munich Post*, fall in the rest of the men,
and return to the Bürgerbräukeller.

" When Hitler returned from his last-minute
activities all over the city he was aghast to find
nobody but General Ludendorff awaiting him in the
room behind the Bürgerbräukeller.

" ' How's this, Excellence ? ' he demanded, ' where
are von Kahr, von Lossow, Seisser ? '

" ' Gone,' replied Ludendorff, ' they gave me their
word of honour—— '

" ' Good God ! ' Hitler exclaimed, ' then the game's
all up ! ' "

.   .   .   .   .

Scarcely indeed had the meeting in the Bürgerbräukeller dispersed ; scarcely had Hitler's almost unarmed columns from places as far afield as Ingold-
stadt and Landshut begun to converge on Munich in
order to take part in the morrow's march ; scarcely
had midnight struck when the whole plan was fever-
ishly frustrated.

Instead of going home for a short while, soon
to return as General Ludendorff supposed, von Kahr,
von Lossow and Seisser betook themselves in haste

to the barracks, and to the Munich Broadcasting Station.

At the very moment when placards were going up all over the city, " Power is in the hands of the new National Government ; Ludendorff, Kahr, Lossow and Seisser are with us," the last three named were already urgently denying their participation in the Hitler *coup d'état*. They called Germany and the world to witness that their consent to the revolt had been obtained at the pistol's point.

Hitler had left the three men under Ludendorff's eye, aware that, despite the enthusiasm of the foregoing proceedings, they were not as yet fully to be trusted.

Instantly he divined the worst. . . .

" We'd revealed our hand too soon," pursued Herr Berchtold, " we hadn't known that they'd been planning some such move themselves, but the time was not quite ripe. They'd even been counting on our support ! At this moment we were unaware that they'd got on to the Radio Station to repudiate our *Putsch* and everything to do with it ! They published that they'd been constrained at the pistol's point to take part in all that had happened an hour or two since.

" Hitler was justified in his profoundest misgivings.

" The Storm Troops bivouacked that night in the garden of the Bürgerbräu. They were joined by detachments of the Bund Oberland and of the ' Freikorps Rossbach,' so that the whole place looked like a camp.

" On the morning of November 9th I received orders to occupy Police Headquarters. The Reichskriegsflagge was already in possession of the Munich Army Headquarters. When my men and I arrived we found the police fully armed and prepared to resist us, so avoiding immediate conflict I went on to the Rathaus. I was aware that a Session was in progress. I flung open the doors and, cocking my revolver, informed the assembled Councillors, Social Democrats and Communists to a man, that they must consider themselves under arrest. Alarmed and startled, they sprang to their feet. We shepherded them from the chamber, and the building, and down the wide flight of steps without.

Here the rest of my men took charge. Each member, accompanied by two troopers, was assisted into a truck. Meanwhile enormous crowds had gathered on the Marienplatz who greeted the appearance of the Councillors with jeers and insults. As a matter of fact it was we Storm Troopers who had to defend them from the onslaught of the people. Otherwise actual fatalities might have occurred. It was quite a job getting them safely loaded into the lorries. So we went on to the Bürgerbräu and shut the whole lot up in the room to the rear from which Ludendorff had released von Kahr and his companions overnight.

" In spite of the way the Commissary, von Lossow and Seisser had double-crossed him, Hitler was by no means eager for the thing to end in a fight.

" He decided to gather his adherents from the more outlying districts, and march upon the centre of the city. He could not believe it, in the face of the temper of the people, that the Government would resort to armed resistance.

" Shortly after eleven o'clock the column got under way. Two standard-bearers led, behind whom, walking loosely abreast, came Hitler, Ludendorff, Goering and one or two others. Twelve ranks of

Shock Troops followed with myself in command ;
then came the S.A. (Sturm Abteilung, i.e. the ordinary
Hitler troops), the United Troops and hundreds of
civilians, workmen, students, all with brassards
showing the hooked cross, by way of a great mass
demonstration. The appeal was to be to the streets,
to the people, to Munich. No arms to be used.
Everything was to be put to the test of popular
feeling.

" By this time all the bridges and public buildings
were held by the regular army, mobilised in the night,
as a result of von Kahr's sudden defection. Nevertheless, all seemed to be going well. Patriotic songs
welled from a thousand throats. At the Ludwig
Bridge leading over the Isar to the centre part of
the city we met with what might have been our
first check.

" A police cordon had been drawn across the
bridge head. The police themselves were armed, and
helmeted. We were within a stone's throw of them
when they raised their rifles. Ulrich Graf, Hitler's
bodyguard, shouted, ' Don't fire ; Ludendorff is
with us,' whereupon they lowered them again, and I
sprang forward at the head of some ten of my
fellows and promptly disarmed them. They were
despatched forthwith to the Bürgerbräu. I myself
convoyed them. Having safely bestowed them in
custody I made the utmost speed to rejoin the
column, which forged ahead meanwhile through the
Marienplatz to the Feldherrnhalle end of the
Odeonsplatz. Taking the shortest cut I sprinted
down the Maximilianstrasse to the Max-Joseph
Platz, and arrived on the spot just as the head of the
column debouched between the Feldherrnhalle and
the Residenz.

THE BEGINNING OF THE S.A. STORM TROOPS IN BAVARIAN DRESS
"STOSSTRUPP HITLER" PARADING PAST CROWN PRINCE RUPPRECHT
A FEW DAYS BEFORE THE PUTSCH, NOV. 9, 1923

" Suddenly everything seemed to be holding up——

" They'd begun singing ' Oh Deutschland hoch in Ehren,' and the crowd was lustily joining in, when there came the hideous racket of a machine-gun! Next second all was horror, agony and confusion. The column broke, the crowd dissolved in wildest panic.

" What in the world, I asked, had happened ?

" It seems that as soon as the head of the column reached the Square the police barred the way. An armoured car was stationed behind them. All along by the Feldherrnhalle machine-guns were in position. As before, someone rushed forward shouting: ' Don't fire, Ludendorff and Hitler are with us!' only to be answered by a murderous volley from the steps of the Feldherrnhalle. The standard-bearer went down, seriously wounded; Hitler's immediate neighbour being shot dead dragged him to the ground in falling, severely wrenching the Leader's shoulder. Everywhere people were going down, writhing on the ground in agony, dead and dying, while the guns still rattled death and murder into their stampeding midst. It was madness and slaughter.

" Goering and Graf fell, badly wounded, fourteen dead were trampled under people's feet throwing the living down; blood flowed everywhere over the grey pavement. The whole thing was a ghastly débâcle. Shrieks and cries rent the air, and ever that insane firing went on until one of the strangest things happened of the many strange things on that day. Ludendorff, still uninjured, detached himself somehow from the rout and went forward towards the Odeonsplatz and planked himself bang before the guns of the police! Nothing happened to him.

He never got a scratch. But presently the firing stopped : no one who saw that will ever forget it or understand how it came about he wasn't riddled !

" Dazed and shocked, one by one the wounded dragged themselves up and contrived to get away. Somebody retrieved the flag from the hand of its fallen bearer. Hitler's chauffeur found him somehow, and with screaming brakes wrenched the car to a standstill beside the fallen Leader. Hitler dragged himself to his knees—and then on to his feet—one arm hung helpless—and was making to get into the car when he blundered over something in the way. It was the body of a boy, bleeding and senseless.

" Hitler caught it up as best he might with the arm still sound, and dragged it to the car, and was shoving it up and in just as the chauffeur flung open the door to receive them, when one of the police sprang forward with his weapon levelled. Hitler thrust the boy behind him, to cover him with his own body. Just in the nick of time he gained the auto which leapt forward in top gear frantically pursued by a great green and yellow armoured car. Away they went, pursued and pursuer, through the affrighted streets. For one hair raising moment Hitler's car shot up a side turning in the effort to escape, and the other went blindly careering by : this just gave the Führer a chance to bestow the wounded boy in hospital before he could make for the outskirts of the city and the open. It was, of course, hopeless for him to try and reach the frontier. Late in the evening he had to leave the car and fly afoot.

" I was in the Odeonsplatz and saw it all. When the crowd broke I made off as hard as I could go, back to the Bürgerbräu where lots of the fellows

soon came trooping in. When most of them seemed
to have turned up we released the Councillors from
the room, where they had been shut up all this time,
and, loading them again into trucks, drove them right
out of the city and away into the woods towards
Rosenheim. When we'd gone some considerable
distance I called a halt. We all got out, and leaving
half my fellows behind I led the other half and our
prisoners deep into the wood.

" The Councillors thought for a certainty that their
last hour had struck. But I had a far less ruthless
purpose. I merely wanted to change an entire suit of
clothes with a couple of them. Each one contributed this that or the other garment, and got the
corresponding one of mine in return. In a few
moments I had transformed myself from a Shock
trooper into a very passable likeness of the ordinary
man in the street. Thereupon we returned to the
cars, and began our journey back to Munich. I
dumped the City Councillors at the first convenient
village and left them to shift for themselves.

" But, dressed as I now was, I could make my way
about without attracting attention. I ventured first
to seek out the hospital to which Goering had been
taken. I even saw him. He was in such pain it
was all he could do to keep his wits about him,
but he managed to give me some details about the
end of the affair. Warrants were out for the lot of us,
Hitler, Ludendorff, Goering and all of us, especially
we of the Shock Troops, as the prime delinquents.

" As a matter of fact they caught me that same
night. But I managed to slip through their hands,
and made off again in the direction of Rosenheim.
In Traunstein they all but had me a second time,
but I doubled back and returned to Munich where

I lay low for a time. There I heard the end of the story."

The Berlin papers arrived boiling over with anger. Hitler and Ludendorff and the Crown Prince Rupprecht all came in for the reproaches and the accusations of the central Government. Von Lossow at the end of that fateful day had telegraphed to General von Seeckt that the *Putsch* was liquidated. " No more troops needed."

Two days later, at Uffing on the Staffelsee, in the house of a German-American friend, whither he had taken refuge, an officer of the Green Police laid his hand on Hitler's shoulder.

.   .   .   .   .

Goering fled to the Tyrol, lying still desperately ill at an Innsbruck clinic, later he went to Italy. Esser, Rossbach and Hanfstaengl, Hitler's foreign press chief, had escaped to Salzburg, the *Völkischer Beobachter* was suppressed ; the Shock Troops and the S.A. generally were disbanded and forbidden ; Hitler, Hess, Kriebel and his principal associates were imprisoned in Landsberg ; nothing whatever remained of the National Socialist Party. Everything had gone down before the treacherous guns on the Odeonsplatz.

" As for me," concludes Herr Berchtold, " I remained on, more or less in hiding, in Munich until the following February (1924), when I managed to get away into Austria. I kept in touch with Hitler as best I could, and when I heard his sentence would gladly have given myself up for a chance of sharing it with him. But by his own wish I stuck where I was, in Austria, until such time as I might return without danger. I stayed until 1926 when Hinden-

burg's general amnesty for political offenders allowed
so many of us, Goering included, to return to
Germany.

" The outlook, however, was pretty miserable.
Our great Movement, everything, was suppressed,
' verboten.' The only thing that remained was
fidelity in many a breast to Hitler and his Idea.
When the hour struck, months and months afterwards, for the resurrection of this idea, we were
all ready . . ."

Anton Drexler concludes the tale :

" They incarcerated Hitler," he said, " to await
trial in the fortress at Landsberg, and I made a point
of going to see him there at the earliest opportunity.
I found him sitting like a frozen thing at the barred
window of his cell.[1] He seemed done, almost broken
up over the deaths of those sixteen of our men on
the Odeonsplatz. Everything seemed all to have
been in vain, all our work and planning and striving,
and stinting and scraping and saving, all our hope
and high endeavour ! I discovered he'd started a
hunger strike right from the first. Every time I went
it was still going on. He'd got thinner and thinner,
and weaker and whiter, every time. Over a fortnight
he carried on this hunger strike until it was hard to
recognise him. The Medical Officer told me it
couldn't last much longer if fatal results weren't to
ensue. If no one could persuade him to take a drop
or a mouthful anyhow he'd soon be past saving.
You can imagine what that meant to us ! I determined to do my utmost to make him call it off.
I went back into his cell one day determined to
succeed if I had to stop there all night. Lord ! how

---

[1] An inscription stands over the entrance to it to-day, recording
Hitler's incarceration here.

I begged and prayed of him, and talked at him and reasoned with him ! I said he'd no right to give up all for lost, however bad things seemed. The Party'd look to him to start it all up again some day. But I couldn't make any impression. He was utterly in despair. So I nearly fell into despair myself, but at last I said how we'd all rather die than try to go on without him. I meant it, too ! Without Hitler and his Movement Germany was doomed. That seemed to rouse him, so I kept on. I said if all did seem to have gone for nothing so far that was no reason why we hadn't yet to do all we could to save the country in her bitter need and humiliation. I talked for a solid two hours. . . . Anyway, I won him round somehow.

" Finally he broke his fast and reconsidered things. He picked up when he got some solid food inside him again, and his old spirit reasserted itself. In fact three months afterwards he was brought back to Munich to stand his trial with Ludendorff and von Lossow and Seisser and the rest. Hitler was as full of force and resolution as ever he'd been in his life. And he made one of the grandest speeches in Court we'd ever heard from him yet."

Hitler was arrested at the country house of his friend, Dr. Hanfstaengl.[1] He allowed himself to be

[1] Dr. Ernst F. S. Hanfstaengl was then as to-day, Chief of the Foreign Press Office of the National Socialist Party. He first came into personal contact with Hitler in 1922.

He was born in 1887, and through his German-American mother is the great nephew of General John Sedgwick of Gettysburg fame. Educated first at Munich and then at Harvard, he also had the advantage of extensive travel. During the War he directed the New York branch of his deceased father's well-known Art Publishing House in Munich. He returned to Germany in 1921, met Hitler in the autumn of 1922 and became his foreign press chief. After the calamity of November 8th–9th he devoted himself to historical study in the University of Munich, and obtained his Degree. His book, *Von Marlborough bis Mirabeau*, is well known in England and America.

taken without resistance, and was at once sent on remand, awaiting trial, to the Prison-Fortress at Landsberg.

The trial began on February 26th, 1924, and lasted for twenty-four days. It was held in the old Munich Infantry School in the Blutenburgstrasse. There is no need, perhaps, to tell the story at length again. It has often been told before. Hitler made a remarkable speech, lasting four and a half hours, in which he set out the aims and principles of his Movement, and in which he endeavoured to take entire responsibility for the events of November 8th and 9th last upon his own shoulders.

The Court was, admittedly, much impressed. The trial was an affair into which none of the judges felt like putting much heart. Public sympathy was largely with the accused. Hitler and his nine companions were the heroes of the day! The State prosecutor had a thankless office. Herr von Kahr was universally execrated as the Judas of the whole affair. But for the sake of saving the Government's face Adolf Hitler, Dr. Pöhner (Chief of Police), Lieut.-Colonel Kriebel, Commander of the *Putsch* troops, and Dr. Weber, Commander of the " Oberland," were sentenced to five years' imprisonment in a fortress. Five other " conspirators " received sentences of a year and three months, and three were immediately set at large. General Ludendorff was acquitted.

CHAPTER X

SOME fifty miles west of Munich lies the small
Bavarian town of Landsberg-am-Lech. Its
inhabitants number only a few thousand. It remains
unspoilt to this day, one of the most beautiful
survivals of the Middle Ages in Germany. The
houses have preserved their old-world character.
Modern times have failed to make any impression
upon Landsberg : the little old town might have
fallen asleep five hundred years ago, and never
since waked up.

It nestles in the little valley of the Lech, an alpine
stream, hemmed in on either hand by steep densely
wooded heights. A mediæval wall still studded with
its watch towers, big and small, wanders over one of
the heights, surrounding the town. My way, however, led me across the stream. I came to the
outskirts of Landsberg down by the river and as I
crossed its old wooden bridge I paused to watch the
babbling, foaming waters below, and then caught
sight of a great conglomeration of grey-white
buildings to be glimpsed through the trees on the
heights before me.

This is the " Gefangenenanstalt und Festungs-
haftanstalt Landsberg."[1]

---

[1] Ordinary prison and fortress for the detention of political
prisoners.

The whole is an imposing place consisting of a number of separate buildings, all enclosed within the usual prison wall. There may be gardens behind those walls, and even orchards ; the situation may be park-like in its peace and verdant beauty ; luxuriant creepers may even do their best to hide the prison walls—but the windows are all barred. Those within can scarcely take much pleasure in the prospect without, however fair it may be, for they are deprived of the greatest boon in the world, their liberty !

I came to the great nail-studded, iron-shod entrance gates, and pulled the bell. Whereupon a rattling of keys was to be heard, and steps on the pavement within. The door groaned on its hinges and opened. A warder in dark blue uniform with chain and keys at his belt, bade me enter. He had been advised of my coming, and showed me in without delay.

We crossed a courtyard and entered the Administration Block where I was ushered in to the Governor's office. This gentleman informed me that at the instance of the Bavarian Ministry of Justice I was to be given every facility to visit the Institution, and to see everything I wanted. I requested that I might have as my guide Chief Warder Franz Hemmrich. This officer had held a position here in Landsberg since 1920, and was, indeed in charge of that portion of the fortress in which Adolf Hitler and his friends were confined after the events of that fateful November 9th, 1923.

For a thumb-nail sketch of Herr Hemmrich— he is a man perhaps at the end of the thirties. The face and especially the eyes are full of alert activity and energy. One gets the impression of an officer who has put in a good many years of responsible and exacting service. He wears a blue uniform with epaulettes, and an official cap.

"Before I start the story of Adolf Hitler's detention here," he tells me, as we prepare to make the tour of Landsberg, "you ought to know something of the place itself. It is, as you can see, fairly modern. It was built in 1909, and originally intended for none but ordinary convicts. It was planned to accommodate five hundred. Only since 1920 have we had political prisoners here—quite a different class. They don't, of course, rank with criminals at all. We had no special accommodation to allot to them, so a wing was set apart for the purpose and called the 'Festung.' In 1920 Count Arco-Valley was sent here. He had been condemned to death for shooting the Bavarian Minister President Kurt Eisner, but his sentence was commuted to penal servitude for life. For a long time he was the only man we had in the 'Festung.' Now and again we got a student in over some duelling affair, but only for a very short stretch.

"During the time Hitler was under detention here —between his arrest and his trial,—the whole place was thoroughly remodelled in view of eventualities. The large generally unused rooms were converted into a series of cells, and quarters were arranged for the military warders. Preparations were made, and precautions taken, for the reception of a large number of political prisoners.

"Then, on November 11th, 1923, I remember, there was a regular storm raging. The wind howled and shrieked round the place and tore at the barred windows. Rain dashed against the panes as if it would break them. At that time I had a room

LANDSBERG ON THE LECH

HOSPITAL AT LANDSBERG. HITLER'S ROOM FIRST STOREY,
FOURTH WINDOW FROM THE RIGHT

within the prison. It was night, and I'd gone to bed.
All was still save for the muffled tread of an officer
going the rounds, or for the ticking when he
clocked in.

"All of a sudden a bell rang through the corridor,
and a moment or two later came a knocking on my
door. 'The Governor wants you. You're to come
at once,' cried a voice without. I jumped into my
clothes with all the speed I could, and hurried to the
office. Herr Oberregierungsrat Leybold was chief
at the time.

"'See here,' he said, and his face was as serious
as his voice, ' Hitler's coming here to-night. He has
been arrested at last, and he'll certainly be sent along
to us. We'll have to be prepared for anything. His
followers may make an attempt at rescue——'

"While we were speaking the telephone rang, and
word came through that a strong detachment of the
local Reichswehr had been detailed to take over
guard in the prison. I received the order to get
ready a cell for Hitler in the fortress division. Now
the only cell in the place which had an anteroom big
enough for the military guard was already occupied
by Count Arco-Valley. So I had to wake him up
and transfer him elsewhere. I was still busy fixing
things to rights for a new occupant when the bell
went which notified me from the gate that the
prisoners had arrived.

"I hastened down to receive them and soon met
a strange enough group of men coming through the
halls with their shadows flickering and dancing in
the darkness before them. First I recognised the
Governor accompanied by the Superintendents of
police, one of whom led a dog on the leash. Between
these came Hitler, very upright, the Iron Cross on his

breast. Over his shoulder was slung the grey trench-
coat he had been wearing in the Odeonsplatz. His
left arm hung in a sling. Bare headed, white and
worn in the face, he marched thus to the place we
had prepared.

" The police and the Governor left him, on reaching
the cell, and I stayed to give him a hand with his
undressing. He was just about all in. He refused
bite or soup, but lay down on the cot. Whereupon
I too went away after securely locking him in.

" The whole place was soon re-echoing to military
tread. The Reichswehr had arrived. Helmets and
rifles glittered everywhere. A detail was assigned as
guard outside Hitler's cell, and the one next to it
was allotted to their officer. Outside in the yard
machine-guns had been mounted, and a supply of
ammunition was brought up, and telephonic communication had been made with the barracks. You
see, we had a case of High Treason to deal with.

" But nothing happened. A grey dawn came at
long length. Both within and without the ' Festung '
it looked like an armed camp. Everywhere rifles
were stacked while the soldiers busied themselves
boiling coffee. Presently, however, for the most
part the soldiers were transferred to an upper floor
within the building : only a small guard remained
without.

" A few days went by and Hitler had to be taken
in to the infirmary. He was in a bad way, generally,
and the injury to his collar-bone made no improvement. But he was allowed to receive visitors, and
these came nearly every day—for the most part
they were the members of his Party, and fellow-
workers. They came to him for directions and
advice at this low ebb of the tide ! One of the

greatest pleasures these visits afforded him was
when a friend brought along his dog ! The meeting
on both sides was touching to behold.

" The days dragged by. The ' Festung ' witnessed
an ever-increasing influx of Hitler's friends and
comrades, one after another of whom were arrested
and sent hither. Among others came Anton Drexler
and Dietrich Eckart. The latter was discharged
after about ten days on account of his health. He
died later from heart failure, his death being
expedited through his arrest and imprisonment.

" On the morning of February 22nd, then, a
number of lorries drove up to the prison gate to
convoy Hitler and his companions for trial in
Munich.

.   .   .   .   .

" About five o'clock in the afternoon on April 1st
Hitler returned to Landsberg. A car drove up to the
entrance. Out of the car stepped three men, Hitler
himself, Lieut.-Colonel Kriebel and Dr. Weber.
Hitler looked more wretched than ever as he once
more crossed the threshold of his well-known cell.
In the meantime it had been refurnished, and now
looked a good deal more inviting than it had done
previously on the night of November 11th. His
cell was No. 7. His neighbour in No. 8 was
Lieut.-Colonel Kriebel, and in No. 9, Dr. Weber.

" The cell remains to-day just as it was then.
You'd like to have a look inside——"

Chief Warder Hemmrich unlocks the door and
swings it open. The furnishing consists of no more
than a simple bed, a table, two chairs, a cupboard
and a bedside table. A glimpse can be caught of the
garden down below out of two high barred windows
in the whitewashed wall.

" Next day," he pursues, " the three prisoners were conducted to the office to have their particulars taken. When they returned to their cells they found a fourth unfortunate in their company. This was an ex-Reichswehr soldier, who for some crime or other had a short stretch to serve at Landsberg. He was earning some remission of sentence by making the mattresses for the new cells in the ' Festung.' Hitler felt sorry for the poor chap, who seemed always hungry and never had any money, and made a point of sharing food with him properly destined for himself.

" A little book of rules hung in every cell. The prisoners were expected to study it meticulously. It mapped out their day for them. Later I'll explain how they were supposed to get through the time. Hitler and his friends put in a lot of reading. Sometimes they'd take a turn in the garden. April 20th that year—Hitler's thirty-fifth birthday—fell just about Easter so that for the first time in its history a really festive sort of spirit held sway here. An incredible number of letters, telegrams and parcels arrived for our most important prisoner that morning. Visitors thronged the gate. His cell was turned into a veritable florist's shop. His presents were heaped upon the table and the chairs. The whole thing was a remarkable demonstration, and I haven't the slightest doubt but that it gave Hitler the greatest joy to realise how his followers were sticking to him through thick and thin.

" There was somebody else who appreciated all those packages of Hitler's—the Reichswehr man ! Hitler turned over all the eatables to him which his friends had fondly imagined would be acceptable to himself. The soldier performed prodigies of valour in accounting for the lot.

" By the beginning of May a large influx of National Socialists came to Landsberg, and during June the number rose to thirty-two. The ' Festung ' was crowded out, despite the fact that some of the cells now contained as many as four or even five prisoners altogether. We were obliged to take over quarters for the politicals in the ordinary part of the Prison which communicated with the ' Festung ' through a corridor. Every new arrival was greeted, naturally, with somewhat of an ovation. Among other new-comers was Rudolf Hess,[1] later Hitler's private secretary.

" You'd like to know a bit about our Bell Scale of the ' Festung ' ? Well, the two night warders went off duty, after clocking in, at six. Then all cell doors were opened and free communication for the day was established throughout the wing. At seven the convicts brought the Politicals their breakfast. This usually consisted of coffee and bread, or porridge, or some cereal. After that the prisoners went to the washroom. At eight the outer doors were opened on to the court and garden, when everybody rushed for the vaulting-horse, or the parallel bars—some gymnastic apparatus had been set up there—to get a bit of strenuous exercise. Some of them had a bout of boxing or did a bit of wrestling. All sorts of sports were provided for. Hitler would have gone in for some of them but for his injured arm. As it was he had to content himself with the job of referee.

" After about an hour of this the prisoners had a turn in the garden. The garden is, as you see, some-

[1] See *Die Männer um Hitler* by Edgar von Schmidt-Pauli for particulars of Hess and many other of the Leader's first companions. To-day Herr Hess is Hitler's " persönlicher Stellvertreter." He qualified for the post by his unremitting devotion and service at Landsberg.

what long and narrow, hemmed in by the prison buildings on the one side and on the other by a twenty-foot wall. The other sides are contained by high wooden fences. Here, you see, is a notice board, ' Bounds.' If anyone overstepped these limits he was looked upon as attempting to escape. My window overlooked the garden and it was my job to keep an eye on our promenaders. You see that long gravel path that runs by the wall ? That was Hitler's favourite walk, up and down, up and down. For the most part Hess was his companion. The rest of them called it ' Hitler's Path.' Sometimes those who had formerly belonged to the Storm Troops would start singing party songs as they tramped along. At first we took no notice, or at least we raised no objection to this, but when the convicts on their side took to yelling in unison and disturbed the peace of the whole neighbourhood, we put a stop to it.

" At ten o'clock it was indoors again, with the gate locked behind. At eleven letters were given out. They had all been opened, in the office of course, and censored. If they contained anything which, in the Governor's judgment, it was unsuitable to communicate they could be withheld. Prisoners had to fetch their own parcels from the parcel room, and all had to be opened and unpacked in my presence. Very often I'd have a look into any of the eatables to see if they were serving to smuggle anything through. It was an interesting job, this parcels inspection, and gave quite an insight into the characters of the recipients. Lieut.-Colonel Kriebel, whom I got to know as a man of somewhat peremptory temper, had a way of wrenching off the wrappings of his parcels, quite characteristic of himself. He always did it like that. He'd whip off the stoutest string in one jerk. Now Dr. Weber was exactly the opposite. He'd undo every blessed knot with the utmost care and patience, no matter how long it took. Whenever a parcel turned up for Dr. Weber I knew what I was in for. I asked him once how he came to take such pains over a little thing like that. He looked up at me, adjusted his glasses and replied: ' When I was a boy I was passionate and impulsive to a degree. My father used to give me a frightful tangle of string to undo, whenever I showed this propensity, and so forced me to learn patience.'

" Now Hitler, again, he did differently. It depended whether the parcel came from a known or an unknown source. In the one case it might have contained sausage, and in the other, an infernal machine! I was always a bit uneasy about those stranger parcels. Hitler'd look 'em over very carefully himself before he cut the string. With the other sort he just took the line of least resistance. If there were a lot of knots he'd cut the string without more ado ; if there were few he'd undo 'em.

" Shortly before twelve o'clock they would spread the cloth for dinner in the common room. This cloth didn't properly come under orders, but the convicts instituted it and we made no demur. They brought the meal in one large vessel and served it to the prisoners. As a rule the meal consisted of but one dish.[1] Everyone waited for Hitler, each standing erect behind his own chair. When the Leader appeared there was a cry of ' 'tenshun! ' and he strode to the top of the table, and remained standing,

[1] Ein " Eintopf-Gericht " foreshadowing, perhaps, the famous self-denying ordinance of last winter in aid of the poor and needy.

until every man in turn came forward with his table-greeting. Then all sat down and fell to. There was seldom any talk of politics. As a rule Hitler himself chatted with his right and left-hand neighbours about such things as the theatre, or art, or even technical matters. He was quite an adept in mechanics, especially motor mechanics. He was always getting plans and specifications from motor works, new designs for the chassis, and sketched out a few himself. (It is well known, of course, that he invented two jolly useful motor gadgets, and patented them. One was for a rearward reflector which would allow the car to travel backwards with facility ; and the other was an adjustable lamp at the driving seat for reading route maps, etc. He made use of both these contrivances later when touring the country at night on his political campaigns.) At the end of the meal Hitler would give the signal ' Mahlzeit,' answered by the rest, and then they would all sit about a bit smoking and chatting while the table was cleared. Perhaps somebody would make him a little present of some fruit—always gratefully accepted by Hitler. After perhaps a quarter of an hour he would lay the plate aside and betake himself again to his room.

" Now came the time for me to make the round of the Politicals' cells to take their orders for any small commodities they might require, always on the understanding that they'd pay for them themselves. At about a quarter to four one or another of the company would brew tea or coffee on the oven in the common room and take the cups round to his companions. At a quarter to five I unlocked the courtyard gate again and all would flock into the open for the second airing of the day—when Hitler and Hess invariably betook themselves to their particular beat.

" At six they returned indoors for supper—a herring or a little sausage and salad, eaten in the cells. Each man was allowed to buy half a litre of beer or wine ; a good many availed themselves of the privilege.

" After this, at half-past six, came a second hour of sport or exercise in the open air once more, then the prisoners reassembled in the common room until nine, when every one was expected to retreat to his own quarters. It was Lights Out at ten. Whereupon the night officers coming on duty were greeted by many a resounding snore.

" Before I can tell you much as to Hitler's own occupations at Landsberg I ought to put in a word or two about his own particular friends and how they carried on here—Lieut.-Colonel Kriebel, for instance. Although like Hitler and the rest, he wore, for the most part, native Bavarian costume, one could always detect the military man. But for all that he was a cheerful soul, and could appreciate a good bit of fun. Dr. Weber was half-sportsman, half-savant. He had served with distinction in the War, and since then, had seen fighting as a volunteer in Upper Silesia. He was rather typically the man of culture and letters. He was particularly interested in astronomy. Once, I remember, when an eclipse of the moon was on, he begged me to open the courtyard door. Hitler and Kriebel were with him : he gave them a wonderful account of the northern hemisphere. It was quite a privilege for me, too, to listen to him. He was a good sports instructor as well, and held regular courses in the gymnasium. On one occasion he arranged a sort of

gymkhana, to which the whole staff was invited.
Hess carried off most of the prizes.

" Hess at that time was still a student. He was
always immersed in his books. He had an energetic
and purposeful character under an exterior as modest
as it was unassuming. Then there was Emil Maurice,
a watchmaker by trade, who helped Hitler in the
beginning with his writing. Afterwards Hess took
this on. In cell No. 2 lived Schneider, the amateur
boxer. He put it up to the authorities to provide him
with a punching ball, and got a sack of sand. A few
of the other Politicals, mostly students, turned
themselves into a band ; one or two possessed
a violin or a lute. The rest fashioned weird instru-
ments for themselves out of tins nailed on to broom
handles, and made them do duty for bass and
'cello.

" A real original was a budding legal light called
Fobke. Although he seriously did his best, somehow,
to keep up his studies here, he was always getting
bright ideas which interrupted their course. He
founded a paper called *Der Landsberger Ehren-
bürger* which circulated privately among the company
and had a good deal of success. It was typed and
hectographed, and consisted of two sections, one
serious and the other comic. Hitler nearly always
wrote the leading article for this production, and
often contributed caricatures. The first part contained political matter, but the second contained
stories about the prisoners themselves and about us
warders. The whole thing remained secret for a
while, until someone wrote home about it, and the
game was up. Because all letters were opened you
know. But our literary aspirants got wind of the
circumstance, and when I raided the editorial office,

Cell No. 11, nothing was to be seen of the paper. Every copy had been burnt.

" Besides the fellows I have named there were a couple of dozen more all thrown together here, so altogether I had a rather hectic time of it.

" Then came Hitler's name day,[1] June 17th. The night officers had scarcely gone off duty when I heard strains of music coming from above. I went up to investigate and found the band had planted itself outside Hitler's door, and was serenading him, if a a serenade can be said to be played at six o'clock in the morning. And upon my word, it wasn't at all bad !

" Hitler got a good many presents which he stored away, this time, in a sort of ditty box proper to cell No. 11. This grub box, or tuck chest, was confided to the care of the senior inmate of the cells, who divided the contents out equally every day. In the evening they held a sort of do[2] in the common room, when the band again distinguished itself. Hitler opened the proceedings with a speech. It was my job to patrol the room to take note that nothing transpired of a revolutionary character. But to-day I can own up that both I and some of the other warders rather exceeded instructions on this occasion. We gathered round the door, all ears, alert for what he was saying about things that concerned our own interests. We were immensely struck by his speaking. He wound up with an exhortation, ' Nun erst recht ! Sieg Heil ! ' And they broke into a song, ' Haken-kreuz und Stahlhelm ' (Hooked Cross and Steel Helmet).

---

[1] Not birthday but baptism day, when the name is bestowed. An observance confined to the Catholic parts of Germany.

[2] Kameradschaftsabend.

' Hat man uns auch verraten,
Trieb mit uns Schindluderei,
Wir wussten, was wir taten,
Bleiben dem Vaterlande treu.
Hitler's Geist in Herzen
Kann nicht untergeh'n,
Sturmabteilung Hitler,
Wird einst aufersteh'n.'

After which they wound up with a few more musical selections, lighter songs and amusing perorations.

" On the anniversary of the Versailles Treaty Hitler gave his followers a longer address, but, here again, we warders were on hand and got the benefit of listening to it from the neighbourhood of the door. And even outside, the sentries had left their posts to gather motionless under the windows and stare up at them, and try to catch the speech.

" Notwithstanding all their efforts to keep their end up, bit by bit the monotony of this existence began to wear down our Politicals. They were obliged to think up something fresh to do, so they hit upon volunteering for garden work. They got the necessary permission and all set to with a will, except Hitler and Hess, who by this time had regularly settled down to the writing of a book—I'll return to that later. There were some horticultural experts among our body of gardeners, so they made no botch of their new-found work. They began by relaying the central path through the garden. They were supplied with overalls, sun hats and the necessary implements and wheelbarrows. Lieut.-Colonel Kriebel, looking like a Brazilian coffee planter in his broad straw, acted as foreman of the works. As soon as a barrow was loaded with gravel, off they went with it at the gallop to the outer postern. I overlooked the whole business from my office

window, and when this detail appeared I would
come down, unlock the gate and accompany the
column to the pit where the stuff was shot. This to
and fro business went on all day : our procedure
became mechanical even for the man on duty at the
postern. The moment my head disappeared at the
window, Kriebel took up his position in front and
the whole outfit moved off.

" We officers at Landsberg had never really looked
upon Hitler and his friends as ordinary ' prisoners '
(political or otherwise), i.e. men sentenced to
punitive detention. On the contrary we had
esteemed them as upright men from the outset,
and now when we had come to know them we
realised how well-founded was this respect and even
admiration. So that one day a queer thing happened.
The guard at the gate opened to Kriebel and his crowd
without noticing that I, for once, was not with them.
The barrow went through, and with it six men
regained their liberty ! There was nothing to
prevent their getting clear away. But after a time
as I shot a glance at the gardeners from my window,
I noticed Kriebel was not to be seen. Worse than
that—five others also were obviously missing !

" I rushed to the outer gate, to the utmost consternation of the warder there who instantly grasped what
was afoot. Good God ! six men had escaped. . . .
I rang up the Administration Block, got on to the
Governor. . . . Warders were immediately summoned from all parts of the prison buildings . . .
word flew round the place like lightning . . . a
posse was despatched in pursuit of the fugitives in
the direction of the town—and then I had a brain
wave !

" I sprinted along to the gravel pit only to

encounter the whole six of the supposed runaways mildly returning with their empty barrow. I could have hugged 'em! They could have made a pretty good getaway among our hills by this time if that had really been their game. But, as I say, we'd always looked upon Hitler and his friends as honourable men, and this goes to prove it. It proves how right we were, too.

" Then another time they put up a rare bit of fun. You know how the peasants here carry on when anyone in the village doesn't quite meet with the approval of the rest ? A dozen of them get together in the evening, disguise themselves so that they can't easily be recognised, arm themselves with pitchforks and threshing flails and things of that sort, and betake themselves to the dwelling of the culprit. There they kick up such a din he is obliged at last to come out and confront them. Then the spokesman ups and gives it to him straight, and lets him know what his neighbours think of him, and tells him jolly well to look out for the future if he doesn't want his roof burnt over his head. Sometimes, even, the churl will forestall what's coming to him, ask for it, and get it over.[1]

" Well, our Politicals arranged to play this game on Hitler. They smeared their faces with oven rust, and black, and what not, enveloped themselves in their bed sheets, and armed themselves with pokers and brooms. Outside Hitler's door they began their row and one of them banged on it with his fists. Hitler opened it, amazed and non-comprehending at first—and then waked to rich enjoyment of the joke.

" ' Adolf Hitler,' demanded the one, ' where are you ? '

[1] This custom is called the " Haberfeld-Treiben."

FORTRESS QUARTERS. HITLER'S CELL FIRST STOREY, FOURTH
AND FIFTH WINDOWS FROM THE LEFT

NTERIOR OF HITLER'S CELL IN THE FORTRESS AT LANDSBERG

" ' Why, here ! ' replied he, laughing.

" ' All right then ! We've come to have it out with you,' and turning to his supporters, ' are you all here, boys ? ' cried the accuser.

" With an immense flourishing of weapons they yelled that they were, in chorus.

" ' Very well,' pursued their leader, ' let's put him through it.' Whereupon he proceeded to a laughable parody of the charges against Hitler at the recent trial, and to the most comical and pointed witticisms at the expense of men like Kahr, Lossow and Seisser who had played such a sorry part in the events leading up to that crisis. The whole thing, of course, was richly interlarded with nicknames and broad Bavarian provincialisms. It ended up with an appeal to the ' Haberer,' ' Are you agreed ? '

" They were, they asseverated, one and all.

" Whereupon sentence must be passed on Hitler.

" He was to be instantly expelled from Landsberg, and condemned to tour Germany in his motor-car and drive the Reds to the devil.

" The assembled Haberer loudly applauded with fresh brandishings and flourishings, and at length withdrew, highly satisfied with the performance, while Hitler laughing still, but shaking his head, went back to his interrupted work.

" It was a good thing both for themselves and for Hitler that the Politicals managed somehow or other to get some fun out of life here, otherwise it would have gone badly for them. There's danger in the monotony of prison. I've seen quite enough of it in my time, I can tell you. Queer things happen.

" But if we're going to talk about Hitler himself more particularly all I can say is that he exercised an influence all his own on everyone, big and little, in

o

the place. He was always an early riser, long before
he came here, and was ready dressed by the time our
' Festung ' day began. He took a good deal of care
of his teeth and mouth. That came of his having
been gassed in the war.

" After breakfast—which he took in common with
the rest, when most times he'd talk a bit about art or
music—anything but politics—he'd retreat into his
room (which had been put to rights meantime by
men from the convict side), and plunge himself for
hours in study, He gathered quite a library about
him of the books sent him by friends and followers
and admirers outside. They were political books, and
scientific books, and what they call *belles lettres*.
He had a lot about his two prime favourites and
heroes—and their pictures—Wagner and Frederick
the Great.

" Then came the courtyard and the garden, when
he could walk about a little and look on at the
gymnastics. Very often he'd have a book in his
hand, and just sit about reading. He formed his
own particular circle, and was the life and soul of it
himself. Very often the morning was all taken up by
visitors, especially on his first coming here. I'll
come back to them later on. They all took their
midday meal together, our Politicals, and then
Hitler would spend the afternoon trying to cope
with his enormous correspondence, or going back to
his books. In the evening he'd be in the garden
again or doing the referee for them at games. But
by special permission Hitler was allowed a light at
night up to twelve o'clock, two hours beyond the time
accorded to everybody else. He never failed to avail
himself of the privilege.

" Hitler's fine personality, in which no trace of

personal vanity was to be detected, made an impression on all around him. He had a remarkable love of order and neatness. He possessed an unquenchable spring of energy within, which, despite his accustomed urbanity, flashed in his eyes whenever a decision had to be made. It stands to reason that when a number of men are penned up together in narrow quarters, against any choice of their own, men, moreover, convinced of the rightness of their actions, the exactions of prison regulations should give rise to endless exacerbations of temper, and necessary clashes with authority. That this was not the case here when we had the National Socialists in Landsberg was due wholly to Hitler's over-ruling influence, and to his sense of soldierly discipline.

" If the rest bore their detention as well as he did, it was because they learnt from him that the Cause for which they stood was well worth what they had to go through in pursuit of it. The uniform politeness with which he treated everyone here, from the Governor to the man who cleaned his cell, excited universal appreciation. He knew, too, what sort of a job we warders had, and understood it. For instance, when one or another of the prisoners would put in for some favour or privilege which I didn't see my way to grant, I'd ask Hitler to my room and put the thing to him. I had my duty to perform, however personally distasteful it might be now and again, and would he please call his friends' attention to the fact ? This, that or the other matter was forbidden : I simply had no option but to see that the rules were kept. Hitler merely returned, ' Quite so, Herr Wachtmeister ; I'll see to it.' And that was the end of the matter. His word simply went with our Politicals, even under the cloud of the present circumstances.

" He was entirely unassuming, and had few personal requirements. He took a real pleasure in all those things people contrived to do to show him their loyalty and sympathy. He gave away the contents of parcels sent to him, and always contrived, if possible, to have something on hand for the children of anyone who came to see him. He bore himself in just that comradely way to his followers which takes no account of difference in position or upbringing, and found full opportunity during their common imprisonment to draw closer the ties which knit them to him. He was always at their command to be of help or service. As a rule he was singularly cheerful, and did his best to make their evenings in the common room go with a swing. He even got Hess to make out a list of their birthdays, so that whenever one of these came round, the individual in question would be specially invited to coffee with him in his room, and they'd sit and talk, and Hitler'd dish up some little present or other.

" Stormy weather, of course, made a difference to everybody's spirits. When it poured and howled outside, it generally fell pretty dull and quiet within. Then it was Hitler grew a trifle thoughtful and anxious. So he did, too, when bad news came. It knocked him pretty hard to realise how things had gone to bits in the Party since his imprisonment— years of labour and endeavour, and struggle, and hopes all gone for nothing ! There were rows and splits in the groups of National Socialists, who still hung together somehow ; the leaderless Movement seemed destined to peter right out. At first he tried, even from here, to keep things going, and to direct the Party as before, but when he found that his instructions were so apt to get themselves misunderstood or misapplied, and often, indeed, failed to reach their destination in the form they had left his hand, he gave up the vain attempt, and withdrew himself altogether from politics. He devoted all his energies to the book.

" It was now that he began to write *Mein Kampf*. All day long and late into the night one could hear the typewriter going in his room, and his voice dictating to Hess. As he finished one section of the book after another he would read it aloud to the others in their evening assemblies. This formed an enormous interest in their lives. They already knew that Hitler could speak : now they were to appraise his writing."

.   .   .   .   .

It may be permitted to digress, for a moment, in order to enter a note or two on *Mein Kampf*.

This book should have for all students of human psychology a quite peculiar interest considering the personality of the man who wrote it, and the circumstances to which it owed its inception and under which it was written. *Mein Kampf* is a human document, if it is neither precisely history nor precisely literature. It has been cruelly criticised. Quite the most bitter things that could have been said about it have come from the side of literary rather than of political criticism. To that extent they are negligible and beside any real point. Hitler's mind teemed in Landsberg as it has teemed since, with a multitude of urgent ideas. It must have been of immense mental service to him to set them down, with the aid of the enthusiastic and devoted Hess, and reduce them to the order and the cogency of ink !

This book, it should be remembered, was addressed to the adherents of the original German Workmen's

Party, and in no way appealed to opponents at home
or to foreigners abroad.

Since the beginning of 1933 when President von
Hindenburg, as a last resort, and faced otherwise
with political and economic chaos, appointed Adolf
Hitler to the German Chancellorship, the Landsberg
writings of the erstwhile prisoner has been the most
widely read work throughout Germany. Had it not
been for Hitler's spectacular political success, *Mein
Kampf* might have had no more and no less of a
public at home than any other literary effort of the
sort. Had it not been for Hitler's appointment to
the German Chancellorship in the January of 1933
it is quite unlikely that the book would have attracted
widespread attention in England.

In this country an idea seems to have gained
ground that every German is obliged at the pistol's
point to buy a copy of *Mein Kampf*. Under such
circumstances, of course, it was bound to be a
redoubtable best seller ! As a matter of fact, it owes
its ubiquity to no such means. The Chancellor,
however, derives a large proportion of his personal
income from its sale. He has no other private
resources. His official salary is wholly diverted for
the relief of poverty and unemployment.

The interest of *Mein Kampf* is not identical in
England with the interest it has for those to whom
it is addressed, and whose lives now are very definitely
set to run upon the lines laid down in it. The interest
of the book for the English reader is something
different. Whether he reads the work (it consists of
two hefty volumes, running into nearly eight hundred
pages of close print), in German or in English, the
first astonishing thing about it is its amazing vigour
and originality.

From this book, written as it was ten years ago, might be inferred or foreseen, the decisive drive and force of National Socialism once it attained to power. The book was written ten years ago, but everything in its pages—with few acknowledged exceptions—holds fast as granite to-day now that it has won. The book was written ten years ago when few perhaps, except its author himself, would really have dared to promise that such a victory as that recorded in the German general election in November, 1933, would ever really happen. The victory of National Socialism could have been won without the book.

The writer himself sets infinitely less store by the pen than by the spoken word. He relied upon it to that end far less than he relied upon his voice. But for those in England, cold to the personal magnetism of the energising German Chancellor, the book is the only key to the riddle of his dominance and power.

To read *Mein Kampf* merely to extract from it the story of Adolf Hitler and the rise of his Movement, is to waive entirely its main content and import. *Mein Kampf* concerns itself least of all with autobiography. It is an immense piece of work, of political, historical, philosophical, psychological, ethnographical, destructive and reconstructive significance for every aspect of the problem of an entire nation's rehabilitation.

The great bulk of all this is beyond the purview of the everyday English reader. Whole tracts of it here and there, of course, bearing upon this, that or the other particular subject—the ethics of twentieth-century art for instance, or the sterilisation of the unfit—are of special interest to any thinking educated man or woman of whatever country ; but for the most part *Mein Kampf* is only for the German national and the highly initiate. Again, merely to extract the narrative of the National Socialist Party would be a piece of superfluous journalism were it not to bring out something of the mentality of one of the most remarkable men of our time.

Adolf Hitler appealed, in fostering his Movement, not to the self-interest of his possible followers but to their self-sacrifice. Those who believed in the Party must be willing to give their all for it—for Germany— their time, strength, money, their blood and life itself. He was asking for nothing more than he was fully prepared to give himself.

The National Socialist must be convinced, enthusiastic, energetic : he must be ready and eager to do his utmost without any necessary wage or return. He must be fanatic for the unity which means strength.

Hitler to this day is, himself, celibate : devoted to one sole aim and end in life. He is ascetic, disciplined ; a vegetarian and a teetotaller. His personal existence is simple. He owns but one unpretentious private house in Berchtesgaden. He sees no point at all in spending public money on official banquets and receptions and on the social amenities of his great position. Something of this passionate self-immolation to a selfless idea emanates from the pages of his book. To appreciate the power of this man to electrify audiences, to vitalise inertia or despair, to direct enthusiasm, to mould the inchoate, to unify the dispersed and antagonistic, to trample down obstruction, and ruthlessly to crush all that might jeopardise his herculean enterprise, one must read *Mein Kampf*. It is all there. The drive, the force, the originality, the fearlessness, the will to frightfulness.

Every development of National Socialist power

which has been witnessed by a world agape since March, 1933, is the logical outcome of plans laid down long before the book was written but which enshrines their inception and their logic.

.   .   .   .   .

To revert to Herr Wachtmeister's story :

" Hitler didn't always write that book in comfort," he assured me. " A cell in the ' Festung ' here was hardly a study ! When the rain came down extra heavily it poured in at the badly fitting window and slopped about on the floor. I've seen Hitler's room like a regular lake for water. He came to me about it once and together we collected rags and pails and returned to mop it up. He shouted with laughter to discover the prison cat perched on top of a stool in the middle of the mess and puddle and licking at it after her own finnicky fashion.

" As I've already told, Hitler had lots of visitors. They came from all over Germany, even from the remotest corners of the country, travelling by motor or by train, many of them trudging it on foot. Every age, every profession, every condition was represented among them. The broad-shouldered, hardy peasant came to Landsberg together with the well-clad city man ; University professors, workmen, clericals, nobles and small craftsmen, everyday citizens, artists, journalists, the most diverse and varied and all-embracing crowd of visitors you can imagine, and all wanted to see and speak with Hitler. Once even a pair of young Hitler followers came all the way on foot, arriving in rags, from remotest East Prussia.

" Prisoners, however, were only allowed one hour a day for visitors, and the minutes of that hour were strictly allotted. Twenty to thirty minutes might be spent on ' next of kin ' and intimately family matters ; ' friends ' merely, got fifteen or twenty minutes, and ' acquaintances ' generally had to be content with five or ten. Every visitor had to report himself to the authorities and submit to interrogation as to whether he was bringing in anything forbidden, weapons or news, or traitorous printed matter. With bureaucratic thoroughness his own particulars were meticulously noted. Every visit, naturally, had to be ' taken ' by an officer who was present the whole time. I used to ' take ' Hitler's visits, in a room set apart for the purpose.

" Many women, too, came to see Hitler at Landsberg. He treated them with uniform courtesy, but I was never able to remark that any single one excited his interest to a particular degree.

" In the course of so many but so brief interviews Hitler developed an extraordinary terseness and fluidity of expression. It often went severely against the grain to me to bring these to a close. The moment, however, I made a sign that time was up, Hitler broke off, and withdrew. I often regretted the necessity ; duty here came sharply in conflict with personal inclination. It was really a wonderful experience to listen to Hitler in *tête-à-tête* conversation. I don't know anyone whose personality was so overwhelming. As a rule when I had to ' take ' one of these visits, I made a point of having a paper on hand, in which, for appearance's sake, I could appear to immerse myself. Very often, though, I just used it to screen the intense interest I myself was feeling in the conversation. Hitler's way of putting things was not mere talking : he made you feel the point come right home : you yourself *experienced* every

word. He put fresh heart into people. Many came
to him in the last stages of discouragement and doubt
about the prospects of National Socialism, but they
went away filled with confidence and vigour. Once
he'd got over his own black hour, here at Landsberg,
Hitler seemed filled with the fresh energy and
purpose that comes from invincible confidence. He
was only abiding his hour to begin the fight all over
again—seen perhaps, now, from a slightly different
angle,—and he managed to infuse the same spirit into
every discomfited Faintheart who sought his support
and advice.

" The summer wore on to its close. Autumn was at
hand. And in autumn Hitler and his friends were
to be set at liberty.[1] By October 1st he would have
done six months. Early in September the following
Report upon him was submitted to the legal authorities in Munich, with a view to his early release.

" ' The political offender Adolf Hitler was
consigned to the Fortress of Landsberg on April 1st,
1924. Up to the present date he has served five and
a half months. By the 1st of October he will have
expiated his offence by ten and a half months'
detention.

" ' Hitler has shown himself to be a well-conducted
man, not only in his own person, but also with
reference to his fellow-prisoners, among whom he has
preserved good discipline. He is amenable, unassuming and agreeable. He has never made complaints.
He has conducted himself in a uniformly quiet and
reasonable manner, and has put up with the deprivations and restrictions of imprisonment very well.
He evinces no personal vanity and has been satisfied

[1] Hitler had been sentenced to five years' imprisonment. But
the Court exercised its prerogative and enjoined that six months
only should be served.

with the care and attention received here. He neither smokes nor drinks. He has exercised a helpful authority over his fellow-prisoners. As a man unused at any time to personal indulgence he has borne the conditions of life in prison better than married men. He received the visits of women friends and followers without particular enthusiasm, and seldom expanded about political matters to this type of visitor. He has been uniformly agreeable, and of no trouble at all, to the warders and officials here. At the beginning he received a great number of visits, but latterly has discouraged them and withdrawn himself from political discussion. He now writes but few letters. These for the most part are merely acknowledgments. He is entirely taken up with the writing of his book. . . . He hopes it may run into a good many editions and so enable him to defray expenses incurred at the time of the trial.

" ' Hitler will, doubtless, return to political life. He proposes to re-found and reanimate his Movement. But for the future he proposes not to run counter to authority, but to make use of all possible permissible means, short of a second bid for power, to attain his ends.

" ' During the last few months he has become much more mature and calmer. He entertains no revengeful purposes and is no longer filled with recriminating reflections. He has no intention to incite strife against the Government; he is fully persuaded that a country without internal order and firm government cannot carry on.

" ' Adolf Hitler is undoubtedly a man of many-sided intelligence, particularly political intelligence, with an unusual power of will, and direct methods of thought.

" ' Taking the above facts into consideration I venture to submit that Hitler should receive the benefit of an early release. . . . It seems to be very generally anticipated that Hitler will be set at liberty on the first of October next.' "

In consequence of this Report, signed by Ober-regierungsrat Leybold, our prisoner, as a matter of fact, was to have been released on October 1st. But objections, possibly inspired by personal dislike, were raised to the leniency, and Hitler had yet another month to drag out here.

The first anniversary came round of the disaster on the Odeonsplatz before the Feldherrnhalle in Munich, November 9th. The day was one of very special import and gravity for our Politicals. They gathered in the evening in the common room and Hitler spoke, with deep emotion of the events of a year ago. **He charged himself with entire responsibility for the whole affair but showed how it was the outcome of the then concomitance of historical and current circumstance. His hearers were profoundly impressed with the Leader's sincerity and deep morality.**

The whole of November went by, when the Governor again submitted considerations to the Court at Munich. It was strongly felt that Hitler's unimpeachable conduct throughout all this time should receive some recognition.

" ' Hitler has not lost his composure. He makes no complaints,' wrote the Governor, ' he has a strong character, and puts constraint upon himself to keep ill-humour and irritability under. He obeys orders, whether they suit him or not. He resorts to no small subterfuges.'

" There was a good deal more yet to be said, and

the Governor said it. ' He is, undoubtedly, the political idealist . . . he has now done thirteen months . . .'

" Nevertheless Christmas drew near with Hitler still in prison. A few of the others were released, leaving those behind very wistful indeed. Hitler bore these repeated disappointments about his own return to freedom with equanimity and philosophy. The remainder prepared to celebrate the season at Landsberg as best they could. They put up Christmas decorations, and found for the Christmas tree a place of honour in the common room. It still awaited dressing. . . .

" Then, like a bolt from the blue, about ten o'clock on the morning of December 20th, came the news, ' Hitler's to be released ! ' Word flew round the cells ; enormous jubilation broke out. He was most loyally and cordially congratulated. But underneath the very real genuine exultation, lay a great sadness. These men had followed him— sixteen of them to death—and the rest to prison : now he was to leave them. They were to lose their Leader——

" But this sort of thing was not allowed to get the upper hand. Time pressed. Hitler had hardly got his things together before the car arrived to take him away. He took cordial farewell of his companions, and then turning to me shook me by the hand and thanked me for what I had done for him (though I am at a loss to know exactly what this might have amounted to). A moment after, he had gone.

" Perhaps it wouldn't be out of place to add a word or two as to the effect his long stay here had had upon me personally. As I told you, when he first came here I hadn't the glimmer of an idea as to what was

CHIEF WARDER HEMMRICH AT LANDSBERG

HITLER'S FOOTPATH SHOWING "BOUNDS" BOARD
AT THE END—LANDSBERG

meant by National Socialism. But throughout his whole ten months Hitler never talked to us officers directly on the subject. Yet I don't think I should be far out if I was to say that before we saw the last of him every one here, from Governor to the furnace man, had become a convinced believer in his ideas.

" How did this come about you'd like to know ? Well, chiefly through two things. First, we'd had the opportunity of hearing him speak so often to his fellow-prisoners on these subjects, and to his numerous visitors, that we had, one and all, come by a fair comprehension of his aim and meaning. Secondly, and perhaps this is even more to the point, we'd seen him living out his theory in his own life, before our eyes. We warders are so used to churlish and resentful behaviour from prisoners generally, that we take that sort of thing all in with the day's work. So that it was a real change and unusual pleasure for us to have Hitler's Politicals in the ' Festung.' Every one of them behaved like a gentleman. Hitler set the tone, that's why. He never made any distinction of persons. He'd offer a peasant who came to see him his own chair to sit on, as readily as he'd offer it to a general. He was as courteous to the least of us officers here as to the Governor himself. That's one of the things we found so tremendously unusual about him : one of the things we liked so much.

" Then, again, I—who'd been in close personal contact with him all that time—can affirm without the least hesitation that he was an exceptionally truthful man. He never lied or prevaricated in any way. He'd even avoid the least dubiousness in what he said. He made our work for us lighter and

pleasanter than any prisoner had ever done before.
We understood each other, he and I, notwithstanding
the fact that it was always my job to insist strictly
on the rules.

" In a word, when Hitler left here, we all held him
in the utmost esteem. It was only in 1932 and 1933
we realised how much we had to thank God for in
having sent us such a man. We had in then a couple
of dozen Communists and we warders had all our
work cut out to deal with them.

" They were a slippery lot, always grousing about
one thing and another. The Press too didn't help
us in any way to carry out what were, after all,
merely our official and routine duties : we were held
up to execration as enemies of the Proletariat. So
I can tell you, looking back upon it, we appreciated
that time when Hitler and his friends were in our
charge.

" The Governor himself turned to me as Hitler
drove away, and remarked, ' Well, if it's anyway
possible to uplift this country again and set her on
her feet, that's the man to do it ! ' "

CHAPTER XI

SECOND FOUNDING OF THE PARTY

WITH Hitler's release begins the second phase of the history of the National Socialist Party. It is a story of ever increasing interest, but now the interest becomes far more political than personal ; the former elements of hazard and even of romance sink into the background. Hitler is no longer an unknown man, struggling under conditions of dire poverty, to force a hearing for a party merely one of many[1] other equally clamorous competitors. He remains individually poor, to be sure, but at least funds enough can now be found to enable him to get about at top speed, everywhere, and to further the work of the Movement at all points.

This second phase lasts from 1925 to the date of the triumph of the Party, and its Leader's accession to power as Chancellor of Germany in January, 1933.

The third phase begins the history of Germany as a National Socialist State. For the purpose of the present book—which is a study more of the Man than of the Movement, and aims rather, to show biographically how and why it was he came by his ideas and principles, (which, as Chancellor, he is translating into action), than to trace the post-war political history of the Reich—I propose to confine

---

[1] There were 36 odd political parties in Germany prior to the dominance of National Socialism.

myself to a necessarily brief review of the progress of the Party after its second founding.

Herr Hermann Esser, Minister of Economics in Bavaria,[1] was good enough to give me the benefit of his personal and first-hand knowledge of this period. Hermann Esser's story is as authentic and as indisputable as any yet recorded. He is, to-day, one of the oldest and staunchest of Adolf Hitler's original friends and fellow-workers. Hitler indeed was Number 7 in the Party : Hermann Esser preceded him—he was Number 2.

" When the authorities in 1923 threw Hitler and his immediate associates into prison," said Herr Esser, " when they took all possible steps to extinguish the Party, they forgot one thing. They overlooked the fact that Ideas are only to be met and combated by other ideas, not by brute force. The authorities in 1923 were at the end of all their ideas. Now the Idea in National Socialism was a living thing. It had set thousands of hearts afire and this fire was no more to be quenched.

" Shortly before the elections of May 4th, 1924, a handful of members of the outlawed Party founded an organisation called the Deutschvölkische Freiheits-partei (German People's Freedom Party), in the hope that it might attract to itself and reabsorb the

---

[1] And holder of many other important positions. Herr Esser was born in 1900. He was still at school when the Great War broke out, but in 1917 he joined the 9th Bavarian Field Artillery. He belonged, at the Front, to the same Division as Hitler. After the War he took to journalism, and soon came under the influence of Feder and Drexler and so joined their movement. After the ill-fated Putsch he fled to Austria, but later became chief of propaganda for the newly founded Party until this work was taken over by Dr. Goebbels. Herr Esser has been tried twenty-one times (and sentenced fourteen times) for breaches of the peace in connection with political campaign work. He was President of the Bavarian Landtag till it was dissolved and he is still one of the Vice-Presidents of the Reichstag.

scattered masses of the National Socialists. This group had the prestige of Ludendorff to commend it. But I wished at all costs to remain true to Adolf Hitler, so I opposed this and organised the Grossdeutsche Volksgemeinschaft instead, not with any idea of refounding his movement, but in order to have something ready for the Führer to begin his own work with again, as soon as ever he should leave Landsberg. (Freiheits-partei won thirty-two seats in the Reichstag that May, but lost eighteen of them at the following election in December. This was in direct consequence of splits and strains within the group itself.) As you know, Hitler in Landsberg had entirely given up any attempt to direct or hold together the members of his former Party—hence my effort."

When at length he was released, he began his work all over afresh. He could only do this in consequence of an assurance he had given, after the trial, to pursue the object of his Party along legalised lines. Many of his firmest friends and adherents were still in Austria, Italy and Sweden—whence they had fled in 1923—and could not yet safely return. The Italian dispersion especially was to prove immensely significant for the Hitler Movement since it brought such personal supporters of the Leader in close touch with Signor Mussolini—a man for whom Hitler had already conceived immense respect.

"Hitler appointed February 27th, 1925," continued Herr Esser, "for this business of refounding the Party. For the first time since that memorable November 9th Hitler appeared in the Bürgerbräukeller, and spoke to his adherents. He restated the aims of the Movement—the liberation of the German people—and made an impassioned appeal for unity and loyalty. Amid great acclamation he declared he would begin over again, however often the powers that were might overthrow him, and he would begin again and again, were he only to begin with one man ! "

Hermann Esser, who had made all the preparations for this meeting, allied himself afresh, unconditionally with Hitler ; as also did Wilhelm Frick (to-day Reichsminister of the Interior), Gottfried Feder, and many old members of the Party. " There had been strains and rifts and strife among us in his absence : that he could heal them all at one stroke, and weld the warring and embittered elements together again, merely shows what a leader he is.

" Now began a hard time again for everybody— perhaps the hardest of all yet ! We lacked every- thing. We had no Party office, no typewriter, practically no money. We were ridiculed, frustrated, boycotted, threatened.

" That first address of Hitler's in the Bürgerbräu was to be his last for a long time. A couple of days later the ' foreigner, Hitler,' was strictly forbidden by the Bavarian authorities to make any more public speeches. Similar action soon followed by the governments of nearly all the other German States."

And then on April 26th, 1925, General von Hindenburg was for the first time elected President of the Republic. A general amnesty was granted for political offenders, of which Hitler's staunchest aides took advantage to return to Germany. Among these was Captain Goering. This time also marked the beginning of the close association between Dr. Goebbels and the Leader. Hitler was much impressed by the capability and ardour of this man and despatched him to Berlin, then a hotbed of Communism.[1] He also appointed him to head the Central Office of the propaganda activities throughout the Reich.

" It was about this time," my informant continued, " that the breach between Hitler and Ludendorff irreparably widened. The latter was making himself conspicuous as an enemy of the Catholic Church and when Hitler finally broke with him in August, 1926, he found himself labelled a Papist by the Nationalists, while the Clerical Centrum Party upbraided him as arch enemy to Rome ![2]

" Little by little the newly risen Party began to gain ground, although Hitler still continued to be forbidden to speak at meetings. In the summer of 1926, however, he was able to address his followers on the occasion of an anniversary celebrated in Brunswick. An audience of twelve thousand followers served to show what progress had been made up to date.

" Through the pressure of public opinion in Bavaria this interdict was lifted from Hitler in the March of 1927, and once more his voice was welcomed with immense acclaim in Munich. The Party there made a great leap forwards, but it was immediately suppressed in Berlin by the half-Jewish, half-Polish Chief of Police Grzesinski, who was to earn such a sinister name for himself later through his enmity to the National Socialist Movement. It was this man who wished to ' drive Hitler out of the

---

[1] The " Red Terror " in Berlin meant that any day, any time, husband or father might fail to return home, might be missing. Then he would be found somewhere, dead, without sign or explanation of any kind.

[2] The Centrum or Catholic Centre Party in Germany was obnoxious to the National Socialists not because it represented Catholicism, but because it meddled in politics.

country with a dog whip.' Dr. Goebbels, however, stuck to his post, all this notwithstanding, and carried on with his work in the capital.

In August, 1927, Hitler reviewed a march past of his adherents numbering thirty thousand men, and over one hundred thousand heard the speech he made on that occasion. They had assembled in Nuremberg from every corner of Germany for this purpose, and dispersed again filled with fresh ardour to promote the Movement and win for it ever more and more support.

After the elections of May, 1928, twelve representatives of the Party appeared in the Reichstag. In August the ban on Hitler speaking in Berlin was removed and he gave a great address there in the Sportpalast.

The following year, 1929, saw an enormous augmentation in the members of the Party. In Berlin it had come to open fighting between the Communists, who erected barricades in the streets, and the police. At the end of the twelve months fully 175,000 people belonged to the National Socialists.

Early in the year 1930 a young National Socialist fell, whose death has come to have a special significance for the Party and the Movement. The shooting of Horst Wessel is one of the landmarks in this story.

This young man, the son of a clergyman, and who wrote a marching song for the Party, which has since gone by his name, was a law student. He embodied in himself the ideal of manly uprightness and modesty, high endeavour, dutifulness and simple living which Hitler desired to impress upon the whole of his following. He had drawn upon himself the enmity of the Communists by having converted a large number of them to his own political creed. One day young Wessel was at work in his room in a lodging house in Berlin when four Communists invaded it and shot him. So bitter indeed was their feeling against him that at the funeral his coffin had to be protected by the police. Even his grave called for protection, and young members of his own Troop still mount special guard, in honour, over it.

The next landmark was the opening of the Brown House in Munich on January 1st, 1931. Hitherto the direction of the Movement had been carried on from a retired house in the Schellingstrasse, but these premises had long been outgrown. They were by now wholly inadequate. Therefore the Party made a purchase in the summer of 1930 of the unoccupied Barlow-Palais in the Briennerstrasse. This mansion was adapted in record time to its new requirements and uses after plans of Hitler's own, by National Socialist volunteer workmen. For the first time the Party beheld an outward sign of the power and strength to which it had attained in the creation of this fine[1] Headquarters, which is now a part and parcel of the very self of Munich. The Brown House stands for everything dear to the heart and purpose of a National Socialist.

Notwithstanding all this progress, opposition was still fierce and obstinate. In the spring of 1931 the wearing of the Brown Shirt was proscribed.

[1] The Brown House, be it noted, is fine as a building rather than fine for splendour and furnishings. The government of the Party has already long outgrown its accommodation, and a dozen other buildings in Munich have been leased for the purpose. Next year two enormous additions will be made to the original Brown House, to install departments of administration for which at present there is no room.

The " Brown Shirts " marched, all the same. They got their clothes torn off their backs in the streets, so they marched bare to the waist. They were flung into prison. Thousands of new members took their places. Bolshevism waged open war on the middle classes, and the Government merely . looked on. **During this period three hundred National Socialists were brutally murdered, one way or another, and over twenty-five thousand sustained serious wounds and injuries.**

A crisis was at hand.

The financial condition of the country was almost as bad as it had been ten years ago. Since the elections of March, 1930, had resulted in triplicating the number of National Socialist deputies to the Reichstag, the President required Chancellor Brüning to dismiss the Reichstag and call for a fresh election. Brüning had always been a determined opponent of National Socialism : his Cabinet was now dissolved. Although the standing of the Party had long been legalised (how could it be otherwise with so strong a representation in the Reichstag ?), shortly before this election it was forbidden for officials in Prussia to give it their adherence and support.

These elections of September, 1930, were preceded by a propaganda campaign such as Germany had not yet witnessed. Hitler flooded the land with Speakers, and organised meetings to be held high and low, near and far, in the most negligible little village as well as in the most important places. At least thirty thousand meetings were held every day for more than two months. The result was the capture of one hundred and seven seats in the

Reichstag, and the Party rose in order of Party precedence from the ninth to the second in Germany.

" The National Socialist March on Berlin has started," announced the N.S. papers. Seven years after the so-called *Putsch* in Munich, Hitler had largely obtained his objective. Out of a voting population of 43,000,000 (36,000,000 went to the polls), the Party, extinguished a few years before, had obtained 107 mandates from 6,500,000 voters.

This was progress. But in the autumn of the same year the trial at Leipzig of three Reichswehr officers, who had shown interest in the National Socialist Party and were therefore accused of aiding and participating in an " outlaw " Movement, enabled Hitler to state his legal aims more prominently perhaps than he had ever done before. It was intolerable that these officers should be sentenced for desiring to belong to the second largest yet most significant political party in the Reich !

The Reich was in a tragic state by the end of 1931. Sixteen million people were earning less than the equivalent of an English pound a week. Emergency measure after emergency measure was passed without any appreciable effect, except that of growing despair, on the outlook for the nation. It was only the National Socialist Party who hammered away with their demand for power, and their confident assertion that they could weld and use it to every sort of public betterment.

No year since the War witnessed a more significant series of political happenings than 1932. No fewer than twelve elections were held. Thanks to the unity of the Party, and to the indomitable energy of its Leader, National Socialism won its way ever more and more to the front. In the spring Brüning endeavoured to postpone the second Presidential election, and sought to come to an understanding about it with Hitler. The latter, however, was anxious for the election to go forward, although there was little hope, at the moment, of his own, personal, victory. Through action taken by the National Socialist Government of Brunswick, Hitler had recently been naturalised in Germany, and was therefore now eligible to stand as candidate himself for the Presidency of the Reich.

This step brought a tragic chapter in the history of German party bureaucracy to a seemly end. It was unheard of that a man born on the very frontier of the country, who had served at the Front in the German Army all through the War, and who had devoted his whole life ever since to the cause of the German people, should be denied German citizenship any longer, and this in the face of the fact that all sorts of East European riff-raff streaming in over the eastern borders could obtain the same privilege, and even entry into all official classes, without further ado!

Prior to this Presidential election Hitler's activities were such as political life in Germany or elsewhere has never before witnessed. To address three or four meetings a day was nothing to him. Most of these were held in the open air, when he might have an audience of anything from one hundred thousand to three hundred thousand men. Everything had to be arranged and brought off strictly to time if his terrific programme, daily, was to be carried out.

While he was speaking in Dresden, for instance, his audience would be already gathering in Leipzig. He flew from place to place throughout the length and breadth of the land, week after week, day after day, and night after night, without rest or intermission, using aeroplane or auto as best might meet the case. He had to sleep where or how he could. He had his own 'plane and pilot, his car and chauffeur, his secretaries and organisers, but all turned in the last resort upon his own indomitable energy and tireless purpose.[1]

At the pre-election in March, 1932, General Hindenburg carried off 18,600,000 votes, and Hitler, 11,300,000. This apparent defeat for the Führer was in reality a great success. He had doubled the number of his electors since the elections of September, 1930.

But now, however, there was to be a second election and all opposing Parties girded themselves up for the final trial of strength. They were fully alive to the dangers that threatened them from the ever waxing Party—dangers which have indeed showered on their heads and extinguished them since January, 1933. Although it was Hitler's design that Catholics and Protestants alike could adhere to his Party, that Catholics and Protestants alike could march in the ranks of his Storm Troops, there was a time when the former were denied the Sacraments and even Christian burial for so doing.

Everything possible was done to crush National Socialism—not because it threatened the people (the people acclaimed it), but because it threatened class interest, privilege, corruption, and everything greedy, small minded and grasping in German public life, everything inclusively stigmatised as " bourgeois." The National Socialists found themselves alone in opposition to the embattled array of all other political bodies. It would require more

[1] Otto Dietrich has given an almost bewildering account of this hectic period in his book, *Campaigning with Hitler*.

space to enumerate the fears each and several of these entertained in the event of National Socialist success. It would require, too, an intimate acquaintance with the chaotic state of German internal affairs to appraise the task before the one Party in the Reich possessed of a single eye, a definite programme, and an unflinching perseverance.

In spite of the fact that even as late as this the north, east and west of Germany were under the sway of the Reds, and that in the Catholic south the Bishops were all powerful, National Socialism forged doggedly ahead. This can only be ascribed to the perfection of its organisation.

The Government monopolised the wireless. All those in power and highly placed felt they had now to fight for their very existence. In spite of everything that militated against him Hitler polled yet another two million votes at this election. It was not enough to return him for the Presidency, but it greatly enchanced his significance in political life.

Chancellor Brüning had scarcely counted on this advancement of Hitler, and was dismayed by it. He resorted to strange measures. On April 13th, 1932, he ordered the demobilisation of the S.A. (Sturm Abteilung) and the dispersal of the Movement known as the Hitler Youth. The homes and property of these organisations were distrained upon.

But all was in vain. At the elections for the Diet (every German State possessed a Landtag), which took place on April 24th, 1932, the N.S.D.A.P. proved everywhere the strongest party. At Oldenburg it returned an absolute majority. The time was ripe for Brüning to retire : Hindenburg let him go, and on June 1st appointed Herr von Papen to the Chancellorship.

At first Hitler contented himself with marking time, and watching von Papen. His own actions depended upon those of the Chancellor. The latter removed the ban on the S.A. and ordered a new election. While the Communists thereupon gave themselves up to fighting in the streets, Hitler made another tour of the country by air, which was a veritable triumph. Shortly before the elections von Papen had the half-Jewish Chief of Berlin Police, Grzesinski, arrested, and also its Jewish Vice-President, Weiss. "Red" ministers were relieved of their offices.

These elections—some of the bloodiest in the whole political history of Germany—ended again in a victory for Adolf Hitler. His Party carried off two hundred and thirty seats in the Reichstag.

Since National Socialism had now become the largest Party in the State, it was only right and proper that the government of the country should devolve into their hands. President von Hindenburg, however, long hesitated to entrust their Leader, Adolf Hitler, with absolute power. For two years the direction of affairs had been, under Brüning, confided to a minority which had done its utmost to suppress the larger Party. But now the time was ripe and over-ripe for a change.

On August 13th, 1932, Hitler found himself involved in weighty conversations between von Hindenburg and von Papen. He was offered the Vice-Chancellorship. But to this he returned an answer in the negative. Compromise or half-measures never commended themselves to Hitler. The day of his refusal has been called Hitler's Black Day, but it was far from being so in reality. He took longer views than his critics. He had no mind to use National Socialism to bolster up a tottering system.

After the world had been relieved of the spectacle of the German Parliament opened by the Moscow agent, Klara Zetkin[1], Captain Hermann Goering was elected its President.

Once more, however, despite its big working majority, Parliament was dissolved, and again in November fresh elections were held. But by this time the public were thoroughly weary of elections, and the results were disappointing to all Parties.[2]

National Socialism itself lost thirty-four seats. There was, however, an overwhelming majority against the Chancellor, and no course seemed open to von Papen but to retire. He was followed in office by a comparatively unknown man, General von Schleicher. However active this man may have been in other capacities and behind the scenes, he was negligible as Chancellor, and soon found himself completely isolated.

At long length—it would serve little purpose to labour this unsatisfactory and confused period for the reader—on January 29th, 1933, von Schleicher's Cabinet was dissolved and Adolf Hitler achieved that for which he had striven with almost unremitting ardour, and all but unshakeable faith from the day when he became the seventh member of an unheard-of little group of political aspirants in one of the poorest restaurants of Munich.

Adolf Hitler became Chancellor of Germany.

[1] The Reichstag was to be opened by its oldest member, only then was the President to be elected.

[2] Prior to the triumph of National Socialism, as has been already noted, there were dozens of recognised political parties in Germany, and the foregoing pages will have done something to suggest to the reader how violent their tactics were, and how thoroughly life in general was at the mercy of political faction, disunion and upheaval.

Hitler's great charge against all the governments which had succeeded each other in Germany since the Revolution was first their shameless venality, and secondly their hopeless weakness.

CHAPTER XII

" NOTHING of importance in life is merely given to man. Everything must be struggled for. Thus the uplifting of a nation does not come lightly, by chance or fate, but must be the outcome of effort."—Adolf Hitler.

For fifteen years Hitler had directed his Movement; during the whole length of this period had he, in thousands of meetings and assemblies, sought to inculcate the masses with his ideas. At length the German people had come to look to him for their resuscitation, for their salvation from the menace of Bolshevism, and they trusted that once in power he could, and would, make good his promises.

When Hitler came to power he did, indeed, proceed at once to carry out the purposes and promises of a programme conceived so many years before. We have seen him working it out, point by point, boiling it down, *pinning* it down under twenty-five " Headings " in Anton Drexler's little Wohnzimmer (living-room) while Frau Drexler gets the frugal supper. We have seen him submitting it point by point to the Munich public in the Hofbräusaal, when hundreds of dissentient beer mugs were hurled at his head. We have seen him pacing up and down his narrow room at Landsberg pouring out the whys and wherefores of it all to Rudolf Hess, who rattles as hard as he can go on the

typewriter to get the teeming content of this energetic brain into some sort of literary order.

And now, after fifteen years of struggle, he saw
himself at long length on the threshold of achieve-
ment.

Together with Hitler two other National Socialists
were included in the new Cabinet, Herr Wilhelm
Frick as Minister of the Interior, and Captain
Hermann Goering as Minister without Portfolio,
and Commissary for Air.

With the coming of this new Government, and the
setting aside of the old duality as between Prussia
and the rest of the Reich, was the basis laid for a
universal German policy, and for the elimination
of all elements inimical to German life.

In his first address to the people the Chancellor
called for a sense of national discipline. He asked
for four years in which to make good the blunders
of the post-war administrators, in which to re-erect
the State, in which to cope with the problem of
unemployment ; in which to redeem German
peasantry from its misery and helplessness.

In the night of February 27th-28th, 1933, the
Communists set fire to the Reichstag. A few days
previously a raid on the catacombs of the Karl
Liebknecht House in Berlin had brought to light a
great quantity of material which proved beyond
cavil that the forces of Bolshevism were girding
themselves for a mass offensive in Germany. The
Chancellor replied by draconian measures to ensure
the safety of the State.

On the evening before the great elections of March,
on the " Day of the Awakened Nation," the Chancellor addressed the entire people by means of the
radio. The result of his speech was to renew in

HAUS WACHENFELD

HAUS WACHENFELD

every heart in Germany the will to succeed, the passion for freedom, the sense of nationality. Everywhere bells were pealed, bonfires were ignited on the hills, flags bedecked the streets in every town and village—as Horst Wessel, indeed, had predicted in his song!

The National Socialists brought off a complete and overwhelming victory on March 5th with a return of 17,300,000 votes, and a win of two hundred and eighty-eight seats in the Reichstag. Adolf Hitler, who headed the voting list, entered the Parliament House, himself, for the first time. The Government could count on a majority of 52 per cent. These results at the poll inducted the "National Socialist Revolution"—perhaps the most bloodless Revolution known in history. The National Socialists, everywhere, "took over."

In Munich the Minister President Held boasted that were Hitler to send a Reichs Commissary thither, he would have him arrested on the frontier. When, however, on March 9th, the Reichs Commissary, in the person of General Ritter von Epp, duly appeared, the Minister President immediately climbed down and withdrew from the scene of action.

Herr Minister Esser, who took part in these proceedings, told me how minutely and exactly all had been arranged beforehand. Everything went by clockwork, according to plan, without the least confusion or miscarriage. "As a matter of fact," he said, "we had been prepared for a good deal more opposition, Held had been so full of threats and fulminations."

The opening of the Reichstag on March 21st was an act symbolising the unity of the entire German

Q

people. Not less historically significant was the hand-clasp exchanged between the aged and revered General Field Marshal von Hindenburg and the new young Chancellor, Adolf Hitler. The dignity of immemorial tradition extended a welcome to the younger generation straining towards a new and happier future. . . . .

At the first session of the new Reichstag an " Enabling Bill " was passed whereby Hitler was made absolute Dictator for a period of four years. The purpose of this was to free him from the shackles and delays of parliamentary procedure in bringing his programme into immediate action. We shall see in a subsequent chapter how, and to what first ends, he availed himself of this measure.

Many noteworthy things occurred in quick succession. On March 12th, a day when flags hung at half mast in honour of those fallen in the War, Hitler issued a decree concerning the German Colours. The old black-white-red flag, bound up with German history, was to be retained, but the new Hooked Cross Flag was always to be flown at the same time.

Next day the Ministry of Propaganda was created, with Dr. Goebbels at its head.

Another important step towards the general weaving together of all the aspects of government was the appointment everywhere of new Reichs-statthalter, i.e. of Provincial Premiers. These, Hitler suggested, should be nominated by the President. The Chancellor himself is Reichsstatthalter for Prussia in order personally to bind that country and the whole Reich together. The duties of these Provincial Premiers, as they may be called, are numerous and important.

In April came the law which would recapture for those of German birth and extraction the majority of representation in the learned professions and in official life. This law, bearing heavily as it did upon the Jews, makes exception in their case for all those who had fought for Germany in the War, and for those whose fathers and sons had so fallen.

Then came ordinances to regulate school matters. In no direction more than in this is the new spirit and bent of National Socialism to be discerned. The High Schools were overcrowded. Their overflow to the Universities had to be facilitated. At the same time Hitler resolved to check the superfluity of girls seeking facilities for the higher education.

An entire book could be written of Hitler's theory of education ; on his estimate of the place and function of woman in the State ; and on the great youth movement resultant from both, known in Germany as Hitler Jugend. He says the most important thing for girls is the right training of the body, next that of character, and third that of the intellect. A striking proof of the self-sacrificing enthusiasm and unanimity with which such data are accepted by the female intelligenzia in Germany to-day has, for instance, been afforded by the willingness of the University women of Heidelberg largely to forgo, at Hitler's behest, and in favour of men, the learned professional careers to which they had looked forward.

To those who imagine that Hitler has set back the clock five hundred years for German womanhood there is this to be answered : If German girls do not retire from competitive life with men, there will be neither work nor food for either in another few decades. A country with a dense and growing population and no colonies, must narrowly restrict its labour market, in the learned professions as well as in the trades. Again, there is no parallel to be drawn between the type of woman and the numbers of women frequenting the Universities in England and America to those in Germany. The German Universities—and their name is legion—were swarming with women. Some went thither for the purposes of serious study. For those who do *not* go thither for the purposes of serious study, it is obvious enough that the quicker they are driven home again the better.

In May the German Labour Front took the place of the old system of Trade Unions. It would require many pages to give an adequate idea of this reorganisation in Germany of the relationships between employer and employé. The idea underlying it was typical of the " Socialism " in Hitler's programme.

By the time summer had come round, most of the previously existing separate (and highly antagonistic) political parties in the State had ceased to exist. The Social Democrats were suppressed, and for the most part the rest extinguished themselves. A law was passed forbidding the formation of fresh parties. The public were relieved at last to be free of the veritable pest of so many parties and groups, and the Gordian knot of German disunity was cut at one blow.

Then came the organisation of the air, both for purposes of ordinary communication and for defence. This Ministry was confided to General Goering.

The lot of the ordinary man in the street, the everyday person, claimed its share of the Chancellor's attention. A law was passed, which, among other things, aimed at making life easier for the weak and unfit, for those impoverished by the War, for War widows and orphans.

Hitler looks to early and healthy marriage, State aid for struggling young families, to assist in stamping out many of those social abominations which St. Paul says should not even be named among Christians, but which have been more hideously rife in the world since the Great War than at any previous period.

Severe measures were enacted to put down immorality, and further, a law was framed with the object of preventing unfit children coming into the world.

Hitler's much discussed Law for the Prevention of Hereditarily Diseased Offspring, passed on July 14th, 1933, is based upon the German policy of[1] " regeneration," which aims at promoting the propagation of valuable, innately healthy children, while preventing an offspring of hereditarily diseased persons in so far as those descendants are likely to be of inferior quality. Considering the fact that the average ratio of children of healthy families to diseased families is from 1 to 2 to 5 to 7, the necessity of such a policy seems clear.

The following statements, taken from the *Zentralblatt für Reichsversicherung und Reichsversorgung* (*Central Gazette for Federal Insurance and Pensions*), show to what extent the German people is affected by hereditarily diseased persons, in the sense of the law, their number being estimated at 400,000 (one-half of them innately feeble-minded). On the average, each diseased person costs the community

[1] These particulars are taken from an article published by the Deutscher Akademischer Austauschdienst, in *News in Brief*, Vol. 2, No. 1, page 5.

which sends him to an institution, RM. 1,482 per annum. Since insane persons live in institutions 7½ years on the average, they require an expenditure of RM. 11,600. It is a conservative calculation that the German communities have to spend more than 170 millions of marks a year on their insane alone.

" This does not include the expenditures for diseased children a part of whom are attending auxiliary schools. Every pupil of an auxiliary school is costing the Government *RM. 573 per annum, compared to a maximum of 230 for a healthy pupil.* For the whole of the Reich the expenditures for auxiliary schools amount to about 40 millions of RM. per annum. Direct expenditures on hereditarily diseased persons in the Reich, states and communities, amount to at least 350 million RM. a year in all. We have to add to that sum all of the expenditures made by charitable organisations and institutions, by churches and by private persons ; also the costs of execution which amount to about 100 million RM. a year. Some institutions, where insane criminals are kept, show quotas of RM. 20 a day for every inmate. The significance of such figures will seem the more evident if we realise that many healthy, industrious families cannot afford such a daily expenditure for their entire household."

One can gather from all this how far-seeing the law is which provides for the sterilisation of the hereditarily defective when so far as medical science can predict, only further severe bodily or mental abnormality is to be anticipated. The absence of the birth of those unfitted for life relieves those upon whom their subsistence would depend from indescribable suffering and unremitting sacrifice.

In spite of all that has been written and said to the

contrary the action of the Chancellor in unifying the Protestant sects of Germany has had no anti-Christian significance. " The rock bed foundation of the German Evangelical Church," says the Instrument which achieves this purpose, " is the Gospel of Jesus Christ, as witnessed for us in the Sacred Scriptures, and as enlightened afresh by the Confession of the Reformation."

The Chancellor sought by a Concordat with Rome to define the relationships and rights of the Catholic Church and the State respectively, so as to secure smooth working in both spheres.

The Party Day in Nuremberg, 1933, witnessed such a demonstration of loyalty to Adolf Hitler as had never yet been seen. For the first time the Party Day had become a State function and had developed into an assembly of the nation.

Hitler can never lay stress enough on the importance of the agricultural classes, of the plough-driving peasant. Upon them, and upon him, is built the superstructure of the State. Agriculture is the source of the country's strength.

All the great cities would soon be nothing but arid deserts of bricks and mortar were they not to receive, year after year, an influx of fresh healthy life from the country. On the other hand, this migration to the towns, if carried too far, is a curse in itself against which the National Socialist theory of the State sedulously sets its face. Hitler envisages for the future not a gathering of the population into endless great cities, but their re-establishment, right down to the roots, in their native soil. National Socialism has already achieved a great deal, and with much success, in this direction.

The law touching hereditary farmland seeks to

relieve the small farmer of many of the uncertainties and troubles which have hitherto weighed him down. His land is to be unalienable and no longer the easy prey of the financial speculator.

On Saturday, October 14th, 1933, Hitler withdrew his country from the League of Nations. There should have been no occasion in this for the universal amazement it has caused. Adolf Hitler had announced his intention of taking this step some months before. Not before Germany has parity of rights does it concern her at all to waste time over disarmament conferences which forever come to nothing.

On the same day President von Hindenburg dissolved the Reichstag, since, in consequence of the dissolution of all parties except the National Socialists, this now had become a mere Rump.

The new electors fully confirmed all former National Socialist gains, and went far beyond. The result of these, held in November, was a victory for Adolf Hitler which even his most ardent adherents had hardly dared hope. From a voting population of 43 millions, 40½ millions supported the National Socialist régime. Six hundred and sixty-one Members returned to the Reichstag. It meant that 95 per cent of the German people had firmly taken their stand behind Hitler.

This result was their thanks to him for all that he had hitherto done for them.

The foregoing brief resumé has concerned itself with little but the political aspect of things. In the following chapter some attempt will be made to show what all this meant translated into everyday terms, brought to bear on the everyday life of the German citizen.

CHAPTER XIII

HITLER, THE WORKLESS AND THE NEEDY

IN the autumn of his first year as Chancellor Adolf Hitler issued what was at once an order and an announcement, " This winter no one must starve or freeze in Germany."

Lots of people scarcely took the words for sober earnest, they saw no possibility of them being made good. Indeed how should this state of things be realised ; the burdens and deprivations of the late War still weighed heavily on all the world ; never had it been possible hitherto that people should neither starve nor freeze to death in winter !

One might safely say that such an ideal never would have been practicable, had not a man directed affairs in Germany who knew how to bring into the sphere of practical politics that simple Christian charity one to another which the churches have been preaching throughout the ages.

Hitler's motto had long been " Love your neighbour *more* than yourself. Be ready, always, for the least of your own, to sacrifice your belongings and your life." It is known, of course, that Hitler accepts no income from his Chancellorship, but directs that this money should go towards the relief of unemployment. It may not equally well be known that during the winter 1933–34, when the sales of his book had reached the peak, the whole of this increment was also ear-marked for the poor.

The Germans have a special gift for organisation. Hence it seemed eminently practical to organise the " Winter Relief Work " (Winterhilfswerk) by means of the Party machine. It was extraordinary to see how everybody took advantage of this to bring his own, personal sacrifice and exertions into line with the Führer's design and behest. No fewer than one and a half million people of position and influence threw themselves whole-heartedly into this great effort, to say nothing of the rank and file who also did their utmost, and of those who willingly gave their mite.

The scope of this, the biggest philanthropic effort ever made at one time by one people, was so all-embracing, that, enlisting as it did the co-operation of great and small alike, it would require three times as much space at our command, merely to outline it. Some idea of it, however, we must endeavour to convey for three reasons, first, to combat the often repeated gibe that Adolf Hitler has no constructive ability, no seizable plans ; second, to show—if it really should need showing—how and why it is that he holds the trust and love of the German people as a whole ; and, thirdly, to claim for him that he lost no time at all after coming to power, in proceeding to make good the promises of his Party programme.

(Since the bulk of this book is, after all, to be limited, it may be that but little space will remain for even the slightest sketch of what more—in a dozen directions—Adolf Hitler has already done under this third heading. Every one of the social enterprises he has undertaken for the amelioration of living conditions and lack-of-outlook in Germany, would require a chapter in itself.)

In no smallest village in Germany, nay, in no poorest cot was something not done, something not spared, to aid this nation-wide work. It was generally estimated that some three hundred million marks were devoted to it in this way. Possibly this estimate is too low. Not, by any means, that the Winterhilfsarbeit (Winter-aid-work) could merely be appraised in terms of money. Nor could it be measured in terms of material comfort. Its value for the union and solidarity of the reawakened German spirit was above all these.

Given, then, this fount of money, let us very briefly enumerate the numerous channels into which its flow was directed.

Adolf Hitler called upon everyone who had a job of any sort, big or small, to set aside weekly or monthly some small saving for the poor. It was a request, not an order, for Hitler knew well enough that very many people were in no position to spare a single pfennig (fifth part of a penny). All who possibly could, came forward with their " bit " for the " Battle with Hunger and Cold." The directors of the whole enterprise set it an excellent example, and the rank and file willingly proved their Socialism in response.

Every Sunday during that whole winter hundreds and thousands of collectors were to be seen selling tags in the street to the same end.

Through this source alone enormous sums were gathered in, and very often other results came from these tag days. Case after case occurred of their leading to employment for the unemployed. For instance, in the Harz Mountains in Thuringia there are little towns whose inhabitants live by glass blowing. At this time unemployment was rife among them. So the directors of the Winter-Aid thought it a good thing to have tags made of glass, and gave this welcome order throughout the district. It resulted in months of work for three thousand poor glass workers in Thuringia.

The whole " brain wave " was so much appreciated by the public that when these glass tags appeared upon the streets there was a rush for them. In three days over twenty-five million were sold out ! Could any better proof be adduced than this of how truly National Socialism concerns itself with the needs of even the smallest of the German workers ?

Dr. Goebbels, one of the most genial and versatile of the men round Hitler, did not fail to bring his bright wits to bear upon the problems of the Winter-Aid. He it was who conceived the idea of the " Eintopfgericht "—the One-Pot-Dinner. Every German, especially everyone blessed with a decent share of this world's goods, was invited throughout the winter on the first Sunday of every month to restrict his main meal to extremely modest (financial) limits, to not more than about 6d., but to give over to a collector, who would call for it next day, the money which would otherwise have been laid out to furnish the table in the ordinary way. It was as if an Englishman saved what he would have spent on his " cut-from-the-joint and two vegs." (to say nothing of sweets and coffee), and gave it away and contented himself with—what shall we say ?—one good old plate of hash or soup instead, and *nothing but that soup*.

All the restaurants and hotels were advised to offer on their menus for that first Sunday, nothing but this one-dish-dinner, but to charge for it according to usual *table d'hôte* or *à la carte* meals. The difference, of course, was to be handed over for the Winter-Aid. The success of this original idea was enormous. Like one man the whole people took it up. The venerable President himself ate a one-dish dinner on the first Sunday of every month.

During the winter over twenty million marks came to hand this way. Again, in this instance, the good of it was not confined to mere material things. The poor saw the Better-off willingly depriving themselves to help them, and the impression it made was of the best for the conception of " national-socialism." Dr. Goebbels hit on the happy slogan : " Don't spend : deny yourself." This went even further. When a rich man gets up from a well-spread table, and gives something to the poor, it is good, but it is not a sacrifice. The sacrifice comes in when a man contents himself with a poor meal instead of a better one, for the sake of giving something away to the man who never feeds well.

Then again—here was a splendid notion ! Very often during that winter there was to be heard a cheerful bugling in the streets, and there was to be seen a truckload of soldiers slowly tooling by, blowing for all they were worth. What was this ? Why—rummage collecting for the needy. Whenever a hand waved, or a door opened, or someone beckoned from window or corner, the truck hastened up, a couple of men leaped down and ran to obey the summons.

Most people had something they could do without for the Winter-Aid. Here it was an old sofa,—quickly handled and bestowed,—here a sewing machine—swung up atop—here chairs needing mending, here a bundle of clothes, here oddments for repairs of all sorts, here crockery, here spare pots or pans—up and down the streets went the truck, fanfaronading everywhere, and loading up cheerfully and dexterously like a furniture van !

Then workrooms were opened for necessitous girls and women, where these second-hand things could be made over, in return for groceries and shoes.

The happiest Christmas Germany had celebrated for many a long year was the first Christmas of Hitler's Chancellorship. It was the first Christmas after these so-called heathen Nazis had come to power. Up to this time Christmas in Germany had largely been a purely family affair. The tens of thousands of those who had no family, no relatives, no home, perhaps, merely looked on from afar.

Such a thing as this had to be put a stop to in the National Socialist State. On Christmas Eve the Party set up, at its own expense, great Christmas trees before many of the church doors, and in many of the open spaces in the cities. These were all aglitter with frost, and burning candles. Tables were spread beneath them. And bands played the immemorial hymns and carols of the season. Speeches were made calling upon those who were keeping up the feast at home, to remember their poorest brethren without, and to show them the good comradeship and brotherliness which was the very essence of National Socialism. This exhortation closed everywhere with the carol " Stille Nacht, Heilige Nacht."

Then came the crush—the rush—the stampede to the tables where hundreds of good folk forced their way to lay their gifts and offerings and contributions and goodies for the poor. Mountains of these things piled up until there wasn't an inch of room left to bestow a single gift more. Even the ground under the table and all round was cluttered with presents. When the donors had really done, and were ready to go back home again, these things were distributed to the lonely and the hungry and the friendless who gladly came forward to receive them. In ways like this National Socialism sought to prove itself not merely a political creed but a practical befriending of the people.

The Winter-Aid was signally supported by peasants, tradespeople and all sorts of industries, whose carts and waggons were daily to be seen in long rows at the doors of the offices of the Organisation, unloading goods and comestibles for the poor. No end of vouchers were issued by means of which the poor could obtain the necessaries of existence without having to expend money. So far as statistics can give any idea of what this amounted to—and statistics take no account of the Christmas presents—the following figures tell their own tale :
Expended—

Coals, about	2,600,000 tons, worth 50,000,000 marks
Potatoes	12,500,000 cwt.
Vegetables & Flour	1,100,000 cwt.
Bread	60,000 cwt.
Tinned Goods	300,000 tins.
Milk	1,000,000 litres.
Shoes	180,000 pairs.
Cloth	250,000 metres.
Garments	1,100,000
Wood	300,000 cwt.
Vouchers	400,000 marks.
Cash	75,000,000 marks, part of it from the One-Dish Dinner source.

The foodstuffs were not always distributed uncooked, but prepared in common kitchens, so that for the equivalent of an English twopence a hungry man could come by a real good meal. In Munich[1] alone that winter daily portions were served from fifteen great communal kitchens to no less than three thousand poor people. Seventeen millions of unemployed, casual labourers, widows and orphans were supported through these efforts of the people as a whole.

It was a tough struggle to do it. But it was the wish of the Führer that this great work should be put in hand, that no one in Germany should starve or freeze, and everyone rejoiced to help in its fulfilment. While everywhere else in Europe the melancholy spectacle was only too often to be witnessed of hunger marchers parading the streets, of the workless and the despairing losing all patience and breaking out into strife and bitter class hatred, in Germany at least Adolf Hitler had united everyone in an unparalleled gesture of fraternal charity.

. . . . .

MOTHER AND CHILD

The winter passed. But the gigantic machinery of its Aid work remained, and Hitler, who could know no rest until he had given every possible demonstration of what National Socialism meant translated into terms of every-day life—Hitler looked round for the next immediate use to which it could be put.

He was already grappling with the problem of unemployment, and now he turned from the consideration of the father of the family, to that of the mother. This matter of maternity and infant welfare had long been comprised in the Party

[1] Population *c.* 750,000.

programme under the heading " It is the duty of the State to ensure the health of the people through due care bestowed upon mothers and children."

So work was immediately set on foot to relieve the terrible burdens weighing so heavily upon the poorer families of the land, and especially upon the toiling housewives. The War and its long subsequent list of privations and bitter hardships had told on this most helpless and defenceless portion of the community as heavily as on every other. This new movement in aid of womankind was at once a recognition of the bravery and suffering of the women of the terrible years gone by, and a beacon of hope for the nameless regiment of brave and struggling women of the present time.

First of all the " Mother-and-Child " Movement undertakes to unearth hidden and secret misery (in order to relieve it), to explore special areas of distress, and to do away with red tape and mistaken economies. The whole thing is to turn upon the personal and individual touch. First the mother of the family is to be supported and helped and then every one of those dependent upon her. The Mother-and-Child work sets itself very few limits.

Needless to say, here again the scope of the enterprise is so wide only the briefest description of it can be given.

The greatest necessity—that of nourishment—calls for the first attention. Better food is to be provided, and sufficient milk for the children. Then comes the question of clothing and adequate laundry facilities. Women with big families swarming round them all day are to receive daily outside help.

The work of the " Arbeitsplatzhilfe "—roughly translated " The Job Finding Agency "—concerns

R

itself largely with placing out the elder children of these numerous broods in suitable posts as soon as they are fit to earn, and help themselves. The hitherto earning mothers of these families are to be enabled at once to leave factory or business and return home where their duty and their most important work obviously lies. The *man* it is who must be enabled to go out and work and keep the home.

Through the " Wohnungshilfe " (Dwelling-house Aid), a mighty attempt is to be made to sweep away the slums and miserable areas in great cities. Either such dwellings as already exist are to be improved and repaired, or entirely pulled down and rebuilt. Property owners who allow their houses to fall into bad condition are to be called to account for it. The unsocial attitude of those who decline to let where there are children is to be sharply corrected.

The Mother-and-Child Aid looks to it that poor families should have at least what furniture is barely necessary, especially beds. A special activity has been set on foot all through Germany whose slogan is " To each child his own bed." And these beds are collected from charitable donors in the same way as similar collections were made from house to house in the winter by the truckloads of trumpet-blowing soldiers.

Another branch of this work is to provide at least four weeks' country holiday or convalescence for mothers who stand in special need of rest and recuperation. The children are meantime to be cared for in kindergarten. For that short space, at least, the mother is to be wholly free. The home, during the interval, is to be kept going by means of the " Frauenarbeitsdienst "—the organisation which provides women's work of this kind for just these purposes, so that the husband and father can go on having his meals as usual, without universal domestic upset, just because the main prop and stay of it all— the wife and mother—has had to go away.

Then there are schools for mothers ; many of these are run by doctors who make it their business to impart all sorts of essential information about food and health in general to these poor women. They can always resort to medical advice without fear or hesitation, since nothing is more important to a nation than its mothers, its children and its health.

All these measures, these undertakings, these departures and these immediate practicalities spring from the text laid down in *Mein Kampf*, the text is ruthlessly worked out in the life story of the Führer himself, " Social work must be tackled from below, not from above."

.   .   .   .   .

UNEMPLOYMENT

" We hold it to be the prime duty of the State to see that the citizen can secure means of livelihood."

Here, once more, we have one of the most important statements of Party undertakings. Hitler has held it of primary importance to combat unemployment by every permissible means devisable by ingenuity and ardent purpose.

This nation-wide struggle postulates immense governmental preparations. It is not one to be tackled piecemeal and by temporary measures. The whole reconstruction is to be built up after Hitler's own scheme and recommendations, schemes which embrace every sphere of industry, of private and public life. Not a struggle merely, but indeed, a mighty campaign against unemployment has been launched in Germany. It is hoped at last to obtain the victory over decades-long misery and ever-recurring industrial crises. Every man in the country must bear his part in this gigantic enterprise. The victory means nothing less than a stable recovery of industry. A strong State is the guarantor of steady business. Every possible means has been co-ordinated to this end.

The State has provided the sinews of war for this struggle, but the German people themselves have also subscribed many millions of marks for the promotion of national industry. In 1933 the Government set aside 4.3 milliards,[1] in 1934 about 5 milliards to finance schemes of work for the unemployed.

Vast plans were put in hand for the making of canals, for the building of power plants. Nearly all the greater rivers of Germany were harnessed to some productive purpose. By the expenditure of one hundred million marks, one million workmen could be kept employed for an entire month. The work on the Weser, and on the Dortmund-Ems Canal will keep twenty thousand men in work for four years. Another gigantic canal, begun in 1933 will provide work for 1,510,000 days. In the same district between Hannover and Magdeburg one hundred and ten square miles will be brought into cultivation which have hitherto been mere waste or swamp.

In order to secure more land for husbandry in Schleswig-Holstein, two great dams are to be constructed across the Eider River. The work will last three years. Thousands will thereby support themselves, and a plain of 225 square miles will be

[1] 4,300,000,000 R.M.

reclaimed. The enterprise can well be compared with that of Signor Mussolini on the Pontine Marshes.

The German Government offers to meet 40 per cent of the cost to everyone who builds a house or who proposes to carry out reparations and improvements. The result of this step is scarcely to be believed. The building trade, hitherto at a very low ebb, has looked up and gone ahead surprisingly. And consequently so have all the allied industries. Factories are at work day and night. In the spring of 1934 in many large German cities not a single skilled man in the building trade was out of work. This flourishing state of affairs repercussed on the machine industry and gave work to again another ten thousand men.

Hitler, himself an ardent motor mechanic, has found the way for a vast revival in the motor-car industry by reducing the tax. The number of cars on the road doubled in 1933. One can judge of the cheerful position of affairs in this direction from the assurances made by motor-car manufacturers that they are in a position to deliver the goods at once.

The most important attack on unemployment, however, was delivered when the building of immense new arterial roads was planned on the direct initiative of the Chancellor. This constitutes the biggest thing ever done yet in this direction. From four to five thousand miles of auto-roads are projected to be built in six directions right across the country. Two will run from north to south, one from Kiel via Hamburg, Bremen, the Schwarzwald to Basle, the other from East Prussia via Berlin and Munich to the Alps. Three of these great roads will run from east to west, one from Frankfurt-Oder, and the other from Breslau to the Rheinland, and

one from Saarbrücken to Salzburg. This last one is
to be called the Nibelungen Road. The sixth of the
whole series will run from Hamburg to Breslau.
All these roads will be built on the most modern lines.

They will be practically all on one grade and in no
way interrupted by crossings. Other roads will be
carried over by bridges. The entire plan will require
many years to carry out. The Government has
earmarked over two milliards of marks a year
towards it. Whole armies of men find employment
on it. The project is a proud one, for it not only
resembles the great engineering feats of the Romans,
but promises to change the face of the entire country
for coming generations.

These are the ideas of young leaders confided to
the might and craft of young workers to carry out,
all working together to reduce—and ultimately to
extinguish—the hideous curse of Unemployment in
Germany.

.   .   .   .   .

WORK CAMPS

The idea of the Work Camp (which was originally
envisaged on volunteer lines, students alone being
obliged to attend), also proposed fruitful means of
combating unemployment. Over five thousand
camps, mostly situated in the country, keep going
three hundred thousand young people between the
ages of seventeen and twenty-five. Many of them put
in no more than half a year of work-service, and are
then free to take employment elsewhere. They go
forth, furnished with certificates, often to places
awaiting them. Very possibly this volunteer service
will develop later into an obligation. Plans are
already in course of construction whereby such an
army of workers can be employed for twenty years.

The produce so raised will value two milliards of marks a year, and at least five thousand new peasant homesteads will be created.

Naturally the work done in these camps is of a supplementary order and is not allowed to compete in the open market with work turned out under ordinary conditions outside. Nor is such work undertaken which could as well be performed by private enterprise. It is the aim and object of these camps to promote facilities for other people, i.e. by the reclamation or improvement of waste land upon which settlements can be founded. The making of new roads, of course, opened up new ground for such a purpose. The settlement building itself is never undertaken by camp workers. The latter confine themselves to forestry, projects of land reclamation from the sea, canals, irrigation and particularly all undertakings which have for their aim the prevention of catastrophic happenings, forest fires, burst dykes, floods and so forth.

All this has proved of great practical utility. The young people in the Work Camps are well trained in the use of their various tools and implements, spades, pikes, shovels, etc., and can be quickly mustered and detailed for a job. Once on the occasion of a huge landslide on the Saale,[1] a serious disaster was only averted by the immediate mobilisation of young navvies from the nearest Work Camp, who immediately set to work to set things to rights. Many a village has been saved from extinction by fire by the exertions of such organised workers, and immense consequent misery avoided.

The campers themselves are willing and devoted enough. Each man knows that his work benefits the community at large, and that he is therefore

[1] A river in Central Germany.

carrying out the fundamental principles of National Socialism. Hitler's worthy pronouncement, " There is only one nobility, the nobility of work," sustains these labourers through the heat and the toil of the longest day.

Life in a Labour Camp is not in the least modelled on the military plan. The workers rise at five in summer, and at six in winter. Half an hour's exercise or sport precedes tubbing and breakfast. Then comes parade and the hoisting of the camp flag for the day. This resembles the Hooked Cross Flag only instead of the hooked cross in the white circle it displays a spade and a couple of ears of wheat. The whole is symbolic and recalls Frederick the Great's fine saying: "He who toils to make two ears of wheat grow where there was only one before, does more for his country than a general who wins a redoubtable victory."

After this parade the workers betake themselves to their various employments ; the volunteers down tools at the end of a seven-hours' spell. Then comes a wash, and the midday meal eaten, naturally, in common. The food is good and everyone can have as much as he requires. An hour and a half's " knock-off " ensues. The afternoon is taken up by a couple of hours of sport, and an hour's instruction in civics. The evening is passed in singing songs, and in reading aloud, etc., etc. Two or three evenings a week each man can call his own up to ten o'clock. Tattoo is at ten : everyone must then be in quarters.

The Work Camp brings all classes together. The student is set just the same jobs as any one else. The hope is that thirty years hence there will be no more intellectuals, or officials in Germany who have not passed through the school of manual work side by side with the everyday workman.

CHAPTER XIV

WHAT THE "SOCIALISM" REALLY MEANS

IT is scarcely necessary to enlarge, here, upon the "Nationalism" in Adolf Hitler's political creed. Enough has already been written about it. It has occupied so much space in the contemporary press and been discussed in so many books it has come to be regarded with a certain degree of Chauvinism. I propose, therefore, to confine myself, in the conclusion of this work, to a few observations under the second heading of our double-barrelled title. It is so completely true that he who studies contemporary Germany with a view to forecasting the future of the country, must study it from inside and not from the outsider's point of view.[1] From outside one mainly perceives the nationalism. From the inside the drive and force of the socialism is most apparent.

German Socialism—Adolf Hitler's Socialism—is a totally different thing from what is generally understood by this term, from the Socialism derived from Marxian and Communistic theory. The first

---

[1] This observation holds particularly good with regard to events in Germany since June 30th, 1934. Germany's political development has been along lines totally different from those in England and America, and has led to a type of political public opinion very different from that of the average Englishman or American. The latters make a great mistake to judge of affairs in another country as if they had happened in their own. This is the universal mistake of the onlooker and critic : perhaps it accounts for two-thirds of the international misunderstanding in Europe to-day.

essential difference between the two consists in this, that the former is strictly national in aim, scope and limit ; the latter is international, without boundaries of race or land. The second vital distinction is that the first has been set up by the wish of the people concerned, the second is imposed upon nations by the will of those who organise and propagate it. A third contrast can be drawn inasmuch as German Socialism tends to draw all sections of the nation closely together, international socialism initiates class war. German Socialism is directed by the country's nationals ; international Socialism is an instrument of the Jews.[1] In the former it is the personality of the Leader which tells ; in the latter we have nothing but the inertia of the mass which is exploited by its organisers.

By the above signs is German Socialism to be recognised and distinguished. When it has completely assimilated Germany to itself, it will extend and become the groundwork for the future development of other countries. Marxism and Communism are finished in Germany. They have played their part and their rôle is over. Long enough have they made their influence felt in every sphere of German life, intellectual, political and economic, to the suppression of the truer socialism. Socialism is not a thing to be apprehended through dreary theory only, but to be tested and proved in action. We have written enough, elsewhere, very fully to show that the present German Government is inspired in its legislation by the spirit of active philanthropy which it calls Socialism. This legislation incorporates the very essence of German Socialism.

[1] *Vide* the period of the Soldiers' and Workmen's Councils in Munich.

As Dr. Goebbels writes : " Socialism, as we understand it, does not reduce men to a dead level, but ranges them in order according to their individual capacity and leading. If I were to try and put our aims and objects in this direction in a nutshell, I should say that it is our endeavour to build up in Germany a people who all possess the same rights in life. We want everyone, high and low, to belong to such a people. We desire that the highest among them shall feel themselves more closely united with the last and lowest of their own kith and kin than with the highest of any other nation. We aim at this **—that the highest of our people would rather be the lowest of his own nation, than the highest of any other nation.** Such an aspiration can only be the outcome of an absolutely unified national will."

   .   .   .   .   .

It would lead us too far afield to instance the many measures in which Hitler has exemplified his conception of true Socialism. We must confine ourselves to a mere sketch of the most important and obvious incorporations of the ideas through which he has restored to the German worker his honour and self-respect.

THE GERMAN LABOUR FRONT

The law of April 10th, 1933, which arranged May 1st as a great Labour Day Holiday initiated the above-named reorganisation of labour in Germany. The first celebration of the new holiday was unanimous and universal : the Germans had never had anything like it before. Thousands of people gathered together at the same time, all over the country, to listen to the Leader's speech, and then to make high holiday. All trades and callings and professions for the first time were assembled in common, symbolising the unity which was henceforth to unite both types of labour—that of the head, and that of the hand, symbolising the necessary equal value to the community of both. German Socialism recognises no discriminating difference between the brain worker and the hand worker.

Quick on the heels of May 1st and its celebrations, came action. The German Labour Front emerged. On May 2nd the premises of all Marxian Labour Unions were taken over and the contents sequestrated.

Abroad, similar Marxist Unions described this action of Hitler's as a theft of the German workman's hardly earned pay, saved up for years and years in the Unions' funds. Such a charge could not be substantiated, since these moneys were not taken from the workmen, to whom they rightly belonged, but from the greedy grasp of union officials to whom they did *not* belong, but who administered them wastefully, or appropriated them in disproportionate salaries.

With the workman himself went his money also, into the Labour Front. Here it could only be put to the best and most legitimate uses on his behalf.

The great object of the Labour Front is to secure German industry from the incessant recurrence of strikes and all their disintegrating consequences. German Socialism utterly opposes itself to strife between employers and men. Here again it shows quite a different face from that of Marxian Socialism which seeks to foment such discord, whereby, moreover, it maintains its own sovereignty.

In Germany to-day a strike is impossible for the reason that no employer dare pay less than the standardised daily wage, or the State would immediately take up the workers' grievance. On the other hand, were the workers to demand more than their due they themselves would bring about the collapse of the concern for which they worked. The standard of wages is arrived at by experts representing the men and concerned to secure their best interests.

Together with wages, the question of hours has also been considered. In Marxist-Socialist Germany after the War, very hard times set in for German working men. Their leaders had every opportunity to show what the theory could accomplish ; they had a majority in the Reichstag, a member of the Party was President of the Reich. Nevertheless, they were all either too lazy or too indifferent to carry out their programme.

So long as the masses went hungry they were easy to inflame, and to excite against capitalism and the wealthy. While six and a half million unemployed hung about the streets while their wives and children were starving, selfish employers exploited this wretched state of things just because they were paying the dole, forsooth ! If a man grumbled he lost his job ; hundreds were only waiting to pounce upon it in his stead. If he sought the assistance of the Secretary of his Union he drew another blank. What cared the employer for the Unions ? Should a strike ensue all he had to do was to close shop or factory as the case might be, and say, " All right. We'll see who can stick it out the longest, you or I."

Days or even weeks might go by, but the result was always the same. The men came back with hangdog mien, glad of the work again at any cost ! This is where the German working man had lost in his own eyes. It was from this sort of victimisation and wretchedness that Hitler designed to rescue him, and give him back his self-respect. Hitherto he had been the prey of vicious circumstances, the slave of an unscrupulous class.

All was altered in a twinkling when Adolf Hitler came to power. A cry of gratitude and relief went up from all ranks of German working men. The Brown Shirts were everywhere welcomed as they made their way into shop and factory and yard to enquire after the needs and circumstances of every employé in the place. Union secretaries were haled to account no less than unsocialistic-minded employers. The German Labour Front was out to accomplish what it promised.

With the exception of peasants and officials, who have their own organisations, the German Labour Front comprises workmen of all kinds, employés, employers and people working on their own account. Hitler is its patron, Dr. Ley is its Leader. The standards of wages are carefully regulated and observed by reliable workers themselves. The Reich is divided up, under this scheme, into Regions, these, in turn, into Districts, there into Circuits or Local Groups, and these latter again into Trade Communes, Cells and Blocks.

STRENGTH THROUGH JOY

Perforce of its iron will, its absolute refusal to compromise and its terrific onset, National Socialism wrenched itself suddenly into power. Long years before this happened its better ideas had attracted people away from those of the old system then in vogue, and so it is readily to be understood how, in March, 1933, the aforesaid old system simply collapsed.

The first and greatest duty before National Socialism lies in winning the German people back to a sense of nationality, and in impressing its own principles upon them. A State that is to endure for centuries ahead must be built upon the very foundations of organic life, upon blood and soil, nationality and home.

In order to replace one kind of State with another, and better one, it is not enough merely to do away with the former : the people themselves must be re-educated. In place of a system full of class enmity and distinctions and pride of place, there is now a commonwealth. The new State, organically designed, is founded upon the principle " The common good before that of the individual."

Under National Socialism the culture of an entire people must not be identified with any particular caste, class, or level : it must characterise and belong to, the mass. Nor must æsthetic enjoyments be only for the few ; they must be common to all. Just as the creation of a united working people has been confided to the German Labour Front, so is it the business of another organisation, that of " Strength through Joy," to make every member of the nation free of its cultural and artistic treasures and resources. The two endeavours are inter-related. By means of the latter every German working man can look to his free evening as a real opportunity for refreshment and " uplift " ; money which had formerly gone merely in organising strikes, can now be spent far more profitably and agreeably.

It is not the object of " Strength through Joy " to

educate the people politically. Few want to attend classes in civics after a hard day's work. Its aim is rather to bring the people together on a broad basis of enlightenment, an effort in which they, too, of course, must concur.

The Director of " Strength through Joy " is also Dr. Ley. His work is comprised under many headings. It is one of his principal endeavours to open up to worker and unemployed alike all the best sources of entertainment, opera, theatre and concert hall. For the fact that a workman in any German city can obtain admission to the finest operas for practically a nominal sum is Hitler himself directly to be thanked. Hitler often starved, in the old days, in order to buy the meanest standing room in the house, to hear Wagner. Now that he is Chancellor, no working man in Germany need be put to such shifts to gratify his artistic longings.

This " Kulturamt " has opened to the people all sorts of intellectual resorts hitherto sacred to the upper ten. It is a mistake to suppose that only such appreciate the best. In Germany Wagner takes precedence, even with the poorest people, over nigger minstrelsy and jazz.

Even the working man's week-ends are provided for. Previously he went for a bit of a walk in the park perhaps, on Sunday, or took a tram out of the suburbs to get a breath of air. If he were a single man he might spend the most part of his leisure in a Bier hall, listening to the band. Although this sort of thing can still be observed, everywhere, nowadays the workman looks to the sort of week-end right away which previously could only be enjoyed by the better to do. For a couple of marks, to-day, he can go thirty miles out of the city, follow a personally

HAUS WACHENFELD ON THE OBERSALZBERG.   HITLER'S
COUNTRY HOME
THE BAVARIAN ALPS FROM THE REICHSKANZLER'S COUNTRY HOME

conducted tour around some beauty spots, and enjoy a good meal into the bargain. When his holiday comes round, it is provided for, lavishly as far as good things are concerned, at equally small cost.

Workmen from Munich can now envisage holidays by the North Sea with all sorts of trips and bathing fun thrown in. Those from Berlin can go to the Alps, do a bit of mountaineering and try what hotel life is like. These are dreams come true which for whole generations past must have ever remained un-realisable. All thanks to Adolf Hitler.

The section of this activity which deals with " Volkstum und Heimat," seeks to revive, for urban populations, the knowledge of and delight in old peasant and traditional customs, songs, dances, costumes. This sort of thing reawakens love of the country and their origins in people long divorced from the land. It bridges the gulf between the peasant and the townsman.

Kraft durch Freude (" Strength through Joy ") looks also to sport to give the working man zest and change in exercise. It is Hitler's keenest desire to see the worker, particularly the youthful worker (Hitler's Germany is all being built for the future— the past must now look after itself, " let the dead bury the dead "——) made " crisis resisting." The young workman goes in for tennis and golf and every other vigorous game that's going.

Through the instrumentality of innumerable exhibitions it is sought to rouse the worker's pride in his own achievements, in his niche in society, in the part he plays in the whole. His craft is displayed before him in its entire interest, or beauty, or significance. Prizes and competitions abound. Each man becomes conscious of the part he takes in the

s

whole, and discovers fresh pride in his trade and in himself.

Cheap classes are held for those who desire to advance in their particular calling, or to study more particularly the trade to which they belong, and for the acquisition of foreign languages. The best teachers are retained and the instruction is given in the buildings of the local University.

People are assisted to acquire their own dwelling-houses. Loans for this purpose can be repaid by instalments over a series of years. In this way it is hoped to promote a cheerful small villadom beyond the limits of the greater cities.

The department for propaganda aims at bringing all these activities and facilities before the people, to encourage them to make the utmost use of them. Only so will they be bringing about the National Socialist State envisaged by Adolf Hitler. There are still more departments in this one Movement alone, but space forbids their description.

.   .   .   .   .

Much, indeed, has been written about the new Germany. In England and America so much attention has been directed to its political aspect, that these others have been neglected. Of that attention, moreover, by far the greater part is highly inimical, highly critical. Few outside Germany yet realise why Hitler is prepared *to go to all lengths* to save this new Germany from being torpedoed either from within or without. He saves it in his own way and from those he considers its enemies, whether his action is understood abroad or not.

Let those disbelieve it who will, Adolf Hitler has done more for Germany since he came to power than any other statesman at any other time, and the wrecking of his work would not only spell the final ruin of Germany, but the ruin of Europe at large. It is not too much that a handful of would-be saboteurs should die, by summary justice, to save a nation-wide, world-wide welter of blood.   It is only time which can be trusted to explain all, to vindicate all, to crown all, and to show the proper greatness of Adolf Hitler.

CHAPTER XV

IN order to round out the picture of Hitler which it has been the attempt of these pages to depict, a few words remain to be said about his private life since 1919.

As has been already narrated, Hitler left barracks in the August of that year, and rented a modest lodging with humble people in the Thierschstrasse, Number 41.

It is interesting to have a look into this poor room where Hitler lived for ten years. A Herr Erlanger is the landlord of the house. He observes to-day: " I hadn't much to do with him myself as he wasn't directly a tenant of mine. His room was a sub-let. And since I am a Jew, I concerned myself as little as possible with the activities of my lodger and the National Socialists. I admit, I liked Hitler well enough. I often encountered him on the stairway and at the door—he was generally scribbling something in a notebook—when he would pass the time of day with me pleasantly enough.

" Often he had his dog with him, a lovely wolfhound. He never made me feel he regarded me differently from other people. He lodged here in my house from the autumn of 1919 to 1929. First he took a little back room, and then an equally small one in the front to serve as a sort of office and study. The back room in which he slept is only eight by fifteen feet. It is the coldest room in the house; there's a passage below it leading to the courtyard. Some lodgers who've rented it since got ill. Now we only use it as a lumber room; nobody will have it any more.

" The only ' comfort ' Hitler treated himself to when he was here, was a hand basin with cold water laid on. The room to the front was a bit bigger, but the small high-set window left much to be desired. It was very scantily furnished."

We have caught a glimpse of the rooms that were his home all these strenuous years in the Thierschstrasse, and now we must have a look at his unpretentious house on the Obersalzberg.

The Obersalzberg is one of the slopes of the Bavarian Alps, above the Königsee, but below the grand, bare snow-flecked summits of the highest mountains near Watzmann. It is a shaggedly pine-wooded region interspersed with wide stretches and spaces of open grass or meadowland threaded by white filaments of winding road. The whole is dotted over with the characteristic Bauernhöfe (peasant farms) of the country, looking much like the chalets of Switzerland with their flower-decked balconies, their green-shuttered windows above the white stonework of the ground floor.

A steep road leads up from Berchtesgaden to the Obersalzberg. Here Hitler and a few chosen intimates found refuge from the stress and strain of life during the time that preceded the disruption of the Party in November, 1923. They forgathered in one of these Obersalzberg farm houses, called the Platterhof, and there took counsel together, and enjoyed brief, but precious, snatches of rest and recreation.

One gets to Berchtesgaden from Munich by train

in about three hours. But by motor one can do the journey a little more quickly. Berchtesgaden is a little town near the Königsee. It does not lie directly on the lake because the mountains there come down so steeply to the water's edge no room remains for the town. The lower flanks of these mountains are covered with hanging pine forests, but the summits are bare rock, snow-clad and glacier-seamed in winter. The Obersalzberg is a single mountain in the neighbourhood of the Königsee (King's Lake). There are houses built upon it.

Lower down the slope of the Salzberg lay a little house, also built in the Bavarian mountain style, called Haus Wachenfeld.

Here the Bavarian Mountains meet the Salzberg Alps; the frontier indeed between Germany and Austria runs athwart these rocky summits. The view from hence is magnificent. Deep down below lies the green valley in which Berchtesgaden nestles. Snow-clad peaks soar into the blue heavens all around; among them König Watzmann and his seven rocky offspring.

Hitler's house, Wachenfeld, here, is in no sense an official ministerial residence like Chequers in England. It is not even a " country seat." It is nothing more than a simple country house.

It consists of two storeys, the lower built of white stone, the upper of brown-stained wood. A wooden balcony with flower-boxes all along the railing runs round the house outside the bedroom windows. The windows have green shutters with white bands; the grey shingled roof is secured against the storms of winter by rows of heavy stones laid upon it. A little belfry, thatched, like a bird shelter, adorns one end of the roof tree. The plateau surrounding the house is laid out for a car park and a garden. There are flower borders, a large green lawn with a wide rectangular path surrounding it, a rock garden, a telescope, garden furniture—gay chairs, tables, coloured sun umbrellas—and a flagstaff with the long red flag and its hooked cross in the central circle of white, hanging from it.

All within is as simple and as well-kept as without. The peasant note is stressed. To describe one of the rooms : the furniture, consisting of little but the table and a few chairs, is of local make, of painted wood. A wooden dado in grey-green panels with a single little bunch of country flowers painted on each, reaches half-way up the cream-washed walls. The window has a vallance, and simple curtains of figured cretonne hang straight at the sides. A wooden bench coloured like the dado amply furnished with variously and gaily covered pillow-shaped cushions runs round the room and forms a window-seat. There are one or two well-hung engravings to be noted, a cupboard with large painted panels, topped with jugs in peasant ware, and the bright notes of here and there a tasteful plate set on the beading of the dado. Such is the Reichskanzler's sitting or dining-room in Haus Wachenfeld. His square bare table has gaily turned and painted legs, and stretchers for foot rests between. All is eminently homelike and simple. A great green tiled oven, surrounded by a bench, takes the place of the English open hearth. Huge rag rugs lie here and there about the floor.

It is this home which is presided over by the Führer's widowed sister, Frau Angela Raubal.

Haus Wachenfeld was built shortly before the War by a Hamburg merchant. Hitler discovered it long before he bought it. His thoughts turned to this spot and this house after the strains and stresses of Landsberg.

He rented it, and asked his sister to come and keep house there, so that he himself could come and go as circumstances might permit. Later on he purchased it outright, and was thankful to withdraw to its peace and privacy during the stressful time of the struggle of the Party.

Later ensued a period during which but the rarest moments of respite could be snatched at Haus Wachenfeld. During the last phases of his struggle for power in 1932 Adolf Hitler rarely was able to resort thither, alone or with chosen companions, for a few hours' relaxation or intensive counsel.

There Frau Angela Raubal directed a household explicitly for this purpose. After a simple but sufficient repast in which fresh milk, black bread, and some sort of cereal were the chief ingredients, the Führer and his friends liked to sit round the table, or around the stove, and in this informal fashion talk over the prospects and the problems of the *Kampf*.

Since his accession to the Chancellorship of the Reich, Hitler's little country place has had to be adapted somewhat to its owner's wider needs. Without losing anything of its unpretentiousness, a motor road approach to it has been constructed, and additional accommodation has been added after the Führer's own plans. It remains, however, much as it was originally, and ever awaits the coming of its master, guarded by three friends of his of whom he has none more loyal and faithful, the sheepdogs, Muck, Wolf and Blonda.

By the year 1929 when Hitler's Party had now become a nation-wide Movement, it was unsuitable that he should remain any longer in the Thierschstrasse, mainly for the reason that he was obliged to receive the visits of highly placed or important people either in his inadequate little room there, or in the back premises in the Schellingstrasse used as Party headquarters. So he removed to an empty apartment in the Prinzregenten—Platz 16. " This bachelor requires nine rooms for himself," wrote one of his critics and opponents, quite failing to add that two families also shared them, one of these consisting of the very people with whom he had lodged in the Thierschstrasse.

Hitler still lives in this house when in Munich. His pretensions have waxed no whit since he became Chancellor.

He generally comes of a week-end to Munich or to Berchtesgaden. The rest of the time he spends in Berlin. He inhabits the old Reichskanzlei of Prince Bismarck. As a rule he takes his frugal meals at home, often in company with a few simple S.A. men who come to him from every quarter, some of whom he may not even know. His adjutant Brückner sees to it, doubtless, that it is not always the same visitors who have the privilege of dining with Adolf Hitler.

Personal comfort, apart from personal cleanliness, never meant much to Hitler. He lives as simply to-day in the Wilhelmstrasse as he lived at Frau Popp's and in the Thierschstrasse in those early beginnings.

He exacts the ideal of " the simple life " from his followers, although this is not the same thing as to say he would, generally, lower the standard of living.

He would raise the standard of living, but *equalise* (socialise) it.

.   .   .   .   .

To-day the whole world demands " Whither Germany ? " The answer is simple. One can only reply, " Germany follows Hitler." Who would predict the course the Fatherland will pursue should study the life of the Führer, mark its consistency from the beginning up to the present, and only so venture on prophecy. It is impossible to foretell what line his policy will take if he is only considered from the angle of politics and diplomacy. Hitler must be estimated from the human side as well.

Anyone who has so studied Hitler's career, especially that period of it in Vienna which preceded his taking up politics, will grant that he has not deviated from the views he formed as a young man either in respect of them or with regard to the conduct of life in general.

And, as has been so often remarked, place and power have not altered the manner of man he was.

So, like Hitler himself, the Party holds straight on its course, and with it, Germany. Hitler is no weathercock, to be twirled this way and that by every wind that blows. Other people's views cannot influence his decisions. He goes direct to his object, without detour. This object is none other than the accomplishment of the Party programme.

The onlookers at the Third Reich often believe they can detect a leaning in Hitler's policy to the " Right " or the " Left " of his Cabinet. The affair at Wiessee, the arrest of Röhm, gave enormous scope for this type of criticism. It overflowed the entire Press. The summary action of the Führer was ascribed most contradictorily either as a " swing to the left," or as one " to the right," according to the way the critics estimated his reaction to the situation and the forces behind it. As a matter of fact it was neither. Hitler went, as usual, straight ahead, straight to his one object—the stabilisation of the Third Reich.

The present writer, who was not only in Munich at the time of the Röhm scandal, but actually in the Brown House itself, had sufficient inside knowledge of the circumstances to affirm that had not Hitler acted with the promptitude and severity that he did, a hideous massacre would forthwith have taken place in the city. All was set for a violent clash between the S.A. Troops and the heavily armed Reichswehr. This piece of treachery was scotched, on the instant, before it could be realised.

But a great part of the non-German Press was loud in its outcry on behalf of the mutineers, stigmatising Hitler's action as that of a murderer. Only a short while previous to the painful events of June 30th no one of these newspapers could sufficiently condemn Röhm and his associates. To the man in the street in Germany the contradiction here is, to say the least of it, extraordinary. He can only conclude that Hitler will always be misrepresented so long as Truth herself suffers the same misfortune.

Germany's foreign policy is directed towards peace and good understanding. Foreign nations make a great mistake when they confuse National Socialism with Imperialism. National Socialism has no designs upon other lands and other peoples. Germany's future lies in its keeping, and, indeed, that of the whole world—in the keeping of the true Socialism of common life, not in that of class war.

Socialism as an international aspiration has practically petered out. It reached its apogee towards the end of the War, and at the moment when it made its bid for power, its failure began.

The future belongs to National Socialism since, like Christianity itself, it is founded on love, and reconciliation between high and low, rich and poor. Herein lies its special creative and effective power. Marxian Socialism, on the contrary, flourishes on class clash and hatred. It is anti-Christian and destructive.

The world will come to the recognition of all this in time. It may be decades will be required before the truth of the contention is established beyond cavil. Later generations will consider the Period of Marxian Socialism as an interlude out of which purgatory the world emerged into the truer and beneficent conception of

ADOLF HITLER

INDEX